SAN MIGUEL DE ALLENDE

THE MEXICAN EXPERIENCE

William H. Beezley, series editor

SAN MIGUEL DE ALLENDE

Mexicans, Foreigners, and the
Making of a World Heritage Site

LISA PINLEY COVERT

University of Nebraska Press / Lincoln and London

Portions of chapters 1, 2, and 3 previously
appeared as "Colonial Outpost to Artists' Mecca:
Conflict and Collaboration in the Development
of San Miguel de Allende's Tourist Industry"
in *Holiday in Mexico: Critical Reflections on
Tourism and Tourist Encounters*, ed. Dina Berger
and Andrew G. Wood (Duke University Press,
2010), 183–220. Portions of chapter 2 also
previously appeared as "The GI Bill Abroad: A
Postwar Experiment in Foreign Relations" in
Diplomatic History 40 (April 2016): 244–68.

Library of Congress Cataloging-in-Publication
Data

Names: Covert, Lisa Pinley, author.
Title: San Miguel de Allende: Mexicans,
Foreigners, and the Making of a World
Heritage Site / Lisa Pinley Covert.
Description: Lincoln: University of Nebraska
Press, 2017. | Series: The Mexican experience |
Includes bibliographical references and index.
Identifiers: LCCN 2016042788
ISBN 9781496200389 (hardback: alk. paper)
ISBN 9781496200600 (paper: alk. paper)
ISBN 9781496201362 (epub)
ISBN 9781496201379 (mobi)
ISBN 9781496201386 (pdf)
Subjects: LCSH: San Miguel de Allende (Mexico)—
History. | BISAC: HISTORY / Latin America /
Mexico. | BUSINESS & ECONOMICS / Economic
History. | POLITICAL SCIENCE / Globalization.
Classification: LCC F1391.S2 C68 2017 |
DDC 972/.41—dc23 LC record available
at https://lccn.loc.gov/2016042788

Set in Whitman by John Klopping.
Designed by N. Putens.

For my mother and father, Lorraine and Alan

CONTENTS

ILLUSTRATIONS

ACKNOWLEDGMENTS

This project has been a piece of me for almost my entire adult life, and I could never adequately thank all of the people and institutions that offered intellectual, financial, and emotional support along the way. I humbly wish to acknowledge some of their efforts here.

The seed that became this book was first planted during the McNair Scholars Summer Research Program at California State University, Long Beach. This program truly changed my life, and it breaks my heart to know that in this era of austerity future generations will not have the same opportunities that I did. Numerous colleagues, faculty members, and staff at CSULB helped me transform this project from an idea into my honors undergraduate thesis, and I especially want to thank Pat Cleary and Jim Green for their time and guidance. Around seminar tables and over coffee, colleagues and faculty members at Yale shared insights and criticisms that shaped my ideas and analysis in so many ways that I surely no longer remember or recognize them all. I am deeply indebted to Gil Joseph, Patricia Pessar, and Seth Fein for the years of support they generously provided. I regret that Patricia will not be able to see the imprints she left on this project and on my life. I am a better scholar and writer thanks to their questions, comments, and words of wisdom, and I strive to follow their example as a mentor and colleague. Adam Arenson, Gerry Cadava,

Sarah Cameron, Amanda Ciafone, Catherine Dunlop, Lillian Guerra, Julia Irwin, Yedida Kanfer, Eden Knudsen, Carmen Kordick, Diana Lemberg, Jana Lipman, Rebecca McKenna, April Merleaux, Laura Robson, Theresa Runstedtler, Stuart Schwartz, Tatiana Seijas, Lisa Ubelaker Andrade, Kate Unterman, Jenifer Van Vleck, Louise Walker, and Kirsten Weld all dedicated precious time out of their own busy schedules to reading and commenting on (some very rough) chapter drafts, in addition to providing their friendship and encouragement. Jonathan Hudson and Angela Pulley Hudson, Kate Reed Hauenstein and Michael Hauenstein, and Ashley Riley Sousa and John Sousa truly made New Haven feel like home.

Many friends and colleagues assisted in the heavy lifting that was required to transform my dissertation into a book. My colleagues at Southern Connecticut State University went out of their way to provide support during a crucial transitional moment in my career. My efforts to revise the project began in earnest once I arrived at the College of Charleston. I owe a debt of gratitude to Rich Bodek, Phyllis Jestice, Rick Lopez, Jason Ruiz, and an anonymous reader for carefully reading and providing feedback on the entire manuscript. I would also like to acknowledge Jürgen Buchenau, Ben Cowan, Oliver Dinius, Ben Fallaw, Ben Johnson (and the other participants in the Newberry Library Seminar in Borderlands and Latino Studies), Jennifer Josten, Andrew Paxman, Scott Poole, and Jacob Steere-Williams, who all generously offered insights on conference papers and chapter drafts. Fredy González read chapter drafts and provided invaluable assistance with key interviews that altered the contours of this project. Raúl Carrillo-Arciniega patiently helped me understand the nuances of Mexican Spanish whenever I bothered him with translation questions. Mitchell Locklear and Bradford Pelletier organized research data into massive spreadsheets, a task that I would never have undertaken without their assistance. Honor Sachs and Erica Buchberger were writing partners at critical stages when I especially needed motivation and camaraderie, as were Sarah Owens, Irina Gigova, and other colleagues at the many College of Charleston Faculty Writing Retreats that benefited this project immensely. Julie Weise, Tammy Ingram, and David Huyssen offered intellectual feedback and provided support in many ways as I navigated the ups and downs of this project (and of life), and I am grateful for their friendship. Bridget Barry believed in this project, and I thank her, along with Emily Wendell, the rest of the editors and staff at the University of Nebraska Press, and Maureen Bemko, for helping me get it across the finish line. Any shortcomings of this book undoubtedly exist because I did not follow the collective wisdom of the people named above.

Countless archivists, librarians, and others who share a passion for history assisted me over the years. I especially would like to thank César Rodríguez, Graciela Cruz López, César Arias de la Canal, Don Patterson, Sue Beere, the interlibrary loan staff at the College of Charleston, and all of the individuals in San Miguel who invited me into their homes and shared their own histories. My deepest gratitude extends to Marina López Flores and her entire family—Ernesto, Luis, Claudia, Juan, and Diego—for the hospitality, advice, connections, and great food during my research trips in San Miguel. Marimar Aguila Sandoval, Sloane Starke de Caloca, Francisco Caloca, Betse Streng, and Vicki Noemí Chanquín Miranda also opened their doors to me and helped me feel at home as I was completing my research abroad. I thank the staff of San Miguel's Biblioteca Pública for providing a beautiful workspace and the staff of El Sindicato for creating a space to share my work with *sanmiguelenses*. Friends, family members, and colleagues continuously inspired me by sending my way a steady stream of newspaper clippings, advertisements, and magazine articles about San Miguel.

In addition I would like to acknowledge the generous financial support from the following institutions, without which this project would not have been possible: the Ronald E. McNair Scholars Program, the California Pre-Doctoral Program, the Yale Graduate School of Arts and Sciences, the Yale Council of Latin American and Iberian Studies, the Yale Center for International and Area Studies (now the MacMillan Center), the Beinecke Rare Book and Manuscript Library, the Society of Historians of American Foreign Relations, the Andrew W. Mellon Foundation, and the Fulbright Foundation. At the College of Charleston I received essential financial support from the History Department, the School of Humanities and Social Sciences, and the Faculty Research and Development fund.

I would like to thank the people who have been there for me throughout my life and who have helped me remember what is truly important. My sisters Angela Pinley and Ashley Pinley Lautman and my dear friend Heather Lien have all given me strength and inspiration even though our paths never seem to cross often enough. My grandmother Majorie Fletcher and my late grandparents, Leroy Pinley and Sam and Cruz Rodriguez, influenced me in profound ways. I especially appreciate the interest my grandfather Sam took in my project, and I will always treasure the memories of our time together in San Miguel. Chris, I thank you for embarking on this crazy journey called life with me, for patiently helping me see this project through, and for enabling me to look forward to an ever-brighter future on the horizon. Jordan and Adam, I am grateful for everything you bring to my life, from the daily reminders of all that is precious and wonderful to the humbling reminders of my many flaws. Through the little things you help me see the big picture. Alan and Lorraine Pinley, I dedicate this book to you because, ultimately, your unwavering love and support made this all possible.

INTRODUCTION

Stirling Dickinson and Emigdio Ledesma Pérez both arrived in San Miguel de Allende, a small town nestled in the folds of Guanajuato's eastern sierra, in 1937. Like many others who journeyed to San Miguel by train during that era, Dickinson and Ledesma recalled being somewhat anxious as they waited on the station platform, straining to see some sign of the town and its inhabitants in the predawn darkness.[1] They arrived during a pivotal time: residents of the town, with a population of just under nine thousand, were searching for a path forward after nearly a decade of violence and economic decline. Both of these men would play an important role in charting San Miguel's new paths. Each would spend the rest of his life there; both became beloved figures in local cultural and civic life.

Yet their trajectories reveal two fundamentally different visions for San Miguel. Ledesma's family arrived after his father had been recruited along with other workers from Mexico City to help boost production at San Miguel's textile factory, Fábrica La Aurora. Ledesma, whose lanky figure belied his nickname, El Gordo, followed in his father's footsteps and also worked in the factory, ascending the ranks as a skilled mechanic and serving as a representative of the textile workers' union. He is perhaps best known for his work to preserve and sustain numerous religious traditions and festivities

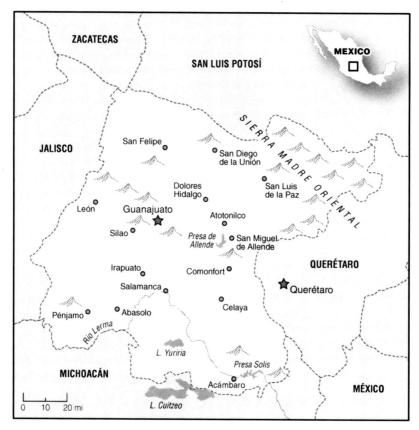

Map 1. Guanajuato. Map by Erin Greb.

that characterized twentieth-century working-class Catholic life in San Miguel.[2] By contrast Stirling Dickinson was an American son of privilege, a Princeton graduate from a wealthy Chicago family who came to San Miguel after a tip from Hollywood film star José Mojica. Dickinson later recalled that San Miguel's historic architecture had immediately enchanted him, and within two weeks of his arrival he had purchased and begun renovating the ruins of an old tannery on a hill overlooking the town. Although he originally intended to winter in San Miguel, he soon became a permanent fixture. Dickinson used his public relations acumen to recruit American students to a new art school that opened in San Miguel in 1938, the first step in the transformation of San Miguel into a world-renowned destination for expatriates and tourists. Until his death in 1998 Dickinson remained a central figure in San Miguel's rapidly growing foreign community and was a tireless advocate for many local civic organizations and charities. Whereas Ledesma's story highlights the hopes for a San Miguel rooted in religiosity and industrialization, Dickinson's story reveals a vision of a small town with grand, international ambitions.

What was this town they stumbled upon, what kind of town did they help shape, and what does it help us to understand about twentieth-century Mexico? Even at first glance the Mexican city of San Miguel de Allende appears to be a study in paradox. The picturesque architecture and cobblestone streets in San Miguel's historic center lend credence to its designation as a nationally protected Zone of Historic Monuments and a UNESCO World Heritage Site. Churches, chapels, and former convents dating to the Spanish colonial period line the central city blocks, and the pealing church bells seem ubiquitous. On weekends Mexican families gather in the tree-lined plazas to people-watch as they snack on *chicharrones* (pork rinds) and mango topped with chili and lime. Plaques and tourist literature draw the visitor's attention to the vital role the town played in Mexico's nineteenth-century struggles for independence, thus staking a claim for the town's centrality in Mexican history. Indeed San Miguel seems to be, as the local tourism office proudly proclaims, the "heart of Mexico."

On the other hand, as a destination for international art connoisseurs, foodies, spiritualists, NGO volunteers, and as home to one of Mexico's largest populations of expatriates, San Miguel has an undeniable foreign presence. On weekday mornings English seems to be the *lingua franca* of the main plaza, also known as the Jardín. The longest-running weekly local newspaper, *Atención*, is bilingual, and its events calendar is filled with bridge tournaments, fundraisers for nonprofits, and film and speaker series intended to appeal to foreign residents and visitors. Tourists line up to get their afternoon caffeine fix at the Starbucks adjacent to the Jardín. San Miguel's foreign residents make up about 10 percent of the total population (an estimated

Fig. 1. A plaque outside the municipal tourism office on the main square in 2007. The municipal government adopted the motto El Corazón de México (The Heart of Mexico) for its tourist promotional materials. Photograph by the author.

16,000 out of 160,383 total residents in 2010), and their concentration in the city's historic center makes their presence all the more striking.[3]

In 2013 *Condé Nast Traveler* readers selected San Miguel as the best tourism destination in the world, and the city consistently appears as a recommended destination in publications such as *Travel + Leisure*, *U.S. News and World Report*, and the *Los Angeles Times*.[4] How did this once small, quiet town near Mexico's geographic center become the object of international accolades? This book explores the apparent contradictions of San Miguel, as both "typically Mexican" and jarringly foreign. It examines how over the course of the twentieth century these seemingly disparate conditions, exemplified by Stirling Dickinson and Emigdio Ledesma Pérez, emerged in tandem.

From the vantage point of the twenty-first century it is clear that various tourism promoters' attempts to secure recognition for San Miguel's historical significance and to attract international tourists have largely succeeded, but for most of the twentieth century this was not a foregone conclusion. Narratives about the inevitability of San Miguel's status as a tourist destination, propagated by Mexicans and foreigners, obscure a more complicated history of conflict, collaboration, successes, failures, and unintended consequences. The most common of these narratives—the myth that the Mexican government declared San Miguel a national monument in 1926—first piqued my own academic interest in the town. In the early 2000s this claim was ubiquitous in tourism promotional materials, in newspaper and magazine articles about San Miguel, and on websites for local hotels and language schools, although since 2008 it has been eclipsed by an emphasis on the city's UNESCO status. Even as a young historian-in-training I found this "fact" problematic on many levels. It seemed implausible that the Mexican government, still working to consolidate power as the proverbial revolutionary dust settled, would have expended energy declaring provincial towns to be national monuments. I considered that perhaps this effort was part of the process of consolidating authority, but no other towns made a similar assertion until the 1930s. No evidence emerged to support this spurious claim.

This led to a more fascinating set of questions. Why would someone fabricate such a story? Why are people so quick to believe it? The myth itself seems to have emerged out of a series of misunderstandings rather than malicious intent. Yet the second part of the problem—why people accept the myth—presents more interesting possibilities that get to the heart of this book. The 1926 myth provides a neat, linear story that simultaneously legitimizes claims about San Miguel's historical significance and frees Mexican proponents of the tourism industry as well as foreign visitors and residents from responsibility for any negative outcomes. If the federal government made this top-down decision, then everyone else was merely a passive observer or simply reacting to make the best of the situation. In this version of history individuals such as Dickinson and Ledesma are largely irrelevant because these processes were set in motion years before they arrived. This narrative also obscures decades of efforts to obtain recognition and resources from the state and federal government, as well as decades of debates about whether tourism was the best economic development strategy. This book unravels that history to show that, far from a foregone conclusion, San Miguel's current status as an international tourist destination is the result of more than fifty years of individual agency, historical contingencies, and even happenstance.

If the details of San Miguel's history are unique, the town's historical trajectory is far from exceptional, which is why San Miguel's struggles help illustrate larger historical processes. This study provides three critical insights into how residents of provincial cities in Mexico and beyond grappled with economic and cultural change. First, it uncovers the decisions, strategies, successes, and pitfalls behind San Miguel's shift from an agricultural economy to a service-based economy between the aftermath of one economic crisis in the 1930s and another in the 1980s. Although it was evident that agriculture alone would not lead San Miguel out of nearly a century of economic decline and stagnation, until the 1930s no clear alternative emerged. By the late 1930s a group of local elites had joined forces with a handful of newcomers to pursue another course. They envisioned San Miguel as a destination for those interested in history and the arts and pursued a number of strategies to bring their vision to fruition, including historic preservation efforts, the founding of an international school for the fine arts, and the creation of basic tourism infrastructure. These elites crafted a narrative about San Miguel that emphasized its central role in the colonial past and Mexico's early struggles for independence. It is important to note that the emerging narrative carefully elided the recent history of decline and upheaval in the postrevolutionary period. To paraphrase an observation of elites in interwar Charleston, South Carolina, San Miguel's elites turned to the past as a means of responding to anxieties and aspirations in the present.[5]

This book examines the hopes and ambitions of political, economic, and cultural elites, as well as those of ordinary *sanmiguelenses* (residents of San Miguel) as they struggled to chart a path for their town's future. Many Sanmiguelenses objected to this strategy and pressed local officials to consider other options. Petitions to government officials, letters and editorials printed in local newspapers, handbills distributed to religious congregations, calls to the local radio station, and successful and failed business initiatives convey a sense of optimism for the town and the nation that was coupled with an awareness of the precarious, fleeting nature of the possibilities on the horizon. Residents contested both the narrative of San Miguel's history that local elites had crafted and the goal—a tourism-based economy—and their objections frequently hinged on competing notions of what it meant to be modern and Mexican. For instance, at the height of the midcentury period of economic growth commonly referred to as the "Mexican miracle," many locals argued that industrialization, rather than tourism, was the real path to Mexican modernity. This story reveals how Sanmiguelenses from different walks of life confronted economic uncertainty and imagined other possibilities in the twentieth century. It contributes to the growing body of scholarship that challenges simplistic characterizations of twentieth-century Mexican economic history.[6] Moreover, a focus on the specific experiences of Sanmiguelenses reveals a history that resonates with towns and cities around the world.[7]

This book also challenges us to rethink how Mexicans debated and defined their national identity and does so by demonstrating how the high economic stakes motivating those debates, the actors involved, and ideas about what it means to be Mexican evolved over time. This is not a story of how individual Mexicans defined their own personal identities but an exploration of how notions about national identity became intertwined with discussions about economic development. For much of the twentieth century Sanmiguelenses sought to link their town to different aspects of Mexican identity, whether through its historic architecture, the contributions of historic figures, or the cultural and religious practices of its residents. As San Miguel's tourism industry expanded and its foreign population grew, this task took on a new urgency as residents attempted to distinguish their town from other Mexican destinations on the one hand and to protect against the encroachment of foreign cultural influences on the other. By the 1980s the limits of these efforts to link national identity and economic development became apparent. Mexico's 1982 debt crisis dramatically reduced government resources and limited the number of Mexicans who could afford to travel, prompting local officials to reframe San Miguel not only as significant to *Mexican* history and identity but also as a place that was *globally* significant. This process culminated in the 2008 designation of San Miguel as a UNESCO World Heritage Site. This study therefore extends the chronology of the scholarly literature on postrevolutionary Mexican state formation and national identity formation to include the neoliberal era.[8]

Finally, this study historicizes midcentury American and Canadian migration to Latin America and demonstrates the implications of those migrants' presence for the surrounding community. The role of foreign influences in San Miguel (whether perceived as potential panacea or pernicious threat) emerges as a central theme in local narratives about Mexican identity. All of Mexico experiences varying degrees of foreign influence, but San Miguel also has a disproportionate share of foreign residents when compared to most places beyond the border region, the beach resorts, and the capital. The foreign population grew from a mere handful in the 1930s to approximately 10 percent of the total population in 2010. The vast majority of these foreigners hailed from the United States and Canada, but others ventured to San Miguel from South America, the Philippines, Japan, Spain, and the Balkans, just to name a few. As a result, debates about Mexican national identity in twentieth-century San Miguel were not based on abstract notions, theories, and ideals but rooted in everyday experiences and interactions with foreigners. This study explores how San Miguel became a "gringo" paradise, who these foreign individuals were, what brought them to San Miguel, and why many decided to stay. It also charts how they navigated and negotiated complex relationships with local residents. Although these foreigners came to Mexico for a variety of reasons and described themselves in different ways, in most cases I refer to them collectively as the "foreign population" or as "expatriates." In chapter 3 I explore in greater detail the challenges these terms pose.[9] The history of San Miguel's foreign population and its relationship with local Mexicans will resonate with communities around the globe as first worlders continue their search for that next, authentic, unspoiled paradise to call home.[10]

Explored through these three lenses, the history of San Miguel in the twentieth century morphs into a story about tourism and economic development, about what happens when the utopian visions of a national revolution come up against competing local aspirations, about the triumph of neoliberal economic development models in the global south, and about the effects an influential foreign population has on ideas about national identity. This study offers key insights into how towns and cities in Mexico and beyond grappled with economic and cultural change over the course of the twentieth century and provides vital historical context for the promise and perils of a shift to a service-based economy. Ultimately the chapters that follow demonstrate how San Miguel de Allende can simultaneously be typically Mexican and palpably foreign, as well as how the histories behind each process were inextricably intertwined.

Scholarly attention to San Miguel de Allende has been surprisingly limited. Historians of Mexico seem to have disregarded this "gringolandia" as too foreign to have anything significant to offer, and although San Miguel has been the subject of many popular histories, newspaper and magazine articles, documentaries, and Internet blogs, most of these are riddled with historical inaccuracies. Scholarship that does exist on twentieth-century San Miguel tends to focus on *either* the Mexicans *or* the foreigners.[11] This book argues that you cannot understand one part of the story without the other because these groups do not exist in separate, distinct spheres. Instead the experiences of Mexicans and foreigners in San Miguel have been deeply entangled and mutually constitutive, codefined through the vast ripple effects of the service economy and through quotidian interactions in homes and businesses across the city. San Miguel's story is indeed a very

Mexican story, rooted in major events, debates, and concerns that resonated across the nation. This history builds upon the long tradition of scholars interested in how ideas about Mexicanness are rooted in specific spaces and local experiences.[12] But it is also a variation of a borderlands history, a story of what happens when different cultures come into contact, often in intimate settings.[13] *San Miguel de Allende* engages current scholarly debates about identity and development in twentieth-century Mexico, but also pushes beyond those debates to connect to broader transnational histories.

The first two chapters examine the origins and early development of San Miguel's tourism industry and lay the groundwork for understanding local responses to foreign tourists in particular. Chapter 1 analyzes how San Miguel evolved from a community on the economic, political, and cultural margins of postrevolutionary Mexico into a typical Mexican town (*población típica*), as designated by the Guanajuato state legislature in 1939. The chapter argues that a coalition comprising local elites and transnational figures such as José Mojica (the Mexican opera singer who spent several years performing in Chicago and Hollywood), Stirling Dickinson (the artist and writer from Chicago), and the Peruvian intellectual Felipe Cossío del Pomar turned to an international solution—tourism—to revive San Miguel's economy and to legitimate its Mexicanness. These efforts provided the foundation for San Miguel's tourism industry and its integration into Mexico's national narrative as a "typical town." Chapter 2 juxtaposes the growth of San Miguel's reputation as a destination for U.S. tourists and artists with the efforts of a parish priest to reinvigorate Catholicism in the region. These parallel developments collided in 1949 as the result of a boycott at San Miguel's art school—an incident that involved Mexico's most famous artists, including David Alfaro Siqueiros, and the highest levels of the U.S. and Mexican governments. The turmoil surrounding the boycott exposed the incompatibility of the conflicting visions for San Miguel's future, while also highlighting the central role foreign visitors had come to play in both local and national economic development strategies.

The next two chapters explore how, even as San Miguel's tourism industry and foreign population expanded, Sanmiguelenses sought out alternative economic development strategies and attempted to limit the perceived detrimental effects of growing foreign influences. Chapter 3 positions local debates over the viability and desirability of tourism as San Miguel's primary economic development strategy within the broader context of the so-called "Mexican miracle." Proponents of the tourism industry argued that tourism, "the industry without smokestacks," was San Miguel's best hope for sharing in Mexico's unprecedented midcentury economic growth. Others, however, argued that the tourism industry truly benefited only a small number of well-connected individuals and forced the town to cater to foreign tastes and whims. Smokestacks were precisely what they wanted, and they pointed to the lone textile factory on the outskirts of town as an example of how unionized industrial jobs provided many local families, including the Ledesmas, with a stepping stone to the middle class. Ultimately, as the downsides of Mexico's economic miracle became more evident, dreams of an industrial San Miguel began to evaporate and future debate focused more on the terms under which tourism would exist rather than whether it should drive the local economy. Chapter 4 focuses on local fears that foreigners might negatively influence San Miguel's youth and, by extension, the future of the nation. But in San Miguel simply scapegoating foreigners for Mexico's problems was no longer a viable solution. Because the economy increasingly relied on foreign residents and visitors, local Mexican business and political elites had to develop a more nuanced relationship with foreigners that drew upon Cold War notions of containment. Through deportations and head-shaving campaigns authorities articulated distinctions between desirable and undesirable foreign influences in San Miguel.

The final chapter assesses the relationship between national identity and economic development strategies in the late twentieth century. San Miguel's 1982 designation as a Zone of Historic Monuments coincided with the onset of an economic crisis and concomitant neoliberal restructuring, and it therefore did not bring the resources that local officials had long anticipated. This chapter nevertheless argues that, because of its reliance upon private investments and foreign visitors, San Miguel's tourism industry emerged from Mexico's various economic crises during the 1970s and 1980s relatively unscathed, thereby becoming a model for future development under a neoliberal economic order. Despite this superficially rosy outlook the service-based economy, combined with the economic crisis, exacerbated the gap between San Miguel's haves and have-nots. This chapter also examines foreigners' participation in local economic debates and their attempts to rationalize their presence through charity, especially when confronted with the region's poverty. As the chapter contends, however, their charitable efforts—what I call San Miguel's other service economy—often reinforced the structural economic conditions that contributed to poverty in the first place. This chapter unveils some of the costs of the economic agenda upon which the Mexican government has staked its twenty-first-century identity.

The epilogue explores how the combination of economic crises and the decay of the country's national revolutionary vision has rendered San Miguel's long-sought national recognition almost meaningless, leaving local promoters to pursue UNESCO World Heritage status and thus to emphasize San Miguel's contributions to a global rather than a specifically Mexican heritage. This shift reminds us of the evolving nature of the relationship between identity and economic development in this typical Mexican town and beyond. The sprawling, bustling San Miguel of the twenty-first century is a far cry from the town Dickinson and Ledesma first encountered in the 1930s, but strangely enough it faces many of the same challenges.

A Note on Methods and Sources

Luis González y González has commented that in the case of the Mexican town San José de Gracia "the number of documents that have been lost seems to be much greater than the number of those that are still available."[14] When I first began this project I feared the same was true for San Miguel. It took me almost two weeks (and several wild goose chases) to locate the municipal archive. My sense of relief upon finding it in a small space tucked behind the stage of the local opera house was soon crushed by dismay. The documents available to consult fit on three bookshelves, and the others, I was told, either did not exist or were in some inaccessible storage unit somewhere. The news became worse. After a few days of beginning to make my way through the documents that did exist, the archivist informed me that the archive would close indefinitely. Little did I realize at the time that this would be a blessing in disguise. While government documents archived in Mexico City, Guanajuato, and College Park, Maryland, served as the backbone of this project, I turned to other sources and methods to reconstruct the local perspectives of this story. I drew upon the anthropological methods of participant observation and formal and informal interviews, tracked down tourism promotional materials and repositories of local newspapers, and applied a cultural studies critical analysis approach to fictional accounts and images. Through these efforts I encountered people, Mexican and foreign alike, who welcomed me into their homes to peruse private archives and manuscript collections in dusty boxes and who gave me permission to consult the archives of religious and educational institutions that were otherwise closed to the public. It turned out that the documents had not been lost; they simply were not where I had expected to find them.

Three local periodicals proved invaluable to this project and merit further explanation. *El Fisgón Anteojudo* (1948–70s), *El Vocero del Norte* (1959–74), and *Atención San Miguel* (1975–present) provide very distinct perspectives on local events, attitudes, and concerns. Manuel Zavala Zavala, whose family rose to local political and economic prominence in the 1930s, wrote *El Fisgón Anteojudo* and mimeographed hundreds of copies from his home every weekend for Sunday morning distribution. *El Fisgón* was more a compilation of gossip, anecdotes, and other tidbits than a traditional newspaper. The pages of *El Fisgón* combined local news with commentary on national and international events. When Zavala took the helm as the main personality of the local radio station XESQ, he continued to combine his trademark humor and commentary so familiar to the readers of El Fisgón. I also obtained access to some transcripts of his radio program from the early 1960s. Antonio Villa Bustamante, brother-in-law of the parish priest in San Miguel, founded El Vocero del Norte in 1959. The newspaper was both more and less provincial than El Fisgón. It focused on local news, gossip, traditions, and sports. A few columns addressed news in the nearby towns of Dolores Hidalgo, San Luis de la Paz, Comonfort, and San Diego de la Unión. Most political discussions centered on local or state politics, with occasional attention to national and international politics as they affected San Miguel. For example, certain events, such as the 1968 Tlatelolco massacre in Mexico City, took several weeks to make the pages of El Vocero, and the Apollo moon landing received no mention at all. By contrast, regional newspapers such as El Sol del Bajío had entire sections dedicated to international events, and El Fisgón addressed international topics and San Miguel's foreign community with greater frequency. Zavala even claimed that his was the first Mexican publication to announce Marilyn Monroe's death.[15] One topic that received substantial coverage in El Vocero was religion, especially the international Catholic Church. The challenges posed by perceived immorality and communism, both of which columnists frequently linked to San Miguel's foreigners, received particular attention. Finally, Atención San Miguel, originally This Week in San Miguel, emerged in 1975 in part to fill the void left when El Vocero ceased publication; it had a completely different perspective and audience, however. From Atención's inception foreigners comprised its editorial staff and the majority of its columnists and reporters, and, although the periodical was bilingual, an overwhelming majority of the readership was foreign. The newspaper covered local political and cultural events as well as the social lives of expatriates and the particular challenges that foreigners faced in Mexico. Together these publications offered essential glimpses of the voices and concerns of individuals often absent from traditional archival sources.[16]

When I thought I had nearly completed this manuscript I found out that San Miguel's municipal archive had been relocated. The new location was almost as strange as the previous one, being in a retail space in a half-abandoned shopping mall on the outskirts of town. The same three bookshelves with neat rows of archival boxes greeted me, but this time a back room housed piles of dusty, haphazardly stacked cardboard boxes—some crushed, others spilling papers out of split sides, some labeled, many not. I only scratched the surface of this bonanza, and it yielded great results that have truly enriched this story. Much work remains, however, and I hope someone picks up where I have left off.

SAN MIGUEL DE ALLENDE

1 Making a Typical Mexican Town

José Mojica's decision in 1935 to purchase an abandoned estate in San Miguel de Allende arguably altered the town's trajectory more than any other twentieth-century event. The Mexican opera singer turned Hollywood star, drawn to the property's orange groves and serene, babbling brook, felt compelled to purchase and renovate the ruin. For him the estate offered the possibility of escape from the chaos of Hollywood life and a peaceful refuge for his ailing mother. When he rechristened the estate Granja Santa Mónica, a nod to the city he had called home in the United States, Mojica probably did not realize how difficult it would be to leave his former life behind. He soon found himself at the center of social and cultural life in San Miguel's elite circles and hosting visitors from around the world. Mojica participated in historic preservation efforts and, in his words, played an "instrumental" role in the establishment of an art school in San Miguel.[1] Indeed during his relatively brief time in San Miguel from 1936 to 1942, when he left for Lima, Peru, to dedicate his life to the Franciscan order, the town underwent an extraordinary transformation.

Although he was not solely responsible for the transformation, Mojica did serve as a catalyst that ignited changes in San Miguel during a moment of transition. Mojica and others have described early twentieth-century San Miguel as a sleepy, timeless town, unburdened

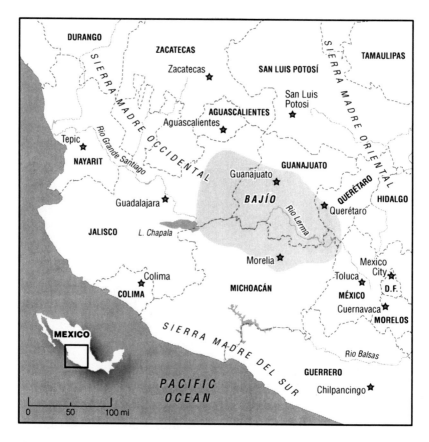

Map 2. Bajío region. Map by Erin Greb.

by the weight of the tumultuous changes in the world around it. But far from sleepy, timeless, and detached, the people of 1930s San Miguel directly grappled with the challenges and opportunities of the time. Church-state conflict in the 1920s and 1930s and the global economic depression established the preconditions for the subsequent reimagining of San Miguel. Both of these factors disrupted local social and economic life, leaving San Miguel on the margins of emerging narratives about Mexican national identity and state and national economic development strategies. Closer examination of the processes that created instability in San Miguel during the early 1930s, however, reveals that they also created an opportunity for local elites to chart a new path for San Miguel. A coalition of local elites and newcomers like Mojica sought international solutions to local economic stagnation. Nostalgia for San Miguel's eighteenth-century past, especially on the part of descendants of the leading families, laid the foundation for twentieth-century claims about its significance. By the end of the 1930s the elites and new arrivals had successfully converted San Miguel from a town that subverted revolutionary change to one that was officially recognized as a typical Mexican town (*población típica*) and destination for international art students. The process by which San Miguel became a typical town demonstrates how debates and ideas about national identity were closely intertwined with economic development strategies in Mexico's postrevolutionary provinces.

San Miguel's trajectory during the twentieth century, including the possibilities for economic development as imagined by its residents, was profoundly influenced by ideas about its past and its location in the state of Guanajuato in a region known as the Bajío. Although scholars have defined the Bajío in different ways, most concur that it is both a geographic and a socioeconomic region in northern central Mexico encompassing parts of the modern-day states of Jalisco, Guanajuato, Michoacán, and Querétaro. The Bajío, often portrayed as a relatively Hispanized region compared to other parts of Mexico, in fact has a history of diverse cultural encounters and dynamism predating the arrival of the Europeans. Historians characterized the region as a "frontier zone" in the pre-Hispanic era, and John Tutino has described the sixteenth-century Bajío as the first "new world," in contrast to Spanish Mesoamerica, which "adapted, changed, and endured despite conquest and colonial incorporation" but was not fundamentally new.[2] In Tutino's formulation the society that emerged in the Bajío was not simply "Hispanized" but a unique and unprecedented amalgamation, "globally linked, commercially driven, ethnically mixed."[3] The persistence of certain indigenous cultural and spiritual practices at least into the late eighteenth century attests to the limits of Hispanization in San Miguel and its environs.[4]

Because of its proximity to some of the world's most productive silver mines, the Bajío had become the richest region in the Americas by the mid-eighteenth century. It sustained dramatic population growth and was highly urbanized and industrialized compared to the rest of New Spain. Towns such as San Miguel produced textiles, leather goods, and other manufactured products to support the booming silver mining industry in Guanajuato and Zacatecas. The mining industries declined in the early nineteenth century after Mexico achieved independence from Spain, sending ripple effects throughout the regional economy. The Bajío reemerged as a significant agricultural and industrial center in the late nineteenth century and continues to be one of Mexico's most economically dynamic regions into the twenty-first century. This is in no small part due to the fact that foreign corporations perceive it as less expensive and safer for manufacturing operations than the violence-plagued northern border region.[5] Despite its economic vitality, the Bajío has also been one of the primary Mexican regions sending immigrants to the United States, making it a pocket of sustained and heightened international contact through informal, and at times formal, channels.[6]

The Bajío is notable for its centuries of economic growth, but it has an equally significant political past. The people of this region historically have resisted attempts at political centralization. This tradition dates back to the indigenous peoples, who long resisted incorporation into the Mesoamerican empires and who subsequently defied Spanish efforts to sedentarize and Christianize them. It includes the *criollo* (creole) conspirators and their followers who rose up against the Spanish in 1810, the counterrevolutionary *cristeros* in the 1920s and 1930s, and the founders of the National Action Party (PAN), which in 2000 successfully challenged seven decades of one-party rule under Mexico's Party of the Institutional Revolution (PRI). Economically and politically, then, the Bajío has been at the forefront of efforts to challenge and redefine the status quo. While this is not a study of the Bajío per se, San Miguel's location along its northern perimeter has

4

influenced the way that *sanmiguelenses*, government officials, and foreigners imagined San Miguel's place in the nation.

San Miguel's own historical trajectory is at once typical of and a departure from the Bajío's broader historical currents. Its foundation and early history as a frontier outpost made it quite similar to other settlements in the region. No evidence exists indicating the precise date that Europeans first established the settlement that would become San Miguel. David Wright Carr explains that 1542, traditionally recognized as the year Franciscans founded the settlement, fits into the regional context well enough.[7] It was a period of extraordinary transition and conflict when not only Europeans but also displaced indigenous peoples pushed northward from the Mesoamerican central valleys. The discovery of silver in Zacatecas in 1546 and in Guanajuato in 1555 accelerated colonization of the region and intensified struggles with the diverse array of sedentary and semisedentary peoples who had been living there. These struggles eventually spiraled into a four-decade-long war known as the Guerra Chichimeca, a name derived from a condescending term akin to "barbarian" that Europeans and their allies used to refer to all indigenous peoples who fought to preserve their autonomy.[8] In the midst of this conflict San Miguel's early settlers moved from the valley to the hills, the location of the present-day city center. In 1559 the viceroy of New Spain recognized San Miguel as a "villa," officially converting the frontier settlement into a formal political entity. The end of the Guerra Chichimeca brought a massive influx of European immigrants to the area.[9] San Miguel's early history was quite typical of the post-Conquest frontier society.

Over time San Miguel's path became more distinct. Three specific factors heavily influenced the town's growth and development in the seventeenth and eighteenth centuries. First, San Miguel (which gained the designation "el Grande" to distinguish it from other towns named after the archangel) became one of the region's most important centers of agriculture and manufacturing. Large ranches undergirded textile, leather, and other industries, all of which found expanding markets in Guanajuato and Zacatecas. San Miguel also earned a reputation for artisanry, with skilled stonecutters, metalworkers, and weavers forming a vibrant working class. The vast majority of workers were indigenous peoples and *castas*, or people of mixed heritage. Rapid commercialization and economic expansion contributed to almost exponential population growth between the mid-seventeenth and mid-eighteenth centuries, when San Miguel's economy reached its colonial-era apex. As Tutino has noted, the population of the entire district grew from fewer than three thousand in the 1630s to more than twenty thousand in the 1740s.[10] This rapid economic and demographic growth set San Miguel apart from most other towns in the Bajío.[11]

The second factor that distinguished San Miguel from other emerging cities in the region was the degree to which a few families controlled local economic and political life. Unlike Querétaro and other regional cities where European and indigenous elites jockeyed for influence, recent Spanish immigrants and their descendants dominated San Miguel's urban population. Three families in particular rose to prominence and cemented their position through intermarriage: the Landetas, the Lanzagortas, and the Canals. Other families, such as the Sautos, Allendes, and Lambarris, increased their influence but never successfully rivaled the dominant clans. The concentration of power meant these families could amass a great deal of wealth in prosperous times, but it also meant that there would be limits to political participation and economic growth for the broader population. These factors contributed to a climate that put San Miguel's so-called "marginal elites" at the center of early struggles for independence from Spain.[12]

The third characteristic that distinguished San Miguel was its religiosity. The historian Margaret Chowning has described eighteenth-century San Miguel as a "pious town," a curious distinction at a time when religion and governance were closely intertwined across New Spain. For Chowning, several factors made San Miguel's religiosity particularly noteworthy. First, the Canal family spent lavishly on religious institutions in the heart of the town, contributing to an already abnormally high density of such entities for a town of that size. Next, the local priest Luis Felipe Neri de Alfaro forged connections across several of San Miguel's religious institutions and oversaw the foundation of another, the Sanctuary of Atotonilco. Father Alfaro encouraged intense penitential devotions inspired by the spiritual exercises of Saint Ignatius of Loyola. These devotional practices included everything from self-flagellation and weeklong religious retreats at the sanctuary, to Good Friday processions that involved the extraordinary theatrics of a man periodically holding Alfaro upside down and driving his head into the ground to press in a crown of thorns, leaving blood to run down his face. Lastly, Chowning attributes the town's unusual religiosity to the large number of artisanal guilds and corresponding confraternities that were responsible for what one colonial official believed to be an "excessive" number of religious celebrations.[13] Together these factors created a religious presence that was unparalleled in the region.

San Miguel el Grande reached its zenith economically and demographically in the late eighteenth century, but changes in the regional economy followed by more than a decade of political upheaval took their toll and the town suffered an equally dramatic decline. As manufacturing increased in cities such as León and Querétaro, San Miguel's share of the market decreased and never quite recovered. A group of Sanmiguelenses led by the second tier of elite families became instrumental in regional conspiracies against Spanish rule, undoubtedly motivated by the combination of economic decline, changing political factors across the empire, and local limits to their power. Spain executed native sons Ignacio José de Allende y Unzaga and Juan Aldama for their participation in the failed 1810 armed uprising, now famous for Miguel Hidalgo y Costilla's rallying cry, the "Grito de Dolores," and for the Virgin of Guadalupe banner that the insurgents obtained from the Sanctuary of Atotonilco. The people of San Miguel then faced harsh repression for their role in the conspiracy until Mexico finally achieved its independence in 1821.[14] The town took the name Allende in 1826 to honor the fallen hero and to mark its role in the nation's independence movement, but it paid a high price for that distinction. Within a matter of decades San Miguel shifted from a bustling manufacturing and religious center to a town facing rapid economic and demographic decline. Liberal reforms and anticlericalism in the mid- to late nineteenth century further affected religious life, leading to the closure and repurposing of many of the town's religious institutions.[15] Agricultural production on the large estates once again drove the economy. It was not until the construction of the rail lines in the late nineteenth century that manufacturing returned to San Miguel, and even then it was at a greatly diminished level.[16]

Old elite families continued to dominate agricultural interests in the area surrounding San Miguel in the nineteenth and early twentieth centuries, but the nature of their influence shifted. Like other large landholders in the Bajío, they avoided various federal attempts at agrarian reform by turning to a sharecropping system whereby workers received plots of land and contracts guaranteeing daily wage labor and access to other resources. Almost half of San Miguel's rural adult male population held sharecropping contracts by 1930.[17] By circumventing land appropriations and swelling their patronage networks, landowners maintained local power and influence, even though urban professionals occupied most government posts. As Tutino argues, this system also likely reduced the appeal of agrarian insurrection that propelled many other regions of Mexico into revolution in the early twentieth century. While many key battles between the factions in the Mexican Revolution occurred in the Bajío, the ranchers and sharecroppers of the region did not mobilize in the same way that peasant communities did in other parts of the country.[18]

Scant research exists on revolutionary-era San Miguel, but the extant studies suggest that the early national revolutionary movements did not have broad appeal. An event in 1911 illustrates how the old political leaders attempted to maintain support and control while the regime of President Porfirio Díaz (1876–80 and 1884–1910) collapsed around them. Francisco Madero led a coalition to overthrow Díaz in 1910, beginning the Mexican Revolution and a decade of violent bloodshed. The *jefe político*, or district prefect of San Miguel, Dr. Ignacio Hernández Macías, organized a rally in support of Madero's revolutionary government, but the rally devolved into a riot. As the historian Mónica Blanco has observed, the nature of the riot indicated that the citizens of San Miguel acted on old grievances: they freed prisoners from the jail, stole funds from the municipal treasury, burned government offices (including the town's archives), and forced Hernández Macías to resign his post.[19] In Blanco's reading, Sanmiguelenses were more concerned with local power dynamics than they were with the national implications of the various revolutionary movements. Indeed while numerous individuals from San Miguel and the surrounding region likely joined one of the revolutionary factions at one point or another, followed the 1917 constitutional convention in nearby Querétaro with interest, and felt the effects of disease, demographic decline, and overall uncertainty wrought by the decade-long violent conflict, the Mexican Revolution was not a defining moment in local historical memory.[20]

During my research I first stumbled upon evidence for this conclusion quite accidentally. I found myself on the doorstep of Genaro Almanza Ríos after a conversation with cab driver José Guadalupe Molina, who insisted that if I wanted to know about the history of San Miguel I had to talk to this man. Although such a comment was usually enough to pique my interest, the driver mentioned something else that prompted me to abandon my plans so he could take me directly to Almanza's home: Señor Almanza had lived through the "revolution." Because it was 2007 at the time, this claim was most unusual. Anyone with any personal recollection of the Mexican Revolution would have been at least one hundred years old. When Almanza opened the door, he was not what I expected. He certainly showed the marks of age, but as he led me through his home, cluttered with wooden masks and the statues of saints, angels, and Jesus Christ that he carved and painted for a living, he seemed too spry and energetic to be a centenarian. When I sat down with him the next evening for the first of many formal interviews, the math did not make sense. He insisted that he was alive during the revolution, but he was born in 1928, thus having missed it by a decade. It was not until I probed a little deeper that I realized the source of my misunderstanding. For Almanza the "revolution" was not the conflict that took place between 1910 and 1917—the war waged by Francisco Madero, and Emiliano Zapata, and Venustiano Carranza. Instead, for Almanza and, as I came to understand, many other Sanmiguelenses, the revolution occurred several years later, during what is more widely known as the Cristiada, or the Cristero War (1926–29).[21] This realization underscored two crucial points. First, the Cristero War remained one of the defining moments in local historical memory for many Sanmiguelenses into the twenty-first century. Second, the most widely circulated accounts of San Miguel's twentieth-century history all but erase this conflict. What follows is an attempt to explain why and how this conflict laid the groundwork for subsequent historic preservation efforts.

A number of provisions in the revolutionary Constitution of 1917 aimed to restrict the power and influence of the Catholic Church in Mexico. Although the Church and the revolutionary government initially maintained a relatively peaceful coexistence, the escalation of religious persecution into the 1920s triggered a wave of violence and fear that persisted in San Miguel for the next decade. The convergence of multiple political, economic, and religious crises during the mid-1920s under President Plutarco Elías Calles, however, ultimately led to his decision to reassert his authority by enforcing the anticlerical provisions of the constitution. In the spring of 1926 Calles advised government officials to expand policies that had already been implemented in some regions since at least 1918: to close convents, monasteries, and parochial schools, to limit the number of priests in each district, expel foreign priests, prohibit public worship, and confiscate ecclesiastical real estate.[22] He signed the Calles Law on June 14, 1926, which ordered the enforcement of these provisions beginning July 31, 1926. The Catholic hierarchy responded by suspending public worship, holding the final masses in Mexico on the evening of July 30, 1926. Reports indicate that San Miguel's churches saw heavy attendance in the days leading up to the closure.[23] The following day the hierarchy canceled services in protest, and Calles ordered government officials to seal church doors and take inventories of church contents.[24] Even though the influence of San Miguel's religious institutions had diminished over the course of the nineteenth century, the town remained deeply religious and the effects of the Calles Law were devastating.

Many Mexican Catholics responded by taking up arms in what became the Cristero War. The majority of Sanmiguelenses were sympathetic to or even outright supportive of the Cristeros, exposing the failures of the postrevolutionary government to build consensus around its policies. As soon as the Calles Law went into effect, the National League in Defense of Religious Freedom (La Liga) organized the local branches of the Knights of Columbus and the Catholic Association of Mexican Youth (ACJM). Members of these organizations, including Donato Almanza, who was Genaro's father and a local sculptor of religious images, often risked their lives by distributing flyers that decried the Calles Law and announced a national economic boycott. Groups met clandestinely to celebrate the Catholic sacraments and plan an armed rebellion, and by September 1926 approximately four thousand men from San Miguel had prepared to join others across the region to fight the federal government in the name of Christ the King. This estimate was substantial considering that according to the 1921 census San Miguel's population numbered barely more than eight thousand. Even if the numbers are not entirely accurate, they reinforce the idea that the vast majority of the population supported the Cristeros.[25] Many of San Miguel's non-Catholic residents fled the town for fear of violent retribution.[26] Local elite families recruited the successful revolutionary general Rodolfo R. Gallegos to lead the Cristiada in the northern region of Guanajuato.[27] The government stationed federal troops in San Miguel's principal plaza and converted the former Conceptionist convent, commonly referred to as Las Monjas, into barracks and stables. This presence provoked attacks

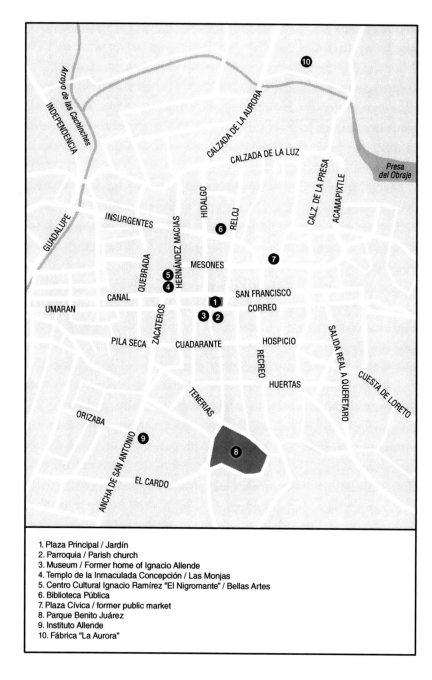

1. Plaza Principal / Jardín
2. Parroquia / Parish church
3. Museum / Former home of Ignacio Allende
4. Templo de la Inmaculada Concepción / Las Monjas
5. Centro Cultural Ignacio Ramírez "El Nigromante" / Bellas Artes
6. Biblioteca Pública
7. Plaza Cívica / former public market
8. Parque Benito Juárez
9. Instituto Allende
10. Fábrica "La Aurora"

Map 3. San Miguel de Allende street map. Map by Erin Greb.

from the Cristero rebels, who descended from their strongholds in the Sierra Gorda and engaged federal troops in the main square. The troops hung the mutilated bodies of captured Cristeros from trees in the town center as a warning to their supporters, an image that continued to haunt eyewitnesses decades later.[28]

Local government officials—frequently torn by their responsibilities as public officials and their devotion to the Catholic faith—walked a fine line between complying with the federal troops and protecting family and friends involved in the Cristiada. Families took turns hiding priests, religious artifacts, and rebels in secret compartments of their homes. While the majority of nuns and seminarians fled to the United States or to their family homes, a number of local priests continued their ministries, usually under the cover of night. Genaro Almanza explained that a priest named José Morales married his parents and later baptized him in secret.[29] One Sanmiguelense proudly claimed that not one person in the town betrayed the priests, because they were all believers.[30] Cristeros from San Miguel often traveled to neighboring states such as Michoacán and Jalisco to fight the government even though they received no compensation and often lacked basic provisions.[31] For San Miguel's Catholics and particularly for families who, like the Almanzas, upheld religious traditions passed down across generations of artisans, the Cristiada was a period of terror and their survival was nothing short of miraculous.

This violent conflict clearly left a mark on the psyche of Sanmiguelenses, but it also had an unintended consequence of laying the foundation for twentieth-century historic preservationists. Popular myth and history have wrongly dubbed 1926 the year that the Mexican federal government declared San Miguel a national monument, a designation it did not actually receive until 1982 (and even then it was technically designated a Zone of Historical Monuments).[32] Due to the unrest in San Miguel and throughout central-western Mexico, historic preservation was not the federal government's priority nor was it realistically within the government's capabilities. However, the promulgation of the Calles Law did set into motion a lengthy process of nationalizing property owned by the Catholic Church, a process that is likely the source of confusion about San Miguel's national monument status.

Nationalizing church buildings took several years and did not originate from the desire to preserve them as part of the national heritage. Rather it reflected the drive to secularize religious spaces during a time of war by converting them into schools, military quarters, and government offices. In November 1926, more than three months after the promulgation of the Calles Law, mayors in the state of Guanajuato received a memorandum from the federal government that requested assistance in developing inventories of what the memo referred to as national property *inside* the churches.[33] Nearly a year after the Calles Law went into effect, in July 1927, San Miguel's municipal government finally assigned monitors for the churches, chapels, convents, seminaries, and parochial schools.[34] Although Article 27 of the Constitution of 1917 technically nationalized the property of all religious institutions in Mexico, the postrevolutionary state was too weak to enforce these measures in the 1920s. Agents from the office of the Procuraduría General de la República (PGR), the Mexican equivalent of an attorney general, had to apply to nationalize each building individually. The first buildings targeted for nationalization were annexes that government officials deemed superfluous and unnecessary for the daily activities and responsibilities of the Church. Because government officials had the burden of proof in nationalization cases, these efforts often turned into battles that lasted for years, even decades, and more often than not government officials failed to prove that nationalization was necessary or within the purview of the federal government.[35] The government closed the case files for the Parroquia and the San Francisco church, two of San Miguel's most recognizable landmarks, in 1957 and 1962, respectively, when it had successfully nationalized them.[36] Therefore the nationalization of ecclesiastical property in San Miguel was not a one-time patriotic act of historic preservation in 1926 but a series of drawn-out, contested actions with different motivations lasting for decades.

Government rhetoric about Church property in San Miguel shifted following the peace accords of 1929 as part of a new strategy for unifying the nation and consolidating federal power. The Mexican government and the Catholic hierarchy ostensibly agreed to coexist peacefully. The government offered amnesty to the Cristeros and the churches reopened. This peace settlement meant that Mexican officials could no longer nationalize Church property with the explicit purpose of secularizing it, and thus a new logic emerged. Memoranda from federal and state officials to the municipal government legitimized continued surveillance of Church property and activities in San Miguel by arguing that the buildings were "monuments of great artistic and historic value" and emblematic of the Mexican national identity.[37] Catholics could use the buildings as long as they preserved them, which meant that they could not post announcements on the walls and had to avoid well-intentioned but historically inaccurate renovations. These poorly enforced and highly subjective restrictions were less about preserving these structures than they were about building a national consciousness that superseded local and religious identities. By continuing to exert some control over religious spaces and by referring to Church buildings as part of the nation's heritage, the federal government was attempting to consolidate authority culturally at a time when it was still too weak to do so politically in provincial towns such as San Miguel.

During the global depression of the 1930s San Miguel's local economy stagnated and the foreign population slowly grew, creating a challenging climate for both economic development and state-led attempts to consolidate a cohesive national identity. The majority of these foreigners were Spaniards, mostly doctors and other professionals who integrated well with the upper classes of San Miguel society.[38] This population was sizable enough for the Mexican secretary of foreign relations to recognize San Miguel resident José de Lema Galván as the Spanish vice-consul in 1933.[39] A small number of foreigners from other parts of the world also settled in San Miguel during this time. The Department of Migration closely monitored non-Spanish foreigners and requested annual updates on their status from the local government. The local chamber of commerce also warned the municipal government about the growing number of peddlers, mostly "[T]urks, Syrians, and Spaniards." According to the complaint, these individuals were undercutting established local merchants in a number of ways: they sold their merchandise after hours, they avoided the additional costs of rent and utilities by carrying their wares along with them, they offered credit to those who could not repay their debts, and they did not pay taxes or licensing fees to the government.[40] Indeed at a time of economic hardship the peddlers and other non-Spanish-speaking foreigners, rather than the Spanish professionals, received the blame for straining the economy.

It was the children of Mexicans repatriated from the United States, however, who captured the most attention from state and federal officials. The state government formed an *ejido*, or communal land grant, named Agustín González outside of San Miguel for the repatriation of families with ties to the state of Guanajuato.[41] Governor Melchor Ortega was certain that the adults would contribute to the local agricultural industry because of their experience in the United States; however, he feared that the children, many of whom were born abroad, had lost their parents' language and culture. The Ministry of Public Education agreed to make special educational arrangements for their linguistic and "spiritual" reintegration into Mexican society.[42]

Although the mere presence of foreigners complicated the consolidation of a Mexican national identity in San Miguel, native-born Mexican residents often posed the greatest challenge by rejecting the central programs of the federal and state governments. As Ben Fallaw's study of the relationship between the Catholic Church and postrevolutionary state formation in Guanajuato demonstrates, resistance to agrarian reform and socialist education from below and differences between two revolutionary factions from above contributed to instability across the state that at times resulted in violence and at other times in a degree of compromise. State and local government officials struggled to placate their constituents while still implementing revolutionary programs, and they relied on local strongmen to serve as intermediaries and rein in the opposition. Indeed the government never fully defeated the Cristeros in Guanajuato, thus leading to a subsequent period of violence known as the Second Cristiada or the Segunda. Fallaw notes that the town of Dolores Hidalgo, approximately twenty miles from San Miguel, was one of the most violent sites of Segunda resistance.[43] Former Cristeros, fueled by contempt for the federal government, threatened by the prospects of losing their sharecropping contracts or individual plots of land, and funded by the large landowners in the countryside, raided newly formed ejidos and schools and protected their patrons' property. As the examples below illustrate, however, *agraristas* (peasants who supported government reforms) were the primary targets of Segunda violence.

The beneficiaries of agrarian reform in San Miguel were mostly marginalized indigenous communities with little stake in the local hierarchy.[44] They eagerly joined agraristas, most of whom were from other parts of the region, in invading privately held property slated for division into communal lands.[45] Between 1930 and 1937 the state government converted one-third of the municipality's remaining large private properties into ejidos.[46] Agraristas often turned to the state and federal governments for assistance when the municipal government failed to act on their grievances.[47] José López, leader of a regional branch of the League of Campesinos, even wrote a letter to President Lázaro Cárdenas asking him to select future municipal leaders in San Miguel from among the residents of local ejidos, so their needs would not be neglected.[48] According to the agraristas' complaints, the municipal government often released people suspected of violence against the agraristas or assisted their escape to neighboring towns so that they could avoid prosecution. The state government rewarded loyal agraristas and attempted to increase their ranks by legislating that when anti-agrarian forces killed a person who requested land from the government, the government would immediately turn over the land in question to the local agraristas.[49] Despite this tough legislation, local authorities had little incentive to protect the agraristas. For the most part San Miguel's local elites obstructed rather than embraced the revolutionary agenda.

Because of local resistance to revolutionary anticlericalism and agrarian reform, there was no obvious place for San Miguel in the emerging national narrative that hailed the revolution's achievements. This narrative, communicated through speeches, art, and public spectacles in the capital, described a nation liberated from the tyranny of Porfirio Díaz and the Catholic Church and where all people, including the formerly marginalized indigenous communities, would stand as equals and share in the fruits of the revolutionary government's programs. Clearly this narrative would have little resonance in San Miguel, where the majority of residents viewed the revolution in negative terms. But Sanmiguelenses also found themselves at the margins of state and national economic development strategies. As violence, unrest, drought, and demographic shifts created instability for the regional agricultural economy, local officials struggled to find alternatives.

The primary concern of municipal officials during the early 1930s was developing local commerce and integrating San Miguel into the regional and national economy. After years of economic stagnation Mayor Gabriel Correa began using several tactics to stimulate economic growth. In 1932 he petitioned the federal government for permission to convert the former convent of San Felipe Neri into a produce-processing factory, emphasizing the number of jobs the new factory would provide. The building was under the jurisdiction of the Federal Property Office as part of the efforts to nationalize Catholic Church properties, and the government garrisoned federal troops there.[50] While questions of jurisdiction between the Federal Property Office and the Ministry of War stalled progress on the factory, the mayor sought assistance from the Ministry of Communications and Public Works for a plan to overhaul the road system in San Miguel. He, along with the local road development committee, argued that San Miguel's economy would not improve without a new road system to connect the town to the state capital and other urban areas in the region. (The existing roads were virtually impassable during the summer rainy season.)[51] Finally, he corresponded with representatives of the Airways Investment Company about the possibility of creating a commercial airfield outside San Miguel. The company ultimately decided against investing in San Miguel because the town lacked substantial commercial traffic and the projected future needs for such an airfield were insufficient.[52] In sum, major local efforts to revitalize San Miguel's economy in the early 1930s did not succeed. The lone exception was the textile factory on the outskirts of town, Fábrica La Aurora. The factory, which first opened in 1902, experienced a period of decline until Manuel Garay Castaños acquired it in 1932, although it was years before the factory made a significant impact on the local economy.[53]

Ironically the combination of church-state conflicts and the failure to revitalize the town's economy through infrastructure and industry created an atmosphere amenable to the complete reimagining of San Miguel's history and its future. A group of local elites and a number of newcomers would draw on government rhetoric about national heritage and preservation and new tourism development strategies in Mexico and abroad to convert San Miguel from a town that subverted revolutionary change to a *población típica*, a typical Mexican town emblematic of Mexico's colonial past.

José Mojica and the Making of a Typical Town

Several newcomers to San Miguel, both Mexican and foreign, proved to be the catalysts that provided the town with economic alternatives and reintegrated San Miguel into the national narrative. Among the figures playing a central role was the international opera and film star José Mojica. Born in San Gabriel, Jalisco, Mojica moved at the age of eight to Mexico City, where he eventually studied music at the Academy of San Carlos. After years of training his tenor voice and multiple minor roles in a Mexico City opera company, Mojica decided to pursue a career in the United States. Lucky breaks eventually led him to Chicago, where he performed with the Chicago Civic Opera company. His reputation grew, especially among female opera fans, and in 1929 Fox Films sought him out to star in a motion picture. Due to the growing popularity of Mexican films and film stars in Hollywood, Mojica enjoyed a successful career. Over a ten-year period he starred in sixteen films and had lesser roles in many others. Mojica first visited San Miguel in 1934 to celebrate the marriage of the bullfighter Pepe Ortíz to the film star Lupita Gallardo. He enjoyed the town so much that in 1935, near the pinnacle of his fame, he purchased and renovated an estate facing Benito Juárez Park.[54]

Mojica was a cosmopolitan figure accustomed to the cultural milieu of large cities, and he led the revitalization of cultural and intellectual life in San Miguel. He quickly earned a reputation for hosting lively parties at his new home, Granja Santa Mónica. Many longtime residents nostalgically looked back on those gatherings as the center of San Miguel's social life.[55] Nationally and internationally renowned film stars, artists, composers, singers, and intellectuals made frequent appearances at these soirees, among them the singer Pedro Vargas, comedian Mario Moreno, actress Dolores del Río, the great Mexican artists of the time, and a host of others from Latin America and Europe, including the Chilean intellectual Pablo Neruda and Russian ballerina Xenia Zarina. Beyond throwing memorable parties Mojica played an integral role in the creation of a theater group called Compañía de Aficionados de San Miguel and a lecture series that brought in speakers such as the Chilean poet Gabriela Mistral and Mexican art historian Manuel Toussaint.[56] Although these activities injected a certain vibrancy and excitement into the town, the relationship that Mojica formed with Toussaint set San Miguel on an entirely new path altogether.

Mojica and Toussaint led an effort by local political leaders and Mexican and foreign artists and intellectuals to obtain government recognition of San Miguel's historic value to the nation and to preserve its ambience. Government recognition was essential because it would legitimize San Miguel's claim to historic and aesthetic importance for outsiders, particularly tourists. Toussaint drew from his extensive background in historic preservation and promotion in the town of Taxco, Guerrero, to assist Mojica and others in the development of a similar program for San Miguel. In 1928 the Guerrero state legislature declared Taxco the first Mexican town protected under preservation law. The law aimed to preserve Taxco's architecture, particularly buildings such as the Santa Prisca church, which dated to the colonial era. Toussaint participated in the efforts behind this legislation by developing a series of arguments for the preservation of Taxco, later published as *Tasco: Su historia, sus monumentos, características actuales y posibilidades turísticas.*[57] While the majority of the book emphasizes the importance of preserving Taxco's historic sites, Toussaint also underscores the potential for tourism development to revive Taxco's local economy.[58]

Toussaint outlined six recommendations for the preservation and development of Taxco, and they became a blueprint for San Miguel. First, he emphasized the need to demonstrate why the town was worthy of preservation by enumerating its attractive natural characteristics and resurrecting its historical significance. The second stage involved the preservation of those natural and historical characteristics so that the town maintained its historic ambience. This stage included writing building codes so that new developments conformed to their historic surroundings. Third, the community was to protect these codes under state or federal law. Whereas the first three guidelines addressed the physical appearance of the town, the last three highlighted the importance of social and cultural life. Toussaint's fourth recommendation was to foster local traditions such as festivals, artisanal industries, and folkloric music. His fifth suggestion was to develop artistic, literary, and historic activities and awareness. Finally, he underscored the importance of providing other recreational activities for tourists, such as horseback riding, swimming, and excursions to nearby attractions.[59]

Toussaint's program for Taxco was quite successful, having placed the town on the regular circuit for artists and other tourists by the mid-1930s. The historian James Oles argues that Taxco appealed to foreign and domestic tourists because of its contrast with the urbanism of Mexico City. To these visitors Taxco represented a more authentic version of Mexico.[60] Among the many artists who spent time in Taxco were the Mexican muralist David Alfaro Siqueiros, American silver designer William Spratling, muralist Marion Greenwood, and art patron Mabel Dodge Luhan. One artist commented that Taxco was likely to become the Taos of Mexico because, for several artists, the New Mexican art colonies were a transitional spot before they proceeded southward.[61] This statement was an obvious reference not only to Dodge, who lived in Taos, but also to artists who, like Greenwood, spent time in New York and Paris and then Taos before going to Mexico. In a memoir of her travels in Mexico Dodge predicted that the people of Mexico would face the same fate as the Pueblo and Navajo in New Mexico. "Mexico," she claimed, "which is now like one vast Indian pueblo full of gentle happy people, will lose its mystery and its lovliness [sic] and gain what is called Progress."[62] To meet the demands of the tourist hordes, she warned, the Mexicans "may even start factories [to manufacture their crafts] as we manufacture Navajo silver jewelry and blankets now, and the 'culture' will soon disappear."[63] Dodge did not recognize her own complicity in the process she described, nor did she understand the economic and social conditions that led Mexicans to seek out and develop industries specifically aimed at attracting people like herself.

Dodge's observations allude to the deeper commonalities that linked places like Taxco and Taos, New Mexico. Since the late nineteenth century people like Dodge had sought out "authentic" cultures and "unmodern" places to ease mounting concerns over what they perceived to be the homogenizing effects of modernization. Outsider artists, intellectuals, and anthropologists attempted to preserve these cultures against the onslaught of what Dodge simply referred to as "progress." While some scholars have argued that these attempts were antimodernist reactions to a rapidly changing industrial society, others have argued that this process was an integral part of modernization itself. By discovering, cataloging, and preserving supposedly endangered cultures, these individuals created an archive for society that romanticized the past while affirming modern advances.[64] Both of these formulations portray outsiders as the primary actors and locals as mere subjects, recipients of outside knowledge and assistance. But the case of San Miguel reveals that this process was in fact collaborative.[65] It is only by recentering the local population that the modernity of such projects comes into full focus. Economic and political rather than romantic or intellectual imperatives often drove local desires to preserve historic architecture or revive "lost" traditions. For example, the case of the Spanish heritage revival in turn-of-the-century Santa Fe, New Mexico, reveals that the debates over New Mexican statehood and the changing local economy drove preservation efforts just as much as did an actual commitment to protecting indigenous traditions and cultures. By designating a local tradition or architectural heritage as authentic, locals and their outside collaborators mark a place as a site that is worthy of state recognition and, ultimately, tourism revenues.[66] Thus the historic preservation efforts in Taxco, and later in San Miguel, emerged within two contexts: a transnational intellectual movement to preserve endangered cultures and a strategy for local economic survival.

Mojica's coalition addressed all of Toussaint's recommendations within four years of his arrival, culminating in San Miguel's designation as a typical town (*población típica*) by the Guanajuato state legislature in 1939. The first step was the initiation of San Miguel's annual patriotic festivals in 1936. Cities and towns across the nation celebrate Mexico's independence from Spain on September 15 and 16 to commemorate Miguel Hidalgo y Costilla's call to arms in 1810. The festivals in San Miguel went beyond the simple performance of patriotism that occurred in many other towns, however. The committee in charge of these festivals consisted of members of San Miguel's most prominent families, such as the Malos and Sauttos, as well as Mojica. They highlighted San Miguel's unique contribution to Mexican independence in the person of Ignacio Allende in order to mark the town as a site deserving of additional government resources.[67]

Nationalist mythology never elevated Ignacio Allende to the status of Miguel Hidalgo, who is widely known as the Father of Mexican Independence or the Father of the Nation. Indeed by 1934 the Ministry of Public Education was already working to preserve Hidalgo's home in the nearby city of Dolores Hidalgo.[68] Through their evocation of Allende in a letter requesting funds from the governor of Guanajuato, San Miguel's patriotic festival committee members reminded the governor of their town's own distinguished place in Mexican history. San Miguel, they wrote, was "the historic place where our Nation's Independence almost began" and the birthplace of Allende was "one of the first to embrace the cause of independence."[69] Although the festival was successful by most accounts, the committee failed to procure substantive support from the state government.

Mojica formalized the efforts of the festival committee by founding the Friends of San Miguel in 1937. Modeled after the successful Friends of Taxco, the group represented a more serious commitment to historic preservation in the absence of material support from the state and national governments. Whereas men like Miguel Malo, with historic familial ties to San Miguel, dominated the old committee, relative newcomers such as Mojica and Leobino Zavala played a greater role in the new society.[70] The most significant difference between the old and new group, however, was that the Friends of San Miguel shifted the emphasis from local hero Ignacio Allende to San Miguel's architecture. This refocusing allowed the group to seek government support for historic preservation by adopting the same rhetoric the federal government had used to justify the expropriation of local church property only a few years earlier. It also positioned San Miguel as a candidate for protection under recent federal legislation advanced by the newly consolidated Department of Artistic, Archaeological, and Historical Monuments (DMAAH) aimed specifically at the preservation of historic or "typical" towns.[71]

The criteria for determining whether a specific building or the zone of a town was worthy of protection under the new law were vague. The legislation decreed that it was in the public interest to protect monuments linked to the nation's social or political history, as well as those towns that possessed a picturesque and typical ambience. As a result the Friends of San Miguel declared that their primary purpose would be to achieve national monument status for San Miguel. The organization also aimed to preserve San Miguel's architectural "gems," train and support local artisans, collaborate with local charitable organizations, and develop recreational activities that would benefit all classes of society.[72]

Demonstrating that San Miguel was a typical town proved to be quite complicated. For a town to qualify as "typical" under federal law it actually had to be atypical in comparison with other towns. The law implied that for a town to be representative or picturesque it needed to be free of the trappings of modernity. Signs, flyers, parking lots, garages, automobile service stations, visible telephone and telegraph lines, electrical transformers, and vendors' stalls were either prohibited outright or subject to the approval of DMAAH inspectors. The law also required that all new construction and any restoration of older buildings conform to the general architectural style of the town. In short the place in question had to appear timeless and unchanging in a rapidly transforming world. State and federal governments did, however, pursue the opposite policy in many other towns and cities across Mexico where drastic modernization projects had altered rapidly urbanizing landscapes.[73] The Friends of San Miguel had to demonstrate that San Miguel preserved some essential, authentic quality that other Mexican towns were losing, thereby justifying San Miguel's protection under federal law.

The law addressed two related goals of new federal agencies such as DMAAH. The first was that these typical towns could represent visually the teleological narrative cultivated in the postrevolutionary period and thus aid in the process of state formation. In other words these typical towns would demonstrate Mexico's idyllic past, and through contrast with more "modern" urban areas they would show how far Mexico had progressed as a nation. The second goal was that the typical towns would satisfy the needs of foreign travelers in search of an idealized Mexico and therefore increase tourism revenues. The law thus provided political and economic solutions to the challenges of political consolidation that continued to hamper the federal government in the 1930s. Despite the government's confident declarations about the success of the revolution, secularization and cultural unity remained unattained goals in places like San Miguel. Historic preservation was a vehicle for achieving these goals because potentially it would give the town's political leaders an economic stake in the federal government's program. By investing in historic preservation the community could receive government recognition and could profit from future tourism revenues. But even though San Miguel seemed to be a perfect candidate for federal recognition and tourism development, the government focused its attention on other sites. The Ministry of Public Education assigned an inspector of colonial monuments to San Miguel, but due to limited resources the ministry left the Friends of San Miguel to shoulder the financial burden of historic preservation.[74]

For San Miguel to fit into the national narrative its claims to a colonial heritage would have to signify typicalness. As Taxco's growing popularity demonstrated, travelers sought both the modern comforts of the capital and towns untainted by that modernity. The postrevolutionary impulse to valorize the indigenous cultures of Mexico while integrating them under a common mestizo identity piqued the interest of foreigners who, like Dodge, wanted to see these cultures before they succumbed to commercialization.[75] The marginalization of indigenous communities in San Miguel meant that the Friends of San Miguel would have to rely on architecture as the town's primary distinguishing feature. Although the postrevolutionary valorization of indigeneity appeared to be in direct conflict with the celebration of Mexico's colonial heritage, they were actually two sides of the same coin. According to the national narrative, colonial missionaries had tamed the barbaric, often nomadic indigenous people in northern Mexico, taught them a sedentary lifestyle, and encouraged the agricultural and artistic production that the postrevolutionary government celebrated as folkloric. Thus San Miguel's architecture, which the state deemed politically significant during the Cristiada, also could play a culturally significant role in government attempts to develop a narrative of national progress. Consequently the colonial town became another archetype on the map of Mexico's diverse cultures.[76]

The Friends of San Miguel therefore recognized the need to demonstrate San Miguel's important colonial and early nineteenth-century past and emphasize that its essence had not changed since. Whereas buildings were the primary focus of the federal legislation, there was an implicit need to prove that the people had also stayed the same— that there had been no history since Allende's involvement in the independence movement. This focus was especially crucial in San Miguel because the town's recent history—riddled with counterrevolutionary violence, instability, and economic decline—contradicted the official national narrative of progress and unity. The Friends of San Miguel had to develop an account of San Miguel's past that minimized recent conflicts.

The Mexican historian Francisco de la Maza, who was Toussaint's protégé, took up this task in the 1939 book *San Miguel de Allende: Su historia, sus monumentos*. De la Maza's account portrayed a linear history of San Miguel's progress and contributions until the twentieth century, when according to de la Maza the city practically went dormant. This depiction of an upward trajectory followed by a period of latency reproduced the structure of Toussaint's work on Taxco and served as the basis for the argument for San Miguel's protection under federal law. The history began in 1542 with the arrival of the Franciscans, whom de la Maza depicted, based on the words of the Spanish chroniclers, as selfless, benevolent individuals who came to civilize the wandering nomads of the region.[77] De la Maza then traced the development of San Miguel's industries, especially the large-scale production of textiles and leather goods, to demonstrate the town's crucial role in the colonial economy. Next he provided the background of many of San Miguel's religious and civic buildings, fountains, and plazas, emphasizing their artistic value and colonial roots. Lastly he detailed the lives of prominent San Miguel residents, including those involved in the independence movement, nineteenth-century religious figures, architects, intellectuals, and even the Friends of San Miguel. Significantly, he glossed over the revolution and avoided mentioning the Cristiada and local conflicts over agrarian reforms and education altogether. In de la Maza's history Sanmiguelenses simply went about their daily lives as the rest of the country experienced violence and chaos. By eliding the conflicts and developments in twentieth-century San Miguel—the movement of people, the attempts to renew the stagnant economy, the corpses hanging in the plaza—de la Maza contributed to the perception that they did not taint San Miguel, and thereby it maintained its typical character.

The Ministry of Public Education did not approve San Miguel for protection under federal law, but the Guanajuato state legislature did.[78] In 1939 the legislature declared San Miguel a "typical town." Leobino Zavala, a state legislator, took credit for writing the decree.[79] The provisions of the decree were essentially the same as the federal law: new construction, restorations, signage, gas stations, garages, parking lots, vendors' stalls, and telephone, telegraph, and electrical lines were subject to the approval of a local vigilance committee. The committee included political appointees and elected members, with the stipulation that at least one member had to be a licensed architect. The decree stated that the municipal government must provide the committee with the support necessary to carry out its functions.[80]

State officials expressed concern over the authenticity of San Miguel's buildings and the local leaders' intentions prior to issuing the "typical town" decree. A report to the governor's office written by the Guanajuato historian Manuel Leal assured the governor that San Miguel remained one of the few cities in Mexico, along with Puebla and Querétaro, that had preserved their colonial heritage, unlike the majority, which had been "stupidly modernized." Leal advocated San Miguel as worthy of preservation, but he cautioned that success in that endeavor would depend on the vigilance committee's competence. The scholar feared that the committee would succumb to personal

Fig. 2. This image, circa 1880, shows the Parroquia and the Plaza Principal prior to the renovations by Zeferino Gutiérrez. Courtesy of the Archivo José Miguel Francisco Malo Zozaya.

tastes and faddish trends when establishing aesthetic standards for San Miguel, rather than preserving its authenticity.[81]

Leal's fears may have been well founded. He was certainly aware that other preservation movements often resulted in ersatz, commercialized tourist sites. Furthermore he recognized the transnational linkages between San Miguel and places such as California and New Mexico. Mojica, the main force behind the preservation efforts in San Miguel, had lived in Southern California while working in Hollywood and was quite familiar with the Franciscan missions that had inspired California's turn-of-the-century architectural and cultural movement known as the Mission Revival.[82] Indeed his friends described his San Miguel home as a California-style ranch house.[83] It is quite possible that California's Mission Revival inspired Mojica's projects in San Miguel, but ultimately Leal should have been more concerned with the fact that many of the San Miguel features he recognized as colonial had been renovated in the late nineteenth

Fig. 3. San Miguel's parish church, the Parroquia, 2007. Photograph by the author.

century. Notably, the most recognizable of San Miguel's "colonial" landmarks, the Parroquia and the plaza it faces, commonly known as the Jardín, had been completely refashioned only a few decades earlier, and the renovation imitated European styles in vogue during the Díaz regime. The local architect Zeferino Gutiérrez, under the direction of the regional Catholic hierarchy, had constructed a pink sandstone neo-Gothic façade for the Parroquia, and it was unlike anything else in Mexico. Uniformly pruned laurels, benches, and a bandstand filled in the previously open plaza.[84] Leal and others were willing to overlook certain inconsistencies in San Miguel's architectural milieu as long as they could continue to claim that it was more authentic than other Mexican towns.

Regardless of authenticity a coalition of local elites and newcomers successfully remade San Miguel into a typical Mexican town. Through a combination of international intellectual trends and local economic needs, this coalition developed a new narrative of San Miguel's history that placed it more squarely within the revolutionary state's narrative of national progress. Even though the federal government did not formally recognize San Miguel's preservation efforts in the 1930s, its new image would galvanize the local tourism industry in ways that the Friends of San Miguel likely never anticipated, beginning with the foundation of an art school.

Bellas Artes and the International Tourism Industry

In the summer of 1938 two men—one Peruvian and the other an American—opened the Escuela Universitaria de Bellas Artes (University School of Fine Arts, or Bellas Artes) in San Miguel. Twelve art students enrolled at the school for its first session. The following summer, enrollments at the art school topped one hundred. Local, state, and federal officials were instrumental in the initial development of Bellas Artes, but ultimately its success or failure depended on the extent to which foreigners bought into the narrative that the Friends of San Miguel had cultivated and the art school's directors had reproduced.

The Peruvian artist and intellectual Felipe Cossío del Pomar moved to San Miguel in 1937. He had originally visited the town several years earlier and eventually returned as Mojica's guest. Peru's governing military junta had forced Cossío del Pomar, a leading member of Peru's leftist American Popular Revolutionary Alliance (APRA), into exile. He crossed paths with Diego Rivera in the artist circles of prewar Paris and had long admired Mexico's relative tolerance for artistic expression and its more recent acceptance of leftist political exiles, particularly those from Spain. Cossío del Pomar envisioned San Miguel as a Mexican Bauhaus, an ideal location for aspiring artists to escape the responsibilities of daily life and to paint. Indeed many prominent artists and intellectuals passed through San Miguel during Cossío del Pomar's early years there, including Pablo Neruda, Gabriela Mistral, Jesús Silva Herzog, Rufino Tamayo, Federico Cantú, Carlos Mérida, Pablo O'Higgins, and José Chávez Morado.[85]

Cossío del Pomar and Friends of San Miguel leaders Mojica and Leobino Zavala met with the governor of Guanajuato, Luis I. Rodríguez, to discuss the establishment of an art school. The governor enthusiastically endorsed their endeavors, just as he would encourage San Miguel's designation as a typical town a year later; tangible support, however, would be minimal. After Cossío del Pomar located a building for his school—Las Monjas, the former convent converted into barracks and stables during the Cristiada—a mutual acquaintance arranged a meeting with President Cárdenas so that the Peruvian could personally ask permission to use the building. Cárdenas agreed to let him convert the building, but the president offered no financial support. Cossío del Pomar assured him that tuition from foreign students would create enough revenue for the school to support itself.[86]

Cossío del Pomar's vision inspired the creation of Bellas Artes, but the Chicago artist Stirling Dickinson was principally responsible for its success. Dickinson moved to San Miguel in 1937 after spending time in Mexico doing research for a book he was to illustrate, *Death Is Incidental*.[87] He too had initially visited San Miguel as Mojica's guest. They first met in Oaxaca, but Dickinson, an avid theater fan, had seen Mojica in films and operas in Chicago several years earlier. Before Bellas Artes opened its doors Cossío del Pomar appointed Dickinson associate director. Dickinson designed Bellas Artes's first promotional materials, in both English and Spanish. Together they distributed ten thousand brochures to universities and art schools throughout the United States, Canada, and Latin America.[88]

Early publicity efforts targeted Dickinson's social circles in Chicago and delineated how people in the United States would imagine San Miguel before many Americans had visited it. Indeed San Miguel did not appear in most tourist guidebooks and itineraries designed for American audiences and published through the 1930s, including *Frances Toor's Motorist Guide to Mexico*, published in 1938.[89] Anita Brenner's popular 1932 guidebook *Your Mexican Holiday* mentioned that San Miguel lacked modern hotels and was therefore "seldom visited."[90] Brief descriptions in railroad company travel guides and maps were the main sources of information for potential tourists. An 1892 Mexican National Railroad guide emphasized San Miguel's fresh springwater and the "modern spires" of the Parroquia, which "contrast strangely" with the rest of the town's architecture.[91] Later publications celebrated the Parroquia, San Miguel's "fine Gothic Cathedral," but focused on its unlikely architect, Zeferino Gutiérrez, "a native of the town who had never been out of his birthplace and had never had an hour of schooling. He could not read and had to draw his plans for the workmen using a pointed stick in plots of sand."[92] Many other travel guidebooks and advertisements have reproduced and elaborated versions of this story, including a 2005 Mexican government advertising campaign that claimed a postcard of a Belgian church inspired Gutiérrez's design.[93] Aside from these tidbits San Miguel was effectively unknown in the United States in the late 1930s.

Dickinson's advertising campaign targeted a very specific audience of foreign art students by placing San Miguel within the narrative constructed by de la Maza and the Friends of San Miguel. His publicity acumen was likely shaped by his father's work with a Chicago advertising agency. A 1937 travel feature in the *Chicago Daily Tribune* quoted Dickinson's description of San Miguel as "one of those 'undis-covered' towns you read about," a "typically Mexican" place where "life moves slowly after the fashion of long ago."[94] Dickinson cast himself as an intrepid explorer and discoverer of a Mexican village that time had forgotten. With this imagery he sought to pique the interest of artists and intellectuals on the lookout for the next bohemian cultural center. By the mid-1930s the most famous art colonies in the United States, such as those in Santa Fe and Taos, were becoming increasingly commercialized and popular as mainstream tourist destinations—and therefore less attractive to those in highbrow art circles.[95]

Dickinson's attempts to recruit this specific segment of the art com-munity became quite direct in 1938. Dickinson returned to Chicago to visit his parents and most likely to promote the school. Shortly after his visit the columnist Judith Cass placed a story about San Miguel and the art school front and center in the *Chicago Daily Tri-bune's* society pages. "San Miguel," Cass wrote, "undoubtedly will be included in the itineraries of many Americans who go to Mexico this summer, for the new art school there is attracting much attention." She also mentioned San Miguel's favorable summer climate and its location, much closer to the U.S. border than Mexico City. Finally, she included the names of two Chicagoans who had already left for the school.[96] With this article Cass (and Dickinson) wove a narrative about a San Miguel somewhat different from the undiscovered town described in the newspaper the year before. Now it was a cultural and tourist center, as well as a destination for well-known Chicago artists. Dickinson cleverly created a destination to appeal to both the bold traveler and the sophisticated artist.

In subsequent years Dickinson's promotional strategies placed San Miguel within the broader context of the Mexican tourism industry. In 1940 the *Chicago Daily Tribune* travel columnist Frederic Babcock wrote two articles after visiting Dickinson in San Miguel. Babcock contrasted Taxco with San Miguel, which, he wrote, was quite sim-ilar to Taxco but "ha[d] not been spoiled by 'invaders' from north of the border." Babcock also suggested that his readers (Chicagoans) had a special opportunity to discover San Miguel while it was "still unknown to most of the tourists."[97] Babcock's second 1940 article on San Miguel likewise framed a visit to the town as an opportunity for people to set themselves apart from average tourists and venture off the beaten path. Although San Miguel would surely "be discovered by the tourists" one day, in 1940, Babcock claimed, "the average American tourist [was] in too big a hurry to get to Mexico City" to explore places like San Miguel.[98]

The number of foreign art students in San Miguel steadily increased, testifying to the success of Dickinson's promotional campaign. The following years brought several changes to the town to accommodate the students—changes that laid the foundation for San Miguel's tourism infrastructure. In order to maintain and increase the numbers of these visitors the art school's founders had to meet numerous challenges, such as a lack of restaurants and limited housing options. During the first year Mojica offered meals for the students at his San Miguel home for a small fee. By the second year renovations at the school were complete. The new building included a fully staffed cooking facility and better studios, which accommodated more artists. Of the one hundred students enrolled at Bellas Artes during 1939 thirty stayed in the brand-new Posada de San Francisco, a hotel owned by a local entrepreneur, Ramón Zavala Camarena, brother of Leobino Zavala. Cossío del Pomar converted the former ranch of the bullfighter Pepe Ortíz into a guesthouse with an Olympic-sized swimming pool and a fronton court for playing jai alai. Many other students stayed with local families.[99]

When Governor Luís I. Rodríguez initially supported the idea of an art school in San Miguel, he anticipated the potential for financial dividends that would benefit the region. Economic challenges threatened the region's stability throughout the 1930s, and the state government eagerly sought new alternatives. Underemployment and low wages drove large numbers of individuals and families to emigrate from the state of Guanajuato, with many heading either south for Mexico City or north to the United States. During the late 1930s the Mexican federal government asked the Guanajuato governor to help repatriate Mexicans deported from the United States and urged him to discourage other Mexicans from leaving the country.[100] The repatriated workers only added to the strain on local economies. Construction work at San Miguel's art school and hotel and income from student boarders provided a boost for some families, but the initial economic benefits from the art school reached relatively few of San Miguel's residents and hardly made an impact on the broader regional economy.

Both state and federal officials saw potential for tourism in the state of Guanajuato beyond economic development. In the midst of escalating violence President Cárdenas sought other means of neutralizing opposition to his agrarian and educational policies, which had failed to take hold in northern Guanajuato. Although Guanajuato's governors during the Cárdenas administration, Enrique Fernández Martínez and Luis I. Rodríguez, were among the president's most loyal supporters, they were in hostile territory and often reacted accordingly. Violent confrontations between Guanajuato's Catholics and agraristas continued into the late 1930s.[101] Confronted with these persistent ideological divisions in the nation, Cárdenas sought other ways to bring the Mexican people together. The Cardenistas used tourism development as a counterbalance to more coercive methods of political control.

Cárdenas's tourism policies were an often overlooked attempt to unify Mexicans during the final years of his presidency. By supporting the development of tourism destinations, the Cárdenas administration provided the promise of economic development and contributed to a growing sense of pride in the Mexican nation and its place on the world stage. Moreover, he found proponents of his revolutionary programs among San Miguel's growing colony of foreign artists and intellectuals, starting with Cossío del Pomar and Dickinson.[102] By supporting the latter's desire to open an art school, the Cardenistas not only offered the community an economic alternative but also created an opportunity to increase the ranks of influential sympathizers.

International events offered additional incentive for Cárdenas's tourism development strategy. After nearly two decades of conflicts and negotiations with foreign oil companies, Cárdenas rallied Mexicans to claim the subsoil rights enshrined in the Constitution of 1917. Mexicans from all walks of life donated money, jewelry, and household items so that the Mexican government could compensate foreign oil companies for their petroleum operations at the values the companies set for tax purposes. Cárdenas nationalized the Mexican petroleum industry, consolidating all operations under the auspices of Petróleos Mexicanos (PEMEX).[103] The international response to the 1938 oil expropriations was mostly tepid. With Europe and Asia on the brink of war, the Roosevelt administration in the United States avoided major confrontations with Cárdenas over the expropriations. However, U.S. oil companies launched a major propaganda campaign warning Americans against travel in Mexico. They declared that widespread anti-Americanism and endemic gasoline shortages made travel south of the border difficult if not outright dangerous. The oil expropriations had a negative effect on tourism, with Nuevo Laredo seeing only half the level of tourist traffic in 1938 compared to the previous year.[104] Therefore Cárdenas's plans for Mexican tourism development also addressed the negative international fallout resulting from the Mexican oil expropriations. These plans culminated in Cárdenas's declaration of 1940–41 as the Mexican Tourism Biennial.[105] If people in places like San Miguel did not take pride in the accomplishments of the revolution, then perhaps, government officials hoped, they would take pride in the nation's tourism industry.

Despite the potential for a nationalist tourism industry that would ignite the patriotism of Sanmiguelenses, tepid government support and Dickinson's promotional strategies resulted in an industry that catered to foreign rather than Mexican tastes. By labeling San Miguel a "typical," "timeless" place, de la Maza, the Friends of San Miguel, the state legislature, and Dickinson overshadowed local histories of triumph and resistance. Just as national officials attempted to legitimate certain histories and claims to power based on the presumed success of the revolution, efforts to preserve San Miguel also privileged certain histories, sites, and traditions over others. As a result, local power shifted to those who crafted the narrative, because ultimately they would determine who would benefit from the new promotional and economic development strategies. The primary beneficiaries of San Miguel's designation as a typical town were the art school administrators and those with the capital to invest in hotels, restaurants, and shops.

Rather than a timeless town without a modern history, San Miguel was part of modern transformations at the national and international levels. But San Miguel's integration into the movements and transformations of so-called modern history had occurred much earlier, with its role in the colonial mining economy that sent silver and gold to Europe helping to spur the colonial and imperial adventures that often characterize the "modern Western world." Before that, San Miguel's pre-Hispanic history involved migratory patterns and trade routes that belie notions of timelessness and peoples without histories. Indeed San Miguel received the labels "backward" and "unmodern" not because it was either one but because it contradicted the revolutionary state's version of Mexican modernity. Even after the Friends of San Miguel incorporated the town into the state's narrative of Mexican history, San Miguel was to represent the nation's past, rather than its present or future.

The urge to preserve an imagined past, whether the effort was led by the state or by individuals, was often an integral component of the modernization process because it reaffirmed the progress of the modern world. "Typical towns" like San Miguel not only constructed a romanticized version of the past for tourist consumption but also served as a point of comparison to show how far Mexico had come. The new "typical town" designation suppressed modern histories of San Miguel with important consequences. It allowed newcomers to inscribe new meanings on the town and create their own histories, which often erased its native actors and the roles they played in opposing the revolutionary agenda. It was only a matter of time before some Sanmiguelenses challenged the dramatic changes unfolding before them.

2 Good Neighbors, Good Catholics, and Competing Visions

A room in the back corner of the eighteenth-century convent now generally known as Bellas Artes contains an intriguing piece of San Miguel history. Motion sensors trigger lights that dramatically reveal an unfinished mural on the vaulted ceiling and walls. The abstract artwork, titled *Vida y obra del Gral. Ignacio Allende*, contains geometric shapes and bold colors that were undoubtedly intended to convey the potency and symbolic virility of one of the fathers of the nation. The mural itself is an important example of mid-twentieth-century experimentation with emerging theories about the integration of architecture and art (*integración plástica*), but the artist behind it is the real attraction. The acclaimed Mexican muralist David Alfaro Siqueiros began and abruptly abandoned the mural in 1949, when the site housed the Escuela Universitaria de Bellas Artes. By most accounts a combination of Siqueiros's notorious temper and the greed and incompetence of the school's director, Alfredo Campanella, contributed to the artist's sudden departure. While these factors certainly played a role, these accounts miss the broader context surrounding the mural. The dispute between Siqueiros and Campanella—two relative outsiders in San Miguel—was a flashpoint in what amounted to a local culture war over the town's very future.

Over the course of the 1940s various groups and actors articulated

Fig. 4. Detail of *Vida y obra del Gral. Ignacio Allende*, David Alfaro Siqueiros, 1949. Photograph by the author, 2010.

different visions for San Miguel in a debate that would come to a head in 1949. On the one hand local boosters and government officials enthusiastically continued to pursue new paths to tourism development. They relied on the new typical town designation and San Miguel's off-the-beaten-path appeal to attract visitors, including a large number of foreigners. Following World War II hundreds of veterans arrived in San Miguel eager to spend their GI Bill stipends at the art school. The local tourism infrastructure steadily expanded to meet these new demands. Although there were bumps in the road, on the surface it seemed as though the vision of the Friends of San Miguel was proceeding according to the group's carefully laid plans. On the other hand the parish priest and many of his devout followers feared that San Miguel was headed in the wrong direction. After decades of religious repression local Catholics fervently pushed to reassert their influence. They viewed an influx of foreign artists and travelers as a threat to their dream for a modern, Mexican, Catholic nationalism. With such conflicting visions for San Miguel's present and future it was only a matter of time before conflict would erupt. The dispute between Campanella and Siqueiros served as a catalyst for a boycott of San Miguel's art school. The boycott divided the town into opposing factions, exposed long-standing grievances, and threatened San Miguel's tourism industry. An examination of the actors and events leading up to this dramatic climax reveals the extent to which San Miguel's identity, and the identity of Mexico as a whole, was subject to debate for much of the 1940s. The resolution of the boycott at the end of the decade, however, demonstrates that the terms of the debate had narrowed significantly, and tourism would prevail.

Foreign Visions of San Miguel

The 1940s were a particularly propitious time for reimagining Mexico's place in the world, with both international and domestic relations in flux. Government officials, tourism promoters, and cultural producers took advantage of this moment to portray Mexico in a new way. Rather than focusing on pastoral representations of indigenous,

41

rural Mexico, these varied interests increasingly emphasized Mexico's modernity and urban cosmopolitanism.[1] In some respects this emphasis was a continuation of late nineteenth-century efforts to make Mexico seem more accessible to foreigners.[2] In the 1940s this changing focus was not merely rhetorical or representational. It also constituted an ideological shift within Mexico's governing political party away from Cárdenas's agrarian-reform–oriented Party of the Mexican Revolution (PRM). Party officials literally institutionalized this shift in 1946 when they adopted a new name: the Institutional Revolutionary Party (PRI). While these efforts repackaged Mexico as a modernizing nation, one that was safe for tourist travel—and, more important, foreign investment—many potential visitors nonetheless sought the experience that only rural, provincial Mexico could provide, as a counterpoint to their own modern, cosmopolitan lives.

San Miguel was one of the provincial Mexican towns that filled this void. While it is undeniable that foreign visitors were more likely to visit San Miguel because of Mexico's new, safe image abroad, these travelers often went to Mexico with motives more similar to those of their predecessors in the 1920s and early 1930s than of typical tourists in the 1940s.[3] They sought out artistic inspiration and intellectual stimulation in the bucolic countryside, as well as adventures on less traveled roads. San Miguel also attracted ordinary Americans who hoped to become informal diplomats through tourism in Latin America, as well as war veterans who studied at the art school on the GI Bill. Through their letters home and articles in the travel sections of local newspapers, these individuals helped perpetuate the image of a quaint, old-fashioned Mexico alongside the ever more prevalent representations of a modern, sophisticated nation.

Located near the geographic center of Mexico, San Miguel had neither pristine beaches nor bright city lights to draw tourists. The town of approximately nine thousand inhabitants was quite literally off the beaten path of tourist traffic in the early 1940s.[4] Uncharted in most tourist guidebooks and on motorist maps in the early 1940s, the route to San Miguel was arduous enough to deter most potential foreign visitors. The few unpaved roads leading to the town were often impassable during the long rainy season, and even during the rest of the year there were steep mountain grades to climb and watercourses to ford.[5] Although the newly touted Pan-American Highway would take motorists part of the way, one guidebook still recommended that travelers first go to Mexico City or Querétaro and then complete their voyage to San Miguel by train.[6] It was not until the 1950s that paved roads connected San Miguel to the Pan-American Highway and to other cities in the region. Indeed the American writer Hudson Strode claimed that San Miguel was the "least visited of all the lovely places in Mexico" and admitted that he had bypassed the town more than three times himself before finally visiting in 1942. Even then Strode did so only because a Mexican friend arranged for him to use a private rail car.[7] The train made its only stop at the San Miguel station in the dark predawn. Like Stirling Dickinson and Emigdio Ledesma Pérez, most visitors found their first impression of the town quite disheartening. The train station was actually just a simple wooden platform. There was nothing in sight—no lights, no buildings, and no people. The only mode of transportation into town was a dilapidated, mule-driven *tranvía*, or streetcar, that sometimes was waiting at the station and other times did not arrive at all. The straw-filled tires lurched and wobbled up the cobblestone hill into town, as the mules labored under the weight of the new cargo. Inevitably, though, the sun would break on the horizon, revealing San Miguel's profile in the soft light. Church bells would peal in a startling but welcome end to the uncomfortable silence. By most accounts this arrival experience provided just the sort of adventure that travelers sought, constituting the beginning of a love affair with the town.[8]

Those who ventured to San Miguel differed from other tourists not only in their choice of destination but also in their overall experience of Mexico. Because most foreign visitors to San Miguel were art students, they usually stayed for several months to complete a summer or winter session at Bellas Artes. Both men and women came bearing large trunks filled with art supplies since paints, brushes, canvas, and easels were scarce in San Miguel. They also packed light clothing and a raincoat for the temperate weather and the seasonal afternoon showers. Most Bellas Artes students were young and single, although some couples also attended. Students typically spent five or six mornings each week in the art studios and workshops, and most also enrolled in the school's afternoon Spanish classes. Art courses ranged from the so-called fine arts of landscape and figure painting to popular arts such as weaving and woodcarving.[9] Many students left their mark on the walls of Bellas Artes by collaborating on one of its murals, including the Siqueiros mural. Some students were beginners, trying their hand at different artistic methods for the first time. Others were accomplished artists and critics who eventually joined the teaching staff. The American Katharine Kuh spent time painting and teaching at Bellas Artes before returning to work at the Art Institute of Chicago. She eventually wrote several books about art and served as the art editor for the *Saturday Review*.[10] The Mexican artist Rufino Tamayo also went to San Miguel to paint and ended up teaching at Bellas Artes, as did Leonard Brooks, James Pinto, and many others. Perhaps it was this distinction—between typical tourists and those in San Miguel whose presence was prolonged, if not permanent—that gave the latter group a sense of ownership over the town and a stake in its future.

Although artists and intellectuals from across Latin America and even Europe gathered at the San Miguel homes of the Peruvian intellectual Felipe Cossío del Pomar and Mexican film star José Mojica in the 1930s, by the early 1940s the largest group of foreign visitors consisted of art students from the United States and Canada. Illinois-native Dickinson's initial promotional efforts in the Chicago area ensured that midwesterners were the overwhelming majority in Bellas Artes's earliest summer cohorts, but knowledge about San Miguel soon spread to artists in other parts of the United States and Canada. The number of articles about San Miguel in three major U.S. newspapers in 1940 alone nearly matched the coverage from the entire previous decade, and media attention continued to expand throughout the

1940s.[11] Despite the difficult travel conditions, demand for the school's summer session quickly exceeded capacity, and by 1940 Cossío del Pomar and Dickinson had decided to initiate a winter session as well.[12] Through a combination of official promotional efforts and word of mouth, San Miguel's international reputation as a tourist destination and cultural center began to flourish.

Alongside Dickinson's efforts the Friends of San Miguel accelerated their own promotional activities in anticipation of the town's fourth centennial in 1942. While Dickinson primarily was concerned with attracting foreign students, the Friends focused on potential domestic tourists. A guidebook the group published, with an English-language section likely written by Dickinson, highlights the different strategies they used to target each constituency. The Spanish-language section draws heavily from de la Maza's history of San Miguel, with an emphasis on the colonial past, the role of Ignacio Allende as the "forgotten hero" of the independence movement, and religious and other historic architecture. The text erases all conflict from the town's past and notably does not address historical events after the 1810 independence movement. The guidebook encourages potential visitors, "No vaya a San Miguel por horas, vaya por días," and with a long list of potential sites to visit and fiestas to attend, it makes a strong case that a day trip would not be sufficient to enjoy all that San Miguel has to offer. The homes of San Miguel's elite families (particularly those with ties to the Friends) receive special mention, as do the hotels, guesthouses, and other travel-related businesses that those families owned. It is clear that the Friends not only shared a sense of patriotism and reverence for San Miguel's past but also had an economic stake in the expansion of the tourism industry and therefore in a very specific version of the past.[13]

The appeal to English-language readers echoed the rhetoric in the art school promotional texts and portrayed San Miguel as historic and, more important, a place conducive to discovery and exploration. In this account the details of San Miguel's history and the history of its buildings are intentionally vague and Mexicans are nearly absent.

Allende receives only a cursory (and inaccurate) mention. One passage glosses over a century of history without including any historical actors aside from the town itself: "Since 1810 San Miguel has seen other revolutions; it has also seen the building of palatial mansions, and their partial disintegration; the erection of fine cathedrals, and the development of great haciendas, many now in ruins."[14] The list of historic homes leaves out the roll call of San Miguel's Mexican elite and instead names the residences of newcomers such as Pepe Ortíz and José Mojica and the foreigners Cossío del Pomar, Dickinson, and an ophthalmologist, Dr. Thomas A. Winslow. According to this account, historic sites and Mexican homes are merely a "starting point," because "San Miguel can best be enjoyed by walking through its narrow cobblestoned streets, climbing its hillsides, poking into its byways and enjoying the hundreds of details which make it Mexico's most beautiful colonial town."[15] For the foreign visitor San Miguel is historic, but the details of that history are insignificant. More important in this rendering is that the detritus of that history was ripe for exploration and adventure.

If foreigners were looking for an adventure, they were likely to find it in 1940s San Miguel. By 1942 there were several long-term housing options available including three hotels and multiple guesthouses with "modern" conveniences, but hotel owners applied the word quite liberally and often did not meet the foreign guests' standards. Hot water and private bathrooms, for example, were luxuries of which few establishments could boast. Only a limited number of cars or telephones could be found in San Miguel, but almost everything was within easy walking distance for those who did not mind the hilly, cobblestoned streets. Students could rent a house with a live-in maid and gardener for the equivalent of about ten U.S. dollars a month, but the accommodations were unlikely to have electricity or indoor plumbing.[16] Like most *sanmiguelenses*, they had to collect water from one of the numerous stone fountains on San Miguel's street corners. Upon describing the challenges that Stirling Dickinson faced with his own San Miguel home, a newspaper columnist quipped, "Perhaps

Dickinson's old home in Chicago's Astor [S]treet has a few more conveniences, but we doubt it was half as much fun."[17]

Foreign visitors willingly traded the material comforts of home for the sense of adventure and an inspiring, picturesque setting. Many U.S. travel writers reproduced the narrative the Friends of San Miguel had developed about San Miguel's architecture, using phrases like "unspoiled colonial town" or "crowned with ancient towers and belfries" to entice potential tourists. They also adopted the trope of the sleepy, timeless town and participated in the erasure of the violence that had plagued San Miguel in the previous decades, insisting that "life in the town has changed little since those early [colonial] days" and that the people always have "a song on their lips and laughter in their eyes."[18] Not all visitors were convinced that the town remained unchanged across the centuries. Hudson Strode, for example, observed, "The town's exterior had not remained wholly a museum, any more than Allende's drawing room," a reference to the fact that the former home of the Mexican independence hero Ignacio Allende was a pharmacy at the time of his visit (and also a direct shot at Anita Brenner's guidebook, which claimed that "the whole town is a museum piece").[19] But Strode was an exception, and his skepticism about the state of San Miguel's historic preservation did not prevent him from being charmed by the beautiful hillside town.

The travel writers' descriptions were specific enough to direct potential visitors yet generic enough to fit San Miguel within the broader understanding of the typical provincial town. Images of San Miguel, specifically the view looking down on the town from the hills above, placed the town squarely within this discursive field. Such a view centered on a prominent bell tower and drew upon a tradition of nostalgia for the serenity of village life. This discursive framework dates to the late eighteenth century and encompasses British landscape artists, French romanticism, and the moving panorama shows that John Banvard popularized in late nineteenth-century America, as well as the contemporary cinematic representations of the Mexican countryside in the films of the Mexican director Emilio "El Indio"

Fig. 5. Women approaching San Miguel. Photograph by Cecil B. Atwater, published in *National Geographic*, 1953.

Fig. 6. Stirling Dickinson, 1957. Photograph by Peter Olwyler, courtesy of Michael Olwyler.

Fernández.[20] While these representations may have invoked nostalgia for some, for others they legitimated the expansion of a "modern" way of life, with foreigners leading the way.[21]

One of the most iconic images of San Miguel is a scenic view with two women walking down a steep, narrow, cobblestoned street in the foreground, with the town, the Parroquia, and the surrounding countryside in the background (see fig. 5).[22] The American photographer Cecil B. Atwater captures the rebozo-clad women from behind and presents them as part of the landscape rather than as actors. Several other foreigners, including Hudson Strode and Peter Olwyler, have

49

attempted variations of this scene. Foreigners play a very active role in most of these images, facing the camera and climbing up the hill as if they were conquering it and, by extension, the entire town.[23] By contrasting the passive, presumably "native" women with the active foreigners, these images visually reinforce the idea that the foreign visitors were discovering, and bringing modernity to, a timeless town.

World War II created an additional incentive for foreigners to travel to San Miguel. As one *Chicago Tribune* columnist noted, schools such as Bellas Artes were an affordable alternative for Americans and Canadians who had hoped to study art in Europe.[24] But more than just a second choice, travel to Mexico in the context of war became a politically charged act. U.S. foreign policy officials encouraged Americans to establish greater bonds with Latin Americans by studying their language and culture and engaging in tourism.[25] These experiences, U.S. officials believed, would foster cultural understanding among the American nations and increase the likelihood of unity in the face of the Axis threat. Schools like Bellas Artes thus became an important front in the war against fascism.

The U.S. government's patriotic call to improve cultural relations with Latin America in the late 1930s became the centerpiece of the Good Neighbor policy. U.S. officials developed the foundations of what would become the Good Neighbor policy in the late 1920s, when they realized that political and military interventions in Latin America were harming the United States' image abroad. In his 1933 inaugural address President Franklin Delano Roosevelt committed the United States to "the policy of the good neighbor," explicitly citing non-intervention as a policy goal. Proponents of the Good Neighbor policy foregrounded the ideals of pan-Americanism, which dated to the nineteenth century and held that the people of the Americas should "stand in special relationship to one another which sets them apart from the rest of the world."[26] U.S. government officials initially understood this "special relationship" to encompass trade agreements and diplomatic relations, but as German economic interests gained influence in Latin America the Good Neighbor policy expanded to include cultural relations. A change in how ordinary Americans imagined their role in fostering hemispheric unity accompanied this shift. Once the realm of diplomats and business people, the work of communicating and cooperating with Latin Americans entered the domain of educators, tourists, and students.[27]

Bellas Artes welcomed its first students to San Miguel in 1938, the same year that the German military mobilized in Europe and U.S. officials debated the extent to which cultural relations should be politicized as part of the larger foreign policy program. By 1940 President Roosevelt had approved a political cultural program under the auspices of the Office of the Coordinator of Inter-American Affairs (OCIAA).[28] Art played a central role from the beginning. The OCIAA sponsored art tours of Mexico, and Nelson Rockefeller, the OCIAA director, arranged the largest exhibition of Mexican art ever seen in the United States, at the Museum of Modern Art in New York.[29] The war converted studying art in a Mexican town into a patriotic experiment in hemispheric relations.

Stirling Dickinson selected promotional language that reinforced the ideals of the Good Neighbor policy. He proclaimed that San Miguel had "already become a center for the cultural union of the Americas" and that it "welcomes those who believe that a true Pan Americanism can only become a reality through sincere cooperation and understanding between the peoples of this hemisphere."[30] He addressed the war more directly in the 1943 Bellas Artes catalog when he reassured potential students that, despite the war, "Mexico has never been safer for travel or study" and that "Mexico's position as an ally of the United States has further cemented the very cordial relations existing between the two countries."[31] One observer commented on the harmonious relationship between tourists and Sanmiguelenses. "The art colony lives side-by-side—and indeed mingles with—the native population," the journalist declared, and "artists and tourists [join] with the townsmen in song and dance and feasting."[32] From these accounts it seemed that the metaphorical Good Neighbor of policy debates could actually exist in San Miguel.

Many Mexicans from San Miguel and the surrounding region had a very different experience of the Good Neighbor policy. While the Friends of San Miguel and Dickinson touted the tourism industry as a panacea for the local economy and a path to inter-American harmony, the number of Mexicans who left San Miguel and other communities in the region in search of better employment opportunities in the United States reached an all-time high. This exodus was mainly due to the Bracero program, through which American employers contracted Mexican labor to meet wartime domestic production needs and depress labor costs. Moreover, Guanajuato sent more migrants to the United States than any other state in Mexico during the Bracero program.[33] For those individuals and the families they left behind, physical labor, rather than art, constituted the core of the Good Neighbor policy in action. The economic benefits of migration allowed many to send money back to their families and to climb the social ladder in Mexico. But migrants frequently faced discrimination and racial prejudice in the United States, and those experiences shaped how they viewed Mexicanness and U.S.-Mexican relations when they returned to Mexico.[34] There was a serious disjuncture between the rhetoric of the Good Neighbor policy and the reality of that policy for most Mexicans.

The exigencies of war further prevented the lofty ideals of the Good Neighbor policy from becoming reality. Although American students increasingly inquired about San Miguel in travel advice columns and in letters to U.S. State Department officials, Bellas Artes recruited more Latin American students and adjusted the course schedule to meet pre–Pearl Harbor enrollment levels.[35] Wartime travel restrictions and censorship laws curbed the flow of tourists across the U.S.-Mexican border.[36] Moreover, the war personally affected both the director and the associate director of Bellas Artes, leaving the school's future uncertain. Dickinson enlisted and served in Mexico as an intelligence agent for the U.S. Navy and later the Office of Strategic Services.[37] Felipe Cossío del Pomar returned to his native Peru after years in exile. In 1945 he sold Bellas Artes and his San Miguel ranch to Alfredo

Campanella, a Mexico City lawyer.[38] Plans for San Miguel to be a model of good neighborliness between Mexico and the United States were temporarily placed on hold.

The U.S. government soon provided San Miguel with another opportunity to foster inter-American relations. In 1944 the U.S. Congress passed the Servicemen's Readjustment Act, more commonly known as the GI Bill of Rights, aimed at providing aid to returning World War II veterans. The Canadian government passed similar legislation. In 1946 the Veterans Administration expanded the program overseas, enabling veterans to use their educational stipends at approved foreign institutions. Dickinson and Campanella, who was the new owner and director of the school, saw the GI Bill as an extraordinary opportunity to attract a steady stream of students who theoretically had a reliable source of income to pay tuition.[39] They revised the curriculum to offer courses year round, meeting the relatively low bar for VA approval. They also continued to offer art courses in English, thereby making Bellas Artes accessible to those veterans with no formal Spanish training, unlike many other approved schools in Mexico. Additionally, because the cost of living in San Miguel was significantly lower than in Mexico City, enrolled veterans could stretch their stipends a little further. Finally, as a veteran himself, Dickinson was well positioned to help them navigate the bureaucracy in the United States and Mexico, giving personalized attention that they were unlikely to find elsewhere. News of the charming Mexican art school quickly spread, and during the summer of 1946 American and Canadian veterans began to arrive in San Miguel.[40]

The veterans made an immediate impression on the town. The GI Bill quickly brought the school back up to enrollments of more than one hundred students per session, and now they were in San Miguel throughout the year. According to Dickinson, in that first year Bellas Artes received more than six thousand applications from veterans, which he and an assistant screened in search of those who seemed the most serious about studying art.[41] A stroll around the small town would have revealed just how pervasive the veterans were. The

Canadian artist and war veteran Leonard Brooks was a fixture in the Bellas Artes studios, first as a student but eventually as an instructor. He and his wife, Reva, originally intended to stay in Mexico for eleven months before Brooks returned to his teaching position at the Northern Vocational School in Toronto. After arriving at San Miguel's train station, the Brookses second-guessed their decision to go to Mexico. Once they reached the town center, however, Leonard proclaimed, "We haven't made a mistake." The Brookses never left San Miguel.[42] The Hotel San Miguel and the Posada San Francisco, both a few blocks from Bellas Artes, were usually the next stop for arriving veterans. During the day veterans spread throughout the town with easels and palettes, trying to capture the local scenery on canvas. The evenings brought most of the art students to the main plaza, where they listened to mariachis or drank at La Cucaracha, a local cantina. At the baseball field and the Frontón Club on the outskirts of town, veterans frequently participated in competitive leagues against local Mexican teams. Some afternoons passersby could witness a truly unusual sight in San Miguel's newly renovated bullring: the young, blonde veteran from Chicago, Dotty Birk, who became a *picador* after a dare. It was scandalous move in a town where single women from "decent" families rarely even wore pants or left their homes without chaperones.[43]

Although the veterans tended to socialize with each other, they also attempted to learn about Mexican culture and integrate into San Miguel society. Most veterans attended the Spanish classes Leobino Zavala taught at Bellas Artes and joined the excursions Dickinson led to the Mexican countryside and nearby towns. In the classroom many students studied with prominent Mexican artists. Perhaps the best evidence of the Good Neighbor policy at work, however, was the number of American and Canadian art students in San Miguel who married Mexicans. Of course marriages between Mexicans and foreigners (particularly marriages between Spanish immigrants and Sanmiguelenses) predated the arrival of the veterans. Matthew and Amalia Beckmann are widely recognized as having had the first marriage between an

American and a Mexican in San Miguel, although they were married in the United States before moving to San Miguel in 1931.[44] However, Felipe Cossío del Pomar recalled that since its earliest days Bellas Artes had functioned as a sort of marriage agency, with few of the female Mexican employees remaining single for more than a year. He also observed that romances leading to marriage tended to flourish in homes that hosted foreign students.[45] Stirling Dickinson reportedly facilitated these cross-cultural relationships by inviting veterans and eligible young Mexican women to cocktail parties at his home.[46] Many of the inquiries he received later on also included requests for him to arrange marriages with Mexican women. One American man, for instance, expressed a preference for a "16 years [sic] old girl" who spoke English and "who wants to get married."[47] Dotty Birk was one of the first American women to marry a Mexican, wedding Francisco Vidargas in 1948. They met at San Miguel's Frontón Club through the bowling league, although the young blonde probably first caught his eye in the bullring.[48] At least fifty marriages between foreigners and Sanmiguelenses occurred in the decade that followed.

By the summer of 1948 nearly one thousand U.S. veterans were studying in Mexico, and nearly 20 percent of those were in San Miguel.[49] A January 1948 article in *Life* magazine was partly responsible for the record number of applications to Bellas Artes that summer session. The piece labeled San Miguel a "GI Paradise" where "veterans go to study art, live cheaply and have a good time." The magazine spread featured several photographs of the students and the town, including a full-page image of two male students sketching a nude female model with the Parroquia in the background. The students worked hard and played hard, the article noted, and "when the parties are too successful, the parish priest floods the village the next day with pamphlets sternly condemning the revelry as unseemly."[50] The article dismissed that parish priest's rants as a comical part of Mexican life, but, as the veterans soon learned, many other Sanmiguelenses shared his sentiments. Bellas Artes students had faced hostilities from locals since the school first opened. Cossío del Pomar recalled asking the governor to send police to protect students who were painting outside from being stoned. The school administrators also had to recommend that female students refrain from wearing pants to avoid offending local sensibilities.[51] Tensions escalated with the influx of veterans. Much like the Good Neighbor policy rhetoric of the war years, the *Life* article portrayed a reality in San Miguel that few Mexicans in the town would have recognized. Moreover, the increased attention the article brought to San Miguel also led to rapid inflation of prices for everything from rentals to food. The dissonance between image and reality eventually led to a conflict that would threaten the students' GI Bill subsidies, not to mention San Miguel's future as a tourist destination.

José Mercadillo's Alternate Vision for San Miguel

Just as the 1940s were an auspicious period for Mexico's tourism industry, the decade was also a stirring moment for Mexican Catholicism. After nearly two decades of government-led anticlericalism Mexican president-elect Manuel Ávila Camacho signaled a shift in official policy through his public declaration of faith. Although the rights of Mexican Catholics were not absolute, the relative détente between church and state allowed Catholics more freedom to practice their faith and participate in public religious rituals.[52] After the violent history of religious repression in San Miguel since the 1920s, this change ushered in a sense of joy and possibility. Parish priest José Mercadillo Miranda used this opportunity to revitalize Catholicism in the region. Employing the language of historic preservation and tourism development that had proven effective at garnering local political and financial support, Mercadillo revived a tradition of religious retreats in San Miguel that drew thousands of Mexican pilgrims. Through these gatherings Mercadillo offered a vision for San Miguel based on intense nationalism and strict adherence to a very conservative interpretation of Catholic mores, an extreme counterpoint to the image propagated by San Miguel's tourism boosters, not to mention the cosmopolitan version of Mexican modernity offered by Mexican government officials.

When Mercadillo arrived in San Miguel in 1933, few probably imagined the influence he would have on the town. State law permitted towns the size of San Miguel only one practicing priest, so the priest already there, Enrique Larrea, charged Mercadillo with organizing the activities of San Miguel's Catholic lay groups. As a self-fashioned worldly Renaissance man, however, Mercadillo had grander ambitions. And at a time when lay groups played a major role in organizing Catholics against the anticlerical regime, Mercadillo was positioned to make an impact.[53]

Mercadillo was a Guanajuato native, born in the state capital in 1908. He entered a seminary in the nearby city of León when he was twelve and came of age during the turbulent Cristiada.[54] According to his nephew, a federal soldier nearly murdered Mercadillo in the town of Irapuato because he was a priest. The soldier supposedly spared Mercadillo only because he recognized him as his son's teacher.[55] Following this incident Mercadillo fled Mexico, traveling by boat from Tampico. He completed his studies for the priesthood in San Antonio, Texas, and traveled in Europe before returning to Mexico in the early 1930s. Over the course of his theological training and travels Mercadillo claimed to have studied English, French, Portuguese, Italian, Latin, and Greek, and he also dabbled in medicine, music, art, and poetry. He opened a medical clinic to serve needy parishioners soon after his arrival in San Miguel. In 1936 Larrea, the parish priest in San Miguel, received permission from state authorities to appoint Mercadillo his assistant because his failing health prevented him from carrying out his duties. By 1939 Mercadillo had assumed full responsibilities as the new parish priest.[56]

Mercadillo arrived in San Miguel around the same time as José Mojica, and it is likely that the historic preservation activities of the Friends of San Miguel inspired Mercadillo's own projects around the city. Mercadillo and the resurgence of Catholicism in Mexico probably also influenced Mojica, who in the early 1940s left Mexico and became a Franciscan in Lima, Peru.[57] In 1940 the new parish priest sought permission from federal officials to restore the interior of the Parroquia to its original grandeur. Mercadillo claimed that altars, arches, and columns inside the church had been whitewashed and that removal of the alkaline material would reveal the true beauty of the *cantera* beneath.[58] Nevertheless, his commitment to historic preservation was questionable. Mercadillo commissioned a mural on one wall that parishioners summarily rejected, and he added his own artistic renderings of biblical stories to several other church walls. The local historian and Mercadillo biographer Antonio Ruíz Valenzuela claims that the priest studied fresco techniques under his distant cousin, Diego Rivera, but Mercadillo never made this claim in his own writings. Moreover, it would not be much of a tribute to Rivera.[59] When federal authorities raised questions as to whether the paintings in the Parroquia would threaten its new protected status, Mercadillo explained that he painted on wooden panels to avoid damaging the original walls. Furthermore, he challenged the judgment of the federal inspector of colonial monuments assigned to San Miguel and claimed that the bureaucrat rarely visited the town and frequently submitted false reports.[60]

Plans for a celebration of San Miguel's fourth centennial in 1942 provided Mercadillo with an opportunity to show off his work in the Parroquia and assert his presence among Catholics in the region. Whereas José Mojica and the Friends of San Miguel focused on restoring San Miguel's dilapidated bullring, the public park, and the main square, Mercadillo led efforts to commission and erect a statue of Fray Juan de San Miguel, the city's Franciscan founder.[61] The process involved much bureaucracy, fundraising, and negotiation about the location for the statue, but Mercadillo seemed to relish the attention and excitement the project generated. He reached out to Catholics around the state for financial support and solicited the regional Catholic hierarchy's opinions on possible sculptors and statue designs.[62] Mercadillo also informed Sanmiguelenses living in Mexico City of the upcoming fourth centennial, and they established committees dedicated to making the festivities as grand as possible.[63]

The celebration took place in October 1942 and, owing to Mercadillo's prominent role, became both a civic and a religious spectacle. Mercadillo organized the Inter-Parish Eucharistic Congress of Christ the King (Congreso Eucarístico Interparroquial de Cristo Rey) to run in conjunction with the festivities, inviting Catholics from across the region to participate in its sessions, which covered religious and secular topics. He even invited the historian Francisco de la Maza to be a guest presenter on San Miguel's historic traditions.[64] The archbishop of Mexico, the archbishop of Morelia, and the bishop of León, as well as several Mexican Supreme Court justices, presided over the dedication ceremony for the Fray Juan de San Miguel statue, which, after much debate, was erected in front of the Parroquia.[65] As the historian Peter Reich has observed, the extraordinary participation of both religious and civil authorities in the ceremony even caught the attention of the Mexico City daily *Excelsior*.[66] The crowd filled San Miguel's main plaza, the Jardín. The fourth centennial celebration was a huge success, and Mercadillo's reputation spread. He used the network he had built around the celebration to fuel his next big project: the renovation of the Sanctuary of Atotonilco.

The sanctuary, located approximately fourteen kilometers outside San Miguel, holds a storied place in the Mexican independence narrative, but it is historically significant to Mexican Catholics for other reasons as well. Best known as the place where Miguel Hidalgo y Costilla obtained the banner of the Virgin of Guadalupe that he used to rally followers against Spanish colonial rule in 1810, it was also the destination for thousands of pilgrims. The Oratorian priest Luis Felipe Neri de Alfaro founded the sanctuary in the eighteenth century as a place of prayer and penitence. The complex included a number of chapels, quarters to house and feed the pilgrims, medical facilities, and administrative offices. The faithful came by the thousands from across Mexico throughout most of the nineteenth century to participate in the Ignatian spiritual exercises led by Alfaro and his successors. Like all other religious buildings, the complex faced closure by the Calles Law in 1926, and after that it served as quarters for federal troops. When the Cristiada ended, "bandits" sacked the buildings and stole many religious artifacts. Although the Mexican government returned the sanctuary to the Catholic hierarchy in the 1930s, there were neither sufficient resources nor a political climate amenable to its restoration during that decade.[67]

According to Mercadillo, Bishop Emeterio Valverde y Téllez of León approached him in 1943 about reopening the sanctuary for seminary retreats. They later agreed to reinitiate the spiritual exercises, and Mercadillo embarked on his largest project yet.[68] Mercadillo eased federal officials' concerns regarding his activities by claiming he was merely restoring an important monument to Mexico's independence. He supervised the restoration of the sanctuary, including its murals, which Alfaro had originally commissioned from the artist Antonio Martínez de Pocasangre. As word spread about the revival of the retreats, Mercadillo received inquiries from parish priests and other Catholic leaders across Mexico. The majority of pilgrims came from the states of Guanajuato, Jalisco, México, Hidalgo, and Querétaro. Mercadillo negotiated special rail rates for the thousands of Catholics who made the trek to Atotonilco. The retreats aimed to strengthen and renew the pilgrims' faith after nearly two decades of religious repression. They typically lasted up to a week, and the visitors paid a small fee for room and board. Mercadillo's writings do not address the retreat program in detail except to state that he followed the spiritual exercises of Saint Ignatius of Loyola. The historian Jorge F. Hernández has observed that with the exception of their attire, modern-day pilgrims at the sanctuary could have been from two centuries earlier.[69] He also speculated that the medical facilities on the premises were not intended to treat random, minor illnesses but rather the complications that emerged from the spiritual exercises, wryly noting "eight days of self-flagellation and little food could logically make anyone sick."[70] During Lent the sanctuary often accommodated crowds of seven thousand to eight thousand people. Mercadillo claimed these were the largest Catholic retreats of their kind in the world.[71] The retreats attract thousands each week to this day.

The prospect of thousands of pilgrims coming to Atotonilco alarmed both Mexican and American political officials. By the 1940s the National Synarchist Union (UNS), which formed in 1937 in León, Guanajuato, had become a threatening presence in central Mexico. The UNS was a right-wing, nationalist, populist, anticommunist Catholic movement that mobilized tens of thousands of Mexicans across the socioeconomic spectrum. Because it emerged in the context of the Spanish Civil War and the rise of Hitler in Germany, opponents in the Mexican government portrayed the UNS as fascist. Scholars have debated whether the organization was actually fascist, and their debate centered on the paradox that, as one study put it, "the sinarquista movement sought a fascist end, but refused to apply fascist means."[72] Regardless of the organization's actual orientation, the UNS was under the constant surveillance of both the Mexican and U.S. governments, especially following the December 1941 attack on Pearl Harbor. Officials in both countries feared that the UNS could form a fifth column in Mexico and exert a strong presence among Mexican and Mexican American populations in the United States. While the organization did count Mexicans in the United States among its largest donors, its influence did not pose a serious danger beyond Mexico's borders.[73]

Although the sanctuary did not have a formal relationship with the UNS, its location in the heart of UNS territory led the Mexican government to consider any mass peregrination of Catholics a potential threat. Most cities and towns in Guanajuato had a UNS presence, although according to the best estimates, the size and participation levels in each place varied widely. San Miguel fell in the middle of the spectrum between the years of 1939 and 1943, with regular UNS demonstrations that averaged about two hundred persons. Celaya had the most events in the state of Guanajuato during this period (forty-three), and León had the largest number of participants.[74] Mercadillo, like most clergy, was not openly a member of the UNS, but he often echoed its rhetoric (see chapter 4) and UNS members undoubtedly were among the pilgrims at the sanctuary.

The UNS leadership articulated foreign policy positions that openly opposed U.S. wartime defense strategies within Mexico. The UNS declared that the Good Neighbor policy, pan-Americanism, and hemispheric defense strategies in general were U.S. imperialism in disguise. The organization also harnessed anti-American sentiments arising from discrimination against Mexicans and Mexican Americans in the United States by idealizing the period when Spanish missionaries spread across the continent from Florida to California, anticipating the calls by the Chicana/o movement in subsequent decades for a return of these lands, later referred to as Aztlán. UNS members envisioned themselves as modern missionaries and attempted to defend Mexico from potential U.S. expansionist ambitions by embarking on utopian colonization schemes in Baja California. Although the UNS leadership preached nonviolence, their rhetoric was extremely inflammatory, especially against Americans, Protestants, communists, and Jews. The organization required militarylike discipline from its followers, demanding the rejection of an easy, comfortable lifestyle and absolute compliance with a strict Catholic moral code.[75] Whereas the Mexican government declared its allegiance to the Allied cause during World War II, the UNS maintained a critical distance from the United States and thus threatened wartime unity. As a result, Mexican government officials attempted to stigmatize these more conservative Catholic elements, even as they renewed their commitment to protecting the privileges of Mexican Catholics more broadly.

Fully mindful of this prevailing political climate, Mercadillo couched the restorations and religious retreats at the sanctuary in secular terms. He insisted that the pilgrims were merely passing through as they had for two hundred years and that he had no choice but to offer them room and board for a small fee. Moreover, he added, the pilgrims benefited the local economy and the railroad company due to the thousands of fares they paid. He also emphasized that the sanctuary provided necessary social services by feeding the hungry, treating the sick, and offering literacy workshops. Mercadillo even drew a correlation between the sanctuary retreats and a recent reduction in crime in the state. Even more important was his consistent reminder to government officials that he was committed above all else to the preservation of this important historic monument.[76] In the process Mercadillo fashioned the pilgrims into a different kind of tourist—weary travelers worthy of compassion.

In reality the pilgrims who traveled to Atotonilco were making a journey that was not an adventure but a demanding act of faith. Their millennial vision for a Catholic Mexico, based on the social Catholicism of the 1891 papal encyclical *Rerum Novarum* and on newer conservative Catholic movements such as Opus Dei, contrasted sharply with the worldview of the foreign art students and tourists who came to San Miguel.[77] The most devoted pilgrims rejected leisurely pursuits and attempted to live up to the strictest interpretations of the Catholic moral code. For example, a handbill distributed by one of Mercadillo's associates blamed alcoholism and immodestly dressed women for threatening the imminent Christian Restoration.[78] The pilgrims traveled not for enjoyment or self-fulfillment but to repent their sins and bring themselves closer to God. Many of the visiting tourists and art students were quick to label Mercadillo and his followers "quaint" or "backward." However, their view of Mexico and of the world, far from being backward, was deeply rooted in current domestic and international events. The vision of society they offered was not simply a reactive, nostalgic look backward but an ambitious alternate Mexican modernity.[79]

A 1946 outbreak of hoof-and-mouth disease (*fiebre aftosa*) in central Mexico provided Mercadillo and the UNS with an opportunity to demonstrate just how modern they could be. The disease spread quickly and threatened the livestock and the livelihoods of people across seventeen Mexican states. Under pressure from the United States to contain the outbreak, the Mexican government adopted a plan in early 1947 to kill all infected and exposed livestock. The Mexican military guarded the mostly American veterinarians as they carried out the unpopular plan, referred to as *el rifle sanitario* (literally, "the sanitary rifle"). The Mexican government also used the outbreak as a pretext for monitoring and controlling the movement of Mexicans, especially large groups such as the pilgrims to Atotonilco. Although the government warned the Catholic hierarchy about the threat pilgrims posed to public health, Mercadillo insisted that the travelers who arrived at the sanctuary would be required to bathe before entering the complex and to disinfect themselves four times a day. He also claimed that he would educate the pilgrims about preventing the spread of disease. The pilgrimages would continue, he argued, but they would help contain the problem rather than spread it.[80]

The UNS leadership took a different approach. Convinced that the U.S. government was trying to decimate the Mexican agricultural industry, the UNS commissioned a study to determine whether vaccination was a viable alternative to killing the infected and exposed livestock. The results confirmed that in similar cases vaccinations had successfully contained the outbreaks. By the end of 1947 the Mexican government had shifted to a vaccination policy, but it had already killed nearly half a million cattle, sheep, and other livestock.[81] The epidemic and the U.S. involvement in the initial containment policy contributed to strong anti-American sentiment among people across the Mexican countryside, but that feeling was particularly intense in the Bajío.[82]

The hoof-and-mouth disease conflict occurred around the same time that the American and Canadian war veterans began to arrive in San Miguel. In just one decade the Mexican government had moved from openly defying the United States through the 1938 oil expropriations to amicably welcoming U.S. soldiers—albeit armed with paintbrushes instead of guns—into Mexican territory. While many Mexican residents of San Miguel welcomed the economic possibilities that these changes portended, Mercadillo and some of his followers saw the foreigners in San Miguel as a threat to their vision for Mexico's future. These conflicting viewpoints finally collided in the summer of 1949.

Paradise Lost at Bellas Artes

In July 1949 a vast majority of the students and faculty at Bellas Artes voted to boycott the art school. What started as an internal quarrel over supplies and studio space eventually escalated into a community-wide conflict over the school's future and finally into an international situation that forced U.S. and Mexican government officials to take sides. An examination of the boycott illustrates the tensions within and between San Miguel's Mexican and foreign populations as it became increasingly evident that the different visions for San Miguel's future would not comfortably coexist.

The problems at Bellas Artes first surfaced during the spring of 1948. Students claimed that the school's owner, Alfredo Campanella, was more concerned with profits than with maintaining the art studios and attracting reputable instructors. Sixty-four students and faculty members signed a petition demanding more administrative control. They called on Campanella to delegate all veterans' affairs to Dickinson and limit his own role to legal matters in which his expertise would be most useful. The petitioners threatened to go to the U.S. embassy if Campanella did not meet their requests. They hoped that the embassy officials would pressure him to acquiesce in order to maintain the school's VA approval.[83] Several months later, when Campanella had yet to act on many of their demands, the students and faculty once again claimed that the approval of the Veterans Administration was at stake.[84] They did not anticipate that this strategy would eventually backfire. Meanwhile Campanella acquiesced to some of the students' demands. It was in this context that he commissioned David Alfaro Siqueiros to paint a mural at the school. Siqueiros began working on the mural in June 1949, assisted by a team of twenty students.

Siqueiros was one of Mexico's most acclaimed artists, but he was also a highly controversial political figure. His artistic and political views emerged in a transnational milieu. He spent time in the United States, Europe, and Latin America developing his understanding of the social realism school of art, which was distinguished by its political content and stood in opposition to the European schools of formalism and abstractionism. Murals were his medium of choice because of their accessibility to the public, but his other work also graces many of the finest museums and galleries in Mexico and around the world. Much of Siqueiros's time outside of Mexico had political motivations as well, whether it was to join the Republican forces in the Spanish Civil War or to live in exile because of his political activities in Mexico. A Marxist, he had both a strained relationship with the Mexican Communist Party (PCM), as well as a rocky rapport with the U.S. government. U.S. officials alternately welcomed him to and prohibited him from entering the country. Siqueiros lectured on the use of art in the war against fascism on an OCIAA-funded "Art for Victory" tour through Peru, Ecuador, Panama, and Cuba, yet he was under constant surveillance by the various American intelligence agencies.[85]

Siqueiros also developed a complicated relationship with San Miguel. The artist first visited the town in October 1948. He was giving a lecture series at Bellas Artes on the Mexican mural movement when a room with a vaulted ceiling at the former convent inspired him. When Campanella later invited him to paint a mural in that same room, Siqueiros gladly accepted the offer. He had turned to portraiture to make ends meet and was eager to work on another mural. The angles in the room provided the perfect setting in which to experiment with emerging theories about the integration of architecture and art, *integración plástica*.[86] The school's owner had agreed to bear the costs for the mural, but, as the expenditures escalated a power struggle ensued between Siqueiros and Campanella.[87] This conflict was the final straw for a vast majority of the students; they began a boycott of Bellas Artes on July 15, 1949, effectively closing its doors.[88] Siqueiros, the other instructors, and Dickinson supported the boycott. The formal boycott announcement declared that Campanella's "total ignorance of each and every aspect of the arts" rendered him incompetent as the school's director. The announcement called for the creation of a Society of Mexican Artists and Foreign Artists Residing in Mexico (Sociedad de Artistas Mexicanos y Extranjeros

Radicados en México) to promote a "true cultural interchange among all nations," an aspiration, it implied, that individuals like Campanella threatened. Fifty-eight of Mexico's most prominent artists and intellectuals agreed to honor the boycott, including Diego Rivera, Dr. Atl, Rufino Tamayo, Frida Kahlo, Miguel Covarrubias, and of course Siqueiros.[89]

Upon hearing news of the boycott, Nathaniel Patterson, the veterans affairs attaché in the U.S. embassy, withdrew the Veterans Administration's recognition of Bellas Artes and encouraged the 125 U.S. veterans enrolled there to transfer to other approved Mexican institutions. However, 75 of the veterans stayed behind with Siqueiros and the instructors in hopes of resolving the situation and regaining the VA's approval.[90] The ensuing tensions revealed a rift in San Miguel over the foreign art students' presence. On one side, Mercadillo rallied his followers to support Campanella and the few foreign artists who did not join the boycott. On the other side, local business interests, municipal officials, and the Mexican art community defended the boycotting students and faculty.

By opening a public discussion over the future of Bellas Artes the boycott provided a space for disgruntled Sanmiguelenses to express mounting frustrations with the foreigners in their town. Concerns voiced to a local audience tended to criticize the foreigners for their allegedly immoral behavior. El Quijote, a local biweekly that emerged on the streets of San Miguel shortly after the boycott began, described what it called a common perception that the veterans were out of control. It is not clear who exactly was behind this publication, but the content suggests that even if Mercadillo did not play a direct role, his sermons were very influential.[91] The August 10, 1949, issue of the newspaper denounced the foreigners, "who under the pretext of being students have turned our town upside down" by converting San Miguel into the "backdrop for their scandalous vices, passions, and crimes." The tirade pointed out the slippery slope of the foreigners' descent into immorality, beginning with "their insolent disregard for decent dress," followed by "their scandalous excesses in the use of alcohol and drugs, and later their repugnant abnormality in their sex relations." The article's authors concluded, "We urge that a halt be brought to the excesses of these morally and physically unbalanced creatures who set a very unedifying example [for] our citizens."[92] This publication apparently aimed to convince local residents that the art students' moral depravity endangered the entire town.

The subject matter of the foreigners' art also provoked a reaction from socially conservative Catholics in San Miguel, who were certainly influenced by Catholic moralization campaigns across the country during the 1940s.[93] El Quijote's writers cited the use of nude models as evidence of the foreigners' immorality. Even more disturbing was a painting by one student portraying a cigarette-smoking Jesus surrounded by nude women, champagne glasses, and a hammer and sickle. News of this painting reached Mexico's minister of the interior, Adolfo Ruiz Cortines, a future Mexican president. He expressed concern in a telegram to Guanajuato's governor, claiming that while people in the capital and other urban areas would consider such a painting a juvenile stunt, in a deeply religious place like San Miguel it could lead to violence that "would be an embarrassment for our country."[94] Gladys Bonfiglio, one of the few Americans in San Miguel who sided with Campanella in the boycott, observed that it was fortunate the artist had left town immediately, "or there might have been violence."[95] That these artistic representations could provoke such a vehement response reveals how certain locals felt deeply threatened by the changes in San Miguel.

The local anxieties were rooted in the foreigners' queer sensibilities, that is, the challenges they posed to patriarchal, heteronormative society, rather than the superficial perils caused by paintings or alcohol consumption. From the unchaperoned single women to the often unconventional living arrangements of students on a budget, foreigners pushed far beyond the limits of traditional Mexican propriety. Moreover, a number of the students and other visitors in San Miguel were likely homosexual, a topic explored further in chapter 4. This threat to patriarchal values, more than any other aspect of the art school or the tourism industry, jeopardized Mercadillo's vision for the restoration of Catholic preeminence.[96]

While some members of the community decried San Miguel's foreigners, business leaders and politicians came to their defense, emphasizing their contributions to the local economy. Dr. J. Jesús Agundis Gallegos, San Miguel's representative to the national legislature, and the mayor, Dr. Anastasio López, both sent telegrams to President Miguel Alemán's secretary, Lic. Roberto Amoros, requesting that the administration take action to help reopen the school without Campanella "for the good of the community." San Miguel's branch of the National Chamber of Commerce warned that if the administration and the Ministry of Public Education failed to intervene on behalf of the striking veterans, the result would be "catastrophic damage to the local economy, as well as the economy of the surrounding area."[97] In a telegram to the president Campanella countered these claims and blamed the boycotting students and faculty for hurting San Miguel's economy, because they were the ones who had closed the school.[98] It was obvious that certain Sanmiguelenses stood to benefit from the art school and the tourism industry, but it was not clear which side the Mexican government would take, if any.

Whereas arguments against the boycotting students centered on morality in local discourse, Campanella sought to discredit them at the national level by appealing to growing anticommunist sentiments in Mexico City. This effort mirrored the strategies of Mexico's Catholic Right during the early Cold War years.[99] Campanella's multifaceted campaign involved sending letters to government officials and Mexican newspapers and holding protests in the capital. A number of U.S. students as well as local Mexican residents who disagreed with the boycott joined his efforts. Campanella requested an audience with President Alemán to discuss the "subversion" that threatened "the cradle of [Mexican] independence."[100] Sanmiguelenses proudly displayed placards on their doors that declared "¡Católicos sí, Comunistas no!"[101] An art student from the United States, Arthur F. Goniewich, made the first direct accusations regarding the boycott's links to communism.

Goniewich, president of a small student group that supported Campanella, warned top Mexican officials that a "Communist Boycott" threatened the well-being of veterans studying in Mexico as well as San Miguel's economy. He asked government officials to consider reinstating the school under Campanella's leadership, a proposition they ultimately rejected.[102]

The boycotting faction received a more favorable response from Mexican officials. They petitioned Carlos Chávez, the director of the Mexican National Institute of Fine Arts (INBA), in the hope that he would reopen the school under the auspices of the institute.[103] Their pleas resonated with Chávez, who submitted a comprehensive memorandum to Manuel Gual Vidal, the minister of public education, who forwarded it to the office of President Alemán (1946–52). Correspondence among Mexican government officials indicated that they took very seriously the threat to San Miguel's economy and, even more important, the international reputation of Mexican art. Marginal notes on the materials Dickinson submitted highlighted the amount of money Bellas Artes and the GI Bill brought into San Miguel. Clearly taking the side of the boycotting students, Chávez emphasized that Bellas Artes in its present state was "threatening the prestige of Mexican arts."[104] Gual Vidal quickly authorized the reorganization of Bellas Artes under the auspices of INBA, placing the school under Dickinson's leadership.[105] Even though officials had been working to reduce foreign influences in Mexico's leading cultural institutions, they seemed eager to end the conflict as soon as possible and keep the foreign students and Mexican artists happy. They thus continued a long tradition of collaboration between the Mexican government and foreign residents.[106]

When it was clear to Campanella and his supporters that Mexico City would support Dickinson's group, they ratcheted up the accusations and addressed further appeals to U.S. officials. Campanella warned the "North American Public" that the conflict demonstrated that "one of the top communists of Mexico . . . can with the support of foreign students take over the private property of a Mexican citizen without due process of law." He continued, stating that it was "a fight our whole continent may have to face some day."[107] Campanella supporter Gladys Bonfiglio reported to the U.S. embassy that "the people of San Miguel, from the head *cura* [priest] on down to the humblest peons from the neighboring ranches, are bitterly opposed to this new school." Citing Pope Pius XII's 1949 decree of excommunication for all communists and their collaborators, Bonfiglio claimed that Sanmiguelenses who sided with the reopened school were receiving death threats, because "to the townspeople it is a fight between communist Siqueiros backed by barbarous foreigners, and good Catholic Campanella backed by the Señor Cura and the respectable pillars of the town." She forwarded the State Department newspaper clippings and book excerpts documenting Siqueiros's long ties to communism and suggested that the UNS in San Miguel considered all foreigners to be communists and that real communists among them would only provoke violence.[108] In fact one incident helped illustrate the danger that Americans faced in San Miguel. One veteran recalled that "religious fanatics" had detonated a homemade bomb in the home of a retired U.S. Army officer, but fortunately no one was injured.[109] Campanella's faction hoped the ominous warnings would cause U.S. officials to distance themselves from the school and, therefore, continue to deny it crucial GI Bill funding.

Dickinson and student representatives of the new Bellas Artes fought hard to defend their reputations and regain VA approval. They sent numerous telegrams and letters to officials in the State Department and the Veterans Administration, to U.S. senators, and to President Harry Truman.[110] Dickinson spent several weeks in Mexico City's Hotel Monte Carlo and visited the U.S. embassy daily to make his case.[111] Despite—or perhaps because of—the pressure applied to officials over this issue, VA attaché Nathaniel Patterson repeatedly rejected their requests. He cited multiple reasons for his refusal: the matter was a conflict among Mexicans, so the U.S. embassy should not intervene; he never received official notification from the Mexican government that the school had been incorporated into INBA (even though the letter announcing that move appears in his case file); the "reorganized" school was in fact a different institution and therefore was not eligible for approval under the GI Bill; and finally that the "reorganized" school did not meet the minimum standards for the education of veterans under the GI Bill.[112] U.S. officials maintained that they had made the correct decision regarding the school in San Miguel. An unsigned State Department memo to the Veterans Administration issued in November 1949 stated that "no useful purpose will be served in acknowledging any further communication . . . from Mr. Dickinson," thus putting to rest any hopes of VA approval for the San Miguel school, even though the Canadian government resumed support of Canadian veterans studying in San Miguel that same month.[113] Many of the veterans who lost their government stipends opted to stay in San Miguel permanently and thus formed the core of what would become one of Mexico's largest expatriate communities.

Although Washington decided to ignore the veterans in San Miguel, the issue was still very much alive in Mexico. Students and instructors at the new Bellas Artes coordinated an art show in Mexico City to raise funds for the veterans who had gone months without subsistence checks. It was not merely chance that the show coincided with the convention of the American Society of Travel Agents at the Hotel del Prado. A shrewd promoter, Dickinson realized that the school needed an influx of students more than ever before, something that the travel agents could surely help arrange. Campanella's supporters distributed anticommunist pamphlets at the convention in an attempt to thwart the veterans' efforts. "Be careful with the deceitful Communists!" the pamphlet warned. "Traitors against Mexico and the United States" were said to be training Americans in communist doctrine at the fine arts school in San Miguel, with the intention of creating communist cells in the United States. "Do not permit yourselves," the handbill concluded, "to be converted into the blind agents of a supposed school which is at the service of communistic interests who are one of the worst enemies of the democracies of Mexico and the United States."[114] This redbaiting effort had little effect on the success of the art show,

Fig. 7. San Miguel's Independence Day parade, September 1949. 103.9992/10-1049, Record Group 59, National Archives and Records Administration.

which sold numerous paintings, woodcarvings, and textiles created by the students, faculty, and their supporters. The show was even extended several weeks at Mexico City's Hotel Geneve.[115]

For the most part Sanmiguelenses eventually supported, or at least acquiesced to, the idea of art school under Dickinson's direction. On September 16 the veterans played a prominent role in San Miguel's annual independence celebration. Without incident they marched in the parade in military dress, some proudly carrying American flags and others displaying signs that proclaimed "Escuela de Bellas Artes" and "Viva San Miguel de Allende!"[116] The image of U.S. soldiers marching down Mexican streets in a parade celebrating the nation's independence was filled with powerful irony. It speaks both to the complicated political relationship between Mexico and the United States in the postwar era and to the paradox that in San Miguel economic independence from the volatile agricultural sector ultimately created a dependence on foreign students and tourists. Both sides of the boycott were right. Even though the majority of Sanmiguelenses did not directly benefit from the art school, the school was responsible for the only significant growth in the local economy over the previous decade.

Campanella, who now found himself without an art school, had one last move. On the morning of August 12, 1950, armed agents arrived in San Miguel and deported eight foreigners affiliated with the new school: Stirling Dickinson, Leonard and Reva Brooks, Jack Baldwin, Howard Jackson, Ruby Martin, and James and Rushka Pinto. The Mexican officials ostensibly deported these individuals because they lacked proper work papers, but the foreigners involved alleged that Campanella had bribed officials to deport them. In the end Dickinson and the others took advantage of their connections to Siqueiros and other prominent Mexicans to secure permission to return to Mexico a week later, proper working papers in hand.[117] Their absence prompted the closure of the art school once again, but it was a pyrrhic victory for Campanella and his supporters. Unable to pay his bills, he left San Miguel soon thereafter. A large crowd reportedly met Dickinson and the other instructors when they arrived at the San Miguel train station.[118] Their return reaffirmed that even though some Mexicans still objected to their presence, foreigners were in San Miguel to stay.

Competing Visions in a Decade of Change

Like many other politicians of the era, former Guanajuato governor Enrique Fernández Martínez had the foresight to use his political connections to invest in Mexico's expanding tourism infrastructure. A key player in the creation of Bellas Artes in the 1930s, he and Felipe Cossío del Pomar cofounded a new art school, Instituto Allende, in 1950. They welcomed Dickinson, the faculty, and students from Bellas Artes with open arms.[119] As the next chapter demonstrates, the Instituto Allende thrived and San Miguel's tourism industry quickly surpassed preboycott levels. The new school's location, on the renovated grounds of the historic estate once owned by the de la Canal family, San Miguel's most generous eighteenth-century religious patrons, was symbolic of a broader shift. The vision of San Miguel as a popular international tourist destination took precedence over the local visions of San Miguel as a modern bastion of the Catholic faith.

The lessons of the 1949 boycott shed light on the economic and political transformations across Mexico during the 1940s. Local government officials and business leaders clearly viewed the art school and international tourism as essential to San Miguel's economic development strategy. National officials, through their support of the boycotting faction, demonstrated their priorities as well. By reincorporating the majority of Catholics into the mainstream national identity over the course of the 1940s, the government effectively marginalized fringe elements such as Mercadillo and the UNS. The response to the boycott also revealed the limits to Mexican anticommunism in the early years of the Cold War. Government officials were willing to tolerate some leftist artists in order to support economic development. For example, when Mercadillo distributed handbills that accused the foreigners of bringing communism to San Miguel in 1950, federal officials' first concern was that Mercadillo's rhetoric would adversely affect the local tourism industry.[120] These priorities reflect government officials' aspirations to transform Mexico into a unified nation with a modern economy. However, the case of the 1949 boycott also demonstrates that even as government officials and tourism promoters embraced this new identity, people still contested it, especially in the provinces. Mercadillo remained an outspoken opponent of San Miguel's foreign presence in the decades to come. While most of Mercadillo's criticisms continued to revolve around protecting San Miguel from immoral foreigners, for many Sanmiguelenses the potential benefits of the tourism industry simply did not outweigh the costs. They continued to search for alternate economic development strategies.

3 Bringing the Mexican Miracle to San Miguel

Ruth Hyba had come a long way since her days as a young student at the Memphis Academy of Art. A self-described introvert, the Tennessee native recalled that she had never imagined herself as the type to travel to foreign places, yet there we sat, in the bright, flower-filled courtyard of the bed-and-breakfast she had opened in San Miguel decades earlier. She explained that she had somehow managed to work up the courage to take a Greyhound bus tour of Mexico during the summer of 1952. After that she was hooked. Hyba returned to Mexico the following May, this time on a guided tour along Mexico's "independence route," which featured stops in Guanajuato, Dolores Hidalgo, and San Miguel. In the fall of 1953 she began taking courses at the Instituto Allende, where she studied watercolor and oil painting and experimented with batik, a fabric-dyeing technique. After returning to Memphis, Hyba received regular letters from José Torres, a Mexican man she had met in San Miguel, and eventually she returned and married him.[1] In some ways Hyba exemplified the growing number of Americans who traveled to Mexico on guided excursions during the 1950s and 1960s. Many would return to Mexico, inspired by their first experience and emboldened to travel independently or stay a little longer. But she is also a great example of the much smaller number of foreigners who eventually decided to stay.

A closer look at Hyba's life in San Miguel reveals why some Mexicans linked debates over economic development strategies in San Miguel to questions of national identity during the 1950s and 1960s. Some might interpret her story as an inspirational model of courage, perseverance, and ingenuity, but through another lens it becomes a cautionary tale of how foreigners might disrupt San Miguel's economic, cultural, and gendered hierarchies. After José and Ruth married they opened a hotel called Vista Hermosa in a prime location near the Jardín with help from a loan from her father. They charged the equivalent of five dollars a day for a room and three meals. Hyba planned the meals and prepared the food, which one guest described as "typical North American meals with a Mexican accent."[2] She received several requests for her recipes from foreign women in San Miguel who had a tough time negotiating the Mexican food landscape. In 2003 she compiled her recipes into a cookbook, *Gourmet My Way*, which continues to sell in San Miguel. Hyba's marriage was short-lived, but after her divorce she exercised her newly acquired business acumen and in 1968 opened her own bed-and-breakfast, La Mansión del Bosque, on a serene corner overlooking Parque Juárez.[3] Hyba's foreignness afforded access to capital, a competitive advantage when interacting with her clientele, and a degree of flexibility from the local taboos of being a divorcée and independent businesswoman.

The number of foreigners like Hyba in San Miguel increased dramatically during the 1950s and 1960s, creating both opportunities and challenges. On the one hand foreigners helped to sustain the local economy, whether they were tourists or part of the growing expatriate community. Many Mexicans developed close ties to the foreign population and considered them a positive social and cultural influence on the town. On the other hand, however, their presence often contributed to a certain discomfort. Few went so far as to call it imperialism, but there was a sentiment that the Americans in particular were invading San Miguel and that they were on the verge of rendering it unrecognizable. Felipe Cossío del Pomar, a foreigner himself, expressed dismay after his own dealings with the Americans at the Instituto Allende. "I tried to sell the Americans culture," he remarked, "and they ran off with the store."[4] This observation would have resonated across Latin America.

As a result, many locals sought other development strategies. The so-called "Mexican miracle," a period of extraordinary economic growth from the 1940s to the 1960s, gave them a reason to be hopeful. The expanding economy created new opportunities, including middle-management positions and unionized jobs in the manufacturing sector, that contributed to the rise of Mexico's urban middle classes.[5] Cultural industries such as film, radio, television, and tourism also contributed to Mexico's economic growth during this period. Many commentators consider these decades to have been a "golden age" of Mexican cultural production.[6] Government officials during this period also committed to developing the national infrastructure, which took the form of new roads, railways, and massive irrigation and energy projects. The new infrastructure facilitated the expansion of both cultural and manufacturing industries.[7] In retrospect it is clear that the Mexican miracle did not come without costs. The majority of wealth remained concentrated in the hands of Mexico's wealthiest families, and economic disparity increased nationally.[8] But at the time, there was tremendous optimism about the possibilities for San Miguel.

During the 1950s and 1960s San Miguel's service-oriented economy was not a foregone conclusion but rather the subject of impassioned local debate. These debates centered on two questions: which industries would best enable *sanmiguelenses* to partake in Mexico's economic miracle and which most represented a specifically Mexican modernity. A number of local government officials, those with a financial stake in tourism, and members of the town's growing population of expatriates argued that tourism, the industry without smokestacks, was San Miguel's best hope for sharing in Mexico's unprecedented midcentury economic growth. They believed that the construction of large factories would detract from San Miguel's supposedly authentic historical ambience, the very quality that secured its designation as a "typical town." They generally viewed the foreign presence as a positive influence. Through their promotional efforts tourism advocates sought to repackage the town as an accessible, cosmopolitan art center. They lobbied the state and federal governments for resources to develop local infrastructure and expand the tourism industry. However, government funding was sporadic, and state and federal priorities often diverged from local interests. Public-private collaboration became the most effective means for securing funding and maintaining a degree of local control, as the case of the Centro Cultural Ignacio Ramírez, a National Institute for Fine Arts (INBA) center that opened in 1962, illustrates. This model would also privilege those local interests with capital to invest, which in turn privileged their vision for San Miguel's future.

Many residents challenged this vision. Opponents argued that the tourism industry benefited only a small number of well-connected individuals and forced the town to sell out to foreign tastes and whims. They claimed that "real Mexico" was not located in San Miguel's architectural ambience but in its people, who increasingly left Mexico to find work in the United States. Smokestacks were precisely what they wanted, and they argued that the true path to prosperity and modernity was industrialization. The Fábrica La Aurora served as a model for this development strategy. By the early 1960s the factory had reached its peak production, employing hundreds of workers in shifts that ran around the clock. The textile workers demonstrated a path for upward socioeconomic mobility.[9] Moreover, because factory workers were instrumental in the development and preservation of various religious traditions, the factory also provided an economic development model that reinforced ideals about a modern, Catholic, patriarchal society and the preservation of Mexican culture and traditions. In the end advocates of the tourism industry triumphed. As the tourism industry grew and the downsides of Mexico's economic miracle became more evident, dreams of an industrial San Miguel began to evaporate, and future debate focused more on the terms under which tourism would exist rather than whether it should drive the local economy.

The Growth of the Expat Community and the Tourism Industry

Tensions surrounding the 1949 art school boycott briefly threatened San Miguel's reputation as a destination for foreigners, but local boosters redoubled their promotional efforts in the 1950s and the results were astounding. By the best approximation San Miguel's foreign population grew to several hundred between the 1950s and the late 1960s, and the number of foreign tourists who passed through the town annually reached the thousands.[10] The largest number of expatriates came from the United States, and they often followed a trajectory similar to Ruth Hyba's: a brief vacation, followed by a longer stay as a student, and then the decision to make San Miguel their permanent home. But people came from all over the world, and their presence altered San Miguel's economic landscape, for better or for worse, depending on your perspective.

Most expatriates envisioned San Miguel as a place where they could realize the American dream or at least a certain version of it. Numerous articles, like a 1956 piece in the magazine *Coronet*, explained that Americans in San Miguel could enjoy "a life of luxury for less than it would cost them to barely scrape along at home." The article listed the low costs of everything from haircuts and a shoeshine to rent and transportation. And whereas live-in maids and full-time gardeners were prohibitively expensive for most "middle-income" American families, in San Miguel these luxuries were easily affordable. The article also emphasized the accessibility of "recreation, sports, entertainment, and a busy cultural program." Life in San Miguel was appealing, according to the article, because it enabled Americans to attain aspects of the "good life" that remained out of reach, such as free time and more disposable income, which could be spent on leisurely pursuits. "Living here," the article claimed, "is so relaxed and inexpensive that it has become the end of the rainbow for hundreds of happy Americans." This sort of lifestyle was possible because Mexico was comparatively cheap, but it was more attractive in San Miguel specifically because of the local beauty and the expatriate population.

Although isolation might characterize other foreign paradises, the article noted that in San Miguel "the fact that you are in the midst of a thriving English-speaking colony eliminates any possibility of loneliness caused by a language barrier."[11] This fantasy erased Mexicans from the scene, except, of course, for their role as cheap labor. In many ways San Miguel seemed like the perfect place to achieve the American dream.

Foreigners moved to San Miguel for other reasons as well. Some came not as students but as instructors at the Instituto Allende. Politics drove others to San Miguel, particularly Spanish Civil War exiles and individuals fleeing McCarthyism in the United States. Others still, like Jaime Morris, an American, moved to Mexico to escape racism.[12] Despite these individuals' diverse reasons for moving to Mexico, it is tempting to refer to and conceive of the "expatriate" or "foreign community" as a monolithic entity. In some ways it is difficult to escape this formulation because many San Miguel residents, both Mexican and foreign alike, used these broad categories as shorthand. But upon closer examination "foreigners" and "Mexicans" do not always break down into such neat, distinct categories. How, for example, do we categorize Mexicans like José Mojica and countless others who spent much of their lives living and working in the United States or Spaniards who tended to blend in with local Mexicans? What about Americans who married Mexicans, spoke Spanish, and maintained very little contact with the United States? And what of their Mexican-born children? So although a distinct expatriate community did (and still does) exist in San Miguel, a better understanding of the members of that community and when and where those lines were blurred adds much-needed nuance to analyses of relationships between foreigners and Mexicans.

Although there were important exceptions, for the most part foreigners and Mexicans moved in separate social circles. Expats established a number of organizations, ranging from theater troupes and fraternal organizations to twelve-step programs and charities, essentially recreating aspects of civic life in the United States. These organizations operated parallel to similar Mexican civic groups, and their members were mostly expats. Language proved to be the primary barrier to more substantive interactions. Many of the expatriates studied some Spanish at the Instituto Allende, the Academia Hispano Americana (discussed later in this chapter), or prior to their arrival in San Miguel, but most did not continue their studies after they achieved a rudimentary proficiency. In other words, they could get by with just enough Spanish to make transactions at the market, give directions to a taxi driver, and communicate basic instructions to their household staff. One long-term visitor observed that maintaining a degree of ignorance about the language allowed foreigners to bend the rules.[13] Charles Allen Smart and his wife bothered to learn only enough Spanish to be polite. "We consider it bad manners," Smart explained, "to remain ignorant or crude in the language of our hosts." Nevertheless Smart enumerated many reasons why he and his wife did not need to master the Spanish language in order to live in San Miguel: "Most educated Mexicans are unsociable, and many are themselves trying to learn English, so it is sometimes rude to insist on speaking Spanish. . . . There is no legitimate theater in this town[;] neither of us is in regular business, or involved in a love affair, with any Mexican."[14] In addition to describing the language barrier Smart's comments divulge a tendency among expats to revert to negative stereotypes about Mexican culture to explain the lack of interaction between San Miguel's foreigners and Mexicans. It was perhaps easier to blame their Mexican neighbors than to acknowledge that their own relatively privileged status as expatriates made possible a lifestyle that gave them the option of whether or not to fully engage with the people and culture around them.

These barriers were not absolute. Another American, Robert Maxwell, claimed that San Miguel's expatriates and Mexicans had more social interactions than did foreigners and Mexicans in the nearby towns of Celaya and Querétaro, where the smaller populations of foreign business people more closely resembled enclaves.[15] Maxwell's perspective on the matter was also undoubtedly influenced by the fact that he was one of many Americans who had married a Mexican. Paulina Hawkins, whose parents were American and Spanish, also recalled that Sanmiguelenses were more courteous toward the foreign population than Mexicans from other parts of the country.[16] Arkansas beauty queen Nell Harris and former Guanajuato governor Enrique Fernández Martínez were San Miguel's most prominent foreign-Mexican couple. Their marriage carried a certain stigma among some sectors of the Mexican population because of Harris's dual sins of being American and having previously been married. There was even speculation that the marriage ended his formal political career, although his son recalled that the erstwhile governor still had significant behind-the-scenes political influence until his death in 1968.[17] The family lived on the grounds of the Instituto Allende and Harris managed the day-to-day operations. They hosted dinners, parties, and other events for almost every Mexican and foreign dignitary to pass through San Miguel, including several Mexican presidents, and they were at the center of San Miguel's social circles.[18] Between Enrique's Mexican political connections and the family's interactions with tourists and expats through the Instituto Allende, the Fernández Martínez–Harris family exemplified the potential for bridging the gap between Mexicans and foreigners in San Miguel.

San Miguel's foreigners quickly made an economic impact on the town through their consumption habits and, perhaps more important, through their entrepreneurship. Whereas in the late 1940s the buildings and establishments on the main square were all owned by Mexicans, by the early 1960s most of the new ventures were either partially owned by foreigners or catered to a primarily foreign clientele. Carmen Masip de Hawkins, who hailed from Spain, and her American husband, Jim Hawkins, opened El Colibrí, a book and art supply store. She and two other Americans later opened Academia Hispano Americana, a school that specialized in Spanish-language instruction as well as classes in literature, history, and sociology. Fred and Sylvia Samuelson joined with other artists to open San Miguel's first art gallery, and Robert and Lucha Maxwell opened a store that sold furniture and other decorative household items. Dotty (Birk) and Francisco Vidargas opened a dairy and sold pasteurized milk products, which were nearly impossible to find outside of the capital. By the late 1950s they had invested in a construction business, and they eventually moved into the increasingly lucrative local real estate market. Others, like Hyba, went into the hospitality business.[19] All of these business owners had the advantage of the insights and cultural capital they accrued as foreigners, which enabled them to adapt to their customers' palates or anticipate their consumer needs more successfully than their Mexican counterparts could. Although most of San Miguel's foreigners would not have considered themselves agents of empire (in fact many would have recoiled at the suggestion), they nonetheless reaped the benefits of the long history of American economic and cultural imperialism in Mexico and continued to extend its reach.[20]

Whether or not they saw themselves as imperialists, San Miguel's expatriates recognized that their presence was changing the Mexican town they had come to love. The foreign community itself became one of the biggest attractions in San Miguel. Once they had settled in the expats invited friends, published articles and stories back home about San Miguel, and hosted foreign literary and political figures at local events. Stirling Dickinson responded to literally thousands of inquiries from Americans seeking information about visiting or moving to San Miguel. He offered advice on everything from immigration rules to home ownership and the cost of living.[21] Dickinson became what the 1956 *Coronet* piece referred to as San Miguel's "unofficial, unpaid information bureau" and made personal connections with potential visitors and residents that probably allayed concerns they might have had about Mexico.[22] The foreigners' very presence and "insider" knowledge made San Miguel seem more accessible to successive groups of foreigners, creating a ripple effect.

Several of the earliest expatriates have expressed regret that they did not keep the town a better secret, and they acknowledge the role they played in converting San Miguel into one of Mexico's largest expatriate destinations. Charles Allen Smart feared that the enthusiasm for San Miguel expressed in his 1957 book, *At Home in Mexico*, would attract other Americans, and he made a point to discourage them from moving to San Miguel. "Although we live well on relatively few dollars," Smart wrote, he wanted to clarify that "life is not as cheap as many newspaper and magazine articles have claimed." Smart wrote that

> the altitude is not good for many heart conditions, and jaundice, dysenteries, and other diseases are common; that the supplies of water and electricity are irregular and disorganized; that the foodstuffs are in general poor quality; that the Spanish language and the Mexican character are not so easy to learn as they are often supposed to be; that the secondary schools do not provide good preparation for American colleges; that the hospital is very poor by American standards; that one must adjust himself mentally and emotionally to the widespread and severe poverty, illiteracy, and ignorance.[23]

Smart's warnings may have deterred some Americans from moving to San Miguel, but nevertheless the number of expatriates gradually grew and their presence expanded across the town.

The number of temporary visitors also increased steadily during this period. San Miguel welcomed visitors across the spectrum, from families traveling by car, to young, single students, to countercultural travelers. For some San Miguel was one of many stops, a random sojourn over the course of a long journey, or a quick detour based on a tip. For others it was the primary destination of a carefully researched and planned trip. Efforts to recruit these visitors began with the Instituto Allende, the art school that the former Guanajuato governor Enrique Fernández Martínez and Felipe Cossío del Pomar founded in the wake of the 1949 boycott and that Dickinson and several of the instructors from Bellas Artes subsequently joined. Like Bellas Artes, the Instituto Allende catered primarily to a foreign clientele. Its affiliation with the University of Guanajuato in the state capital enabled students to earn a master's degree in fine arts, which attracted serious artists in addition to the more casual art student. Cossío del Pomar had envisioned a school oriented more toward the popular arts and Latin American youth. He eventually allowed Fernández to buy him out, fearing that the emphasis on foreigners and tourism would compromise the school's integrity.[24] With Dickinson and Fernández at the helm the art school did in fact become the driving force behind San Miguel's tourism industry. Dickinson drew upon his experiences promoting Bellas Artes in the 1940s to create a buzz about the Instituto Allende through advertisements in newspapers across the United States and Canada.[25] They also opened a hotel located on the school grounds and offered traditional rooms as well as apartments and houses for long-term visitors. Hotel Instituto Allende boasted tennis courts, a swimming pool, and a restaurant staffed by a chef and waiters recruited from Cuernavaca.[26]

The Instituto Allende's directors developed a multifaceted strategy to refashion San Miguel as a cosmopolitan cultural center. This promotional strategy differed from the rhetoric used in the 1940s to portray San Miguel as being off the beaten path. Instead it resonated with President Alemán's own attempts to rebrand Mexico, specifically through tourist sites such as Acapulco.[27] Promotional pieces in *Travel* magazine, a U.S. publication with an upper-middle-class readership, illustrate these efforts. The magazine mentioned San Miguel in seven out of twelve issues in 1957 alone. This regular coverage was due in no small part to *Travel*'s Mexico correspondent, Peter Olwyler, a photographer who moved to San Miguel in 1955 and at various times served as the Instituto Allende's director of public relations. Short items in the magazine cast San Miguel as a vibrant destination for jet-setters and included the latest gossip on people who passed through the town, such as the Hollywood screenwriter and director John Huston, the Tony Award–winning writer and director Josh Logan, and the Mexican tenor Carlos Puig. Olwyler described the town as a "colony of literati," a "center for literati and artists," and the "old colonial culture-center."[28] His articles, which also appeared in other publications across the United States, constituted part of a comprehensive effort to attract mainstream tourists in search of a cosmopolitan Mexican experience.

San Miguel's increasing accessibility to ordinary tourists aided the Instituto Allende's promotional efforts. The Mexican government dedicated substantial resources to infrastructure across the nation during this period—tangible evidence of the economic miracle. For instance, the section of the Pan-American Highway that runs through Mexico was completed during the 1950s, and the completion of Route 57, an express highway from Texas to Mexico City, made the trip even faster.[29] Paved roads that branched off the main highways provided direct access to San Miguel for the first time. The city began to appear on more sample Mexico travel itineraries and travel agency advertisements than it had in the previous decade, and travel features in U.S. newspapers mentioned these newly paved roads, positioning San Miguel as "off the beaten track yet easily accessible."[30] In 1953 *National Geographic* showcased a full-page image of San Miguel opposite the title page of a story about college students who spent the summer in Guanajuato (see fig. 5 in chapter 2). Aside from that image San Miguel received a brief mention in the article that contributed to the idea of San Miguel as being both accessible and an important center for the arts. The students took a weekend trip to the town from their base in Guanajuato, a journey made easier by the newly paved roads. Their main destinations in San Miguel were "several of the famous handicraft shops" and "the fine arts school where artists from all over the continent study Mexican arts and crafts."[31] The combination of the article and associated images marked San Miguel as a beautiful, welcoming place where the arts flourished. San Miguel was literally more accessible, not just because of road improvements but also because it began to occupy a discursive space that was more familiar to potential foreign visitors.

Another important, and likely unintentional, development occurred during this period that undoubtedly contributed to San Miguel's appeal to foreign audiences. Several writers began to refer to San Miguel as a

Mexican national monument, probably stemming from a misinterpretation of the *población típica* designation. It is unclear who first made this error, but by the 1960s travel journalists and guidebook authors had repeatedly reproduced the false characterization, thus reinforcing it in the public imagination. The writer Norman D. Ford used the point to underscore how the town had "successfully resisted change" yet also had a growing number of modern amenities. He declared in a 1962 *New York Times* article that "San Miguel de Allende is a National Monument," and thus "the purity of its colonial architecture has been preserved for posterity."[32] Another writer, James Norman, confidently asserted that "the federal government long ago declared the entire town of San Miguel de Allende to be a national colonial monument."[33] While foreigners were mostly to blame for propagating this myth, Mexicans were also guilty. For example, Simón González's *Síntesis histórica de San Miguel de Allende* makes this claim on the first page of both the Spanish section and the English translation.[34] The misrepresentation certainly broadened San Miguel's appeal, and, although it is mostly harmless, it served to reinforce a very specific narrative about San Miguel's past that benefited those with a stake in expanding tourism.

Although the Instituto Allende attracted the largest numbers of visitors, new schools that extended San Miguel's appeal beyond the art community later emerged. In 1959 the Spanish-born Carmen Masip and her American husband Jim Hawkins opened the Academia Hispano Americana. Masip had offered private instruction for several years to supplement her income and recognized the growing demand for a more formal educational setting. A few years later another American, Harold Black, founded the Escuela Ecuestre, a school that offered horse-riding lessons and excursions. Black first became acquainted with horseback riding in San Miguel. The region is steeped in equestrian culture dating back to the ranching days of the colonial period, and it also has a long tradition of bullfighting and *charreada*, a Mexican version of the rodeo. The riding school provided another venue in which foreigners could experience San Miguel.[35]

Finally, efforts to attract more domestic tourists also continued. Mexico's economic growth meant that more families had disposable income for travel, and Sanmiguelenses recognized that an increase in the number of domestic visitors could help mitigate fears about foreign influences.[36] In 1963 the National Institute of Anthropology and History (INAH) published a version of a San Miguel guidebook that was originally published in 1958 by the Instituto Allende. The book, coauthored by Miguel Malo Zozaya and F. León de Vivero, was largely derivative of Francisco de la Maza's 1939 history of San Miguel and the Spanish version of the guide published by the Friends of San Miguel to celebrate the fourth centennial in 1942. It narrated the sixteenth-century foundation of San Miguel and included descriptions, histories, and images of San Miguel's religious and civic architecture. This guidebook also featured a calendar of local events and "traditions," consistent with INAH's overall mission of raising awareness about Mexican folk practices.[37] The majority of the "traditions" listed were of recent vintage, such as the holiday processions known as *posadas* that the Friends of San Miguel initiated, and the Alborada, a celebration that textile workers from Salvatierra brought to San Miguel when they came to work at the Fábrica La Aurora in the 1920s.[38] The rhetoric invoked to lure domestic tourists was slightly different from promotional materials used to attract foreigners. For example, Spanish-language materials rarely mentioned the art school, emphasizing instead San Miguel's history and pleasant atmosphere. This emphasis suggests that tourism promoters did not think that the Spanish-speaking population was likely to come to San Miguel because of its artistic community, whereas the art scene was the main draw for foreign tourists, who could find a good view, gardens, nice rooms, and haute cuisine in other parts of Mexico or even in their own country. Both foreign and national tourists did arrive in increasing numbers. During 1968 the local tourism commission identified more than thirty-five hundred tourists from the United States, more than fourteen hundred domestic tourists, and approximately five hundred others from around the world. These numbers certainly undercount

Fig. 8. Sara Montiel and Mario Lanza during the filming of *Serenade* at Atotonilco, 1955. Photograph by Peter Olwyler, courtesy of Michael Olwyler.

the actual number of tourists, especially Spanish-speaking visitors who might have been less likely to stop in the tourism office for information.[39]

The promotional efforts were working, but there was still a gap between the infrastructure and the resources needed to accommodate these visitors. New hotels and guesthouses helped. The Instituto Allende published a bilingual guidebook in 1958 that contained advertisements for at least ten hotels, including "one of Mexico's finest," Hotel Instituto Allende, located "on the grounds of the internationally famous arts, crafts, and writing center."[40] In addition to Hotel Instituto Allende and Posada de San Francisco, which were both primarily Mexican-owned establishments, the Maycotte family from Mexico City opened Rancho Hotel El Atascadero on the estate once occupied by bullfighter Pepe Ortíz and later by Felipe Cossío del Pomar. These hotels offered what is known as the American plan, which included three meals with the price of a room. Although these hotels relied on foreign art students for the majority of their income because students usually stayed for several months at a time, they also welcomed both foreign and domestic tourists. Many smaller hotels and guesthouses, mostly locally owned, also took advantage of business from the art school and tourism. Some, such as Hotel Colonial and Casa Sautto, emphasized their family-friendly atmosphere. Others, like Casa Arias, served foreign food in addition to Mexican cuisine. Hotel San Miguel appealed to tourists with cars and travel trailers by advertising its ample parking facilities. By contrast Hotel America attempted to attract those traveling by air by providing guests with transit between San Miguel and Mexico City. Most of these accommodations were Mexican-owned converted homes located near the center of town. While some properties had been in certain families for decades and even centuries, newcomers acquired others.[41] More and more people were attempting to translate the tourism industry into personal financial gain.

The cosmopolitan image the Instituto Allende cultivated, the efforts to preserve the town's "historic" ambience, and the expanding tourism infrastructure captured the attention of the transnational film industry. During the 1950s and 1960s San Miguel frequently served as the backdrop for Mexican and Hollywood films.[42] In these films Mexican and U.S. directors deployed San Miguel and the surrounding countryside in their portrayal of "typical" Mexican scenes for audiences in Mexico, the United States, and beyond.[43] Production crews and actors enjoyed the hotels and restaurants that had initially emerged to cater to art students and tourists. As early as the 1930s, when Pepe Ortíz welcomed José Mojica to San Miguel, the town served as an inspirational getaway for actors and screenwriters. In 1950 crews from Columbia Pictures began filming San Miguel's first Hollywood picture, *Brave Bulls*, starring Mel Ferrer and Anthony Quinn. Locals claim that the 1953 Disney animated short, *For Whom the Bulls Toil*, featuring the character Goofy as an accidental bullfighter, was inspired by Walt Disney's time in San Miguel.[44] The town was the primary backdrop for the 1955 Disney film *The Littlest Outlaw*. José Mojica set his own autobiographical film, *Yo pecador*, in San Miguel in 1959. In 1968 scenes for the Mexican telenovela *Los caudillos*, about the conspirators in Mexico's 1810 independence movement, were filmed in San Miguel. By the late 1960s U.S. studios also had begun to use San Miguel as a setting for western films, such as the MGM western *Guns for San Sebastian* and *Hour of the Gun*, a 1967 movie about Wyatt Earp. Nearly all of the major Hollywood studios spent time filming scenes in San Miguel, and the presence of several Mexican and Hollywood stars, including Mario Lanza, Robert Mitchum, Pedro Armendáriz, Mario Moreno (better known as Cantinflas), James Garner, and Jason Robards, lent credence to the town's cosmopolitan reputation (see fig. 8). Both Mario Moreno and Anthony Quinn eventually bought homes in San Miguel. It seems unlikely that people decided to visit San Miguel because they recognized it as a backdrop to these dramatizations. Nevertheless the film industry contributed substantially to the local economy through the money film crews spent while they were in town and the publicity San Miguel received as it hosted famous film stars, even if accommodating film folk was not a reliable economic development strategy.[45]

In order to improve the long-term viability of the tourism industry Sanmiguelenses sought small-scale, local solutions. Proposals usually involved organizing the industry according to modern conceptions of hygiene, professionalization, and spatial orderliness. Some of these efforts originated with local officials. For example, in 1961 San Miguel's municipal government inaugurated the Tourism Commission to coordinate efforts to accommodate tourists and distribute information. The commission included local political leaders, business people, intellectuals, and expatriates. One of its first projects was to open a tourism information office on the main square, the Jardín.[46] Officials at the local and state levels also responded to complaints and feedback from tourists, especially concerning trash and noise. One such letter from the state tourism director in 1969 informed municipal president Antonio Gil Vega that tourists complained of trash in San Miguel and gently suggested he not forget that "tourism is a source of wealth."[47] Gil diligently reminded individuals around town to clean up garbage in public areas. Municipal officials also asked local schools to postpone band practice until the afternoon so as not to disturb tourists.[48] Residents offered their own solutions for improving the tourism industry, and the local weekly *El Vocero del Norte* became one of the primary means for discussion. For example, one journalist suggested that in order for San Miguel to become a more attractive tourist destination, local residents needed to stop urinating in public.[49] Another criticized the proliferation of *chiquillos*, or youths who offered to guide tourists arriving by train into town or who offered to guard and wash the vehicles of tourists arriving by automobile. The journalist recommended that the city designate specific locations for the chiquillos to gather so that they would not become a nuisance.[50] Yet another *El Vocero* article encouraged municipal officials to make trained tourist guides available to visitors so that they would not have to rely on poorly educated guides and potential thieves.[51] Local business owners petitioned the municipal government to reverse regulations that forced businesses farther from the Jardín to maintain shorter hours, arguing that it gave other establishments an unfair advantage when it came to attracting tourists.[52] Each of these recommendations and initiatives implied a desire for centralized control over the tourism industry at the municipal level. They also reveal increasing preoccupations with class, particularly the fear that presumably lower-class individuals would cheat, misinform, or otherwise scare off the tourists.

Despite these steps, the municipal government still lacked the resources to implement all of the desired changes and turned to state and federal officials for help. Requests and the responses (or lack thereof) from state and federal officials reveal where the priorities of different levels of government diverged. For instance, while the state tourism official seemed preoccupied with garbage in San Miguel, he did not offer more funding for sanitation services. Local efforts to appeal to various Mexican presidents are also revealing. In 1951, for example, Mayor Julian Malo Sautto sought resources from President Alemán for historic preservation and improvements for the local market and roads. Mexico City awarded San Miguel an eighth of the money that Malo Sautto had requested, allocating all of it to historic preservation projects.[53] When President Adolfo López Mateos (1958–64) toured Guanajuato state in the early 1960s, San Miguel's town council (ayuntamiento) petitioned him to fund ten specific projects that addressed a variety of local needs: a new primary school, a new public market, athletic fields, regular flights to a local airfield, a bus station, subsidized housing for government employees who could no longer afford to live in the city center due to tourism-related price inflation, a highway directly connecting San Miguel to the state capital, better tourism promotional efforts for the region, funding for artisanal production, and access to credit for communal (ejidal) and small-scale independent farmers.[54] The president's itinerary, which focused on the industrial parts of the state such as León, Celaya, and Irapuato, demonstrated the federal government's own priorities. It would be decades before the municipal government would complete some of the proposed projects, with or without federal assistance. The federal Ministry of Hydraulic Resources did construct a large dam just outside of San Miguel, completed in 1968 and named Presa Allende, although the project was more of a boon to the large-scale agricultural producers in the Bajío than to Sanmiguelenses.[55] The state government funded other projects, such as a highway and a school.[56] The proposed airline service operated intermittently, offering flights to Guadalajara and Mexico City.[57] Some of the projects, such as subsidized housing for government employees, never came to fruition.

Perhaps the most notable affront was San Miguel's exclusion

95

from the 1966 Plan de Guanajuato—a statewide strategy to improve infrastructure and spur economic growth. Former governor Enrique Fernández Martínez considered himself a longtime ally of the plan's main proponent, Governor José Torres Landa, and took the snub quite personally. His son, Jaime Fernández Martínez, recalled that his father even prohibited the family from mentioning Torres Landa's name in the house once the Plan de Guanajuato had been unveiled.[58] While it is conceivable that Torres Landa's personal ambitions led him to distance himself from Fernández Martínez, it is likely that San Miguel's exclusion had more to do with the prioritization of the industrial southern part of the state.[59]

Local officials and tourism promoters once again attempted to recenter San Miguel in the narrative of the struggles for Mexican independence with the expectation that patriotic sentiment would inspire Mexicans to visit and government officials to finance local public works projects. Numerous attempts to solicit government resources during this period highlighted the local hero of the Mexican independence movement, Ignacio Allende, who for various reasons was never quite elevated to the same status as the more famous national hero Miguel Hidalgo y Costilla. Sanmiguelenses hoped that an emphasis on Allende would attract the attention of government officials and give the town a competitive advantage over other towns also vying for resources. The schemes to raise Allende's profile, including erecting a statue of Allende in the newly renovated Plaza Cívica and declaring the entire year of 1969 a jubilee in honor of the bicentennial of Allende's birth, did catch on with U.S. journalists and tourism promoters. Several travel writers placed San Miguel "in the region in which Mexican independence was born" and linked Allende directly to the independence movement.[60] One U.S. journalist described Allende as the "Mexican Paul Revere."[61] However, in terms of the Mexican audience the town's efforts on this front fell short. The jubilee did not result in broader Mexican recognition for Allende and did not attract substantial numbers of new domestic tourists.[62]

The most enduring effect of the 1969 jubilee seems to have been that it turned many local residents against the tourism industry, revealing the limits of patriotism and national identity when it comes to economic development. Whereas proponents touted the celebration of Allende as something that would benefit the local economy, for many it proved to be a nuisance, if not an outright disruption of their economic activities. Two consequences stemming from jubilee preparations highlighted what was at stake with local developments in the tourism industry. First, the renovation of the plaza for the Allende statue served as an excuse to demolish the public market that had previously occupied that space. The displaced vendors were promised space in a new market building a block away from the old site, but that facility did not open for several years. When it finally did open in 1972, the modern space with fixed stalls required an application process and usage fees and thus excluded many vendors, who were consequently dispersed throughout other parts of the city. Meanwhile municipal authorities also forced street vendors (many of whom were likely displaced when the old market closed) to vacate portals on either side of the main plaza. The removals were ostensibly to conduct repairs, but the timing coincided perfectly with the beginning of the 1969 September patriotic festivals, raising concerns that this signaled a new policy.[63] These cases demonstrate how the 1969 Allende jubilee became a pretext for imposing a very specific vision for San Miguel's tourism industry: a top-down, centralized, and orderly industry that had no place for street vendors and other participants in the informal economy.

Questions about whether tourism would deliver the promised economic windfall began to mount. Although tourism industry proponents proudly peddled tourism as the industry without smokestacks, many Sanmiguelenses wanted that type of heavy industry. Residents frequently left San Miguel to find work in other industrialized cities in the region such as León, Salamanca, and Celaya or in the United States because the tourism industry did not provide sufficient employment opportunities. Within the halls of government and the pages of the local newspapers the debate over whether tourism and other industries could coexist in San Miguel intensified.

Bringing the Mexican Miracle to San Miguel

A growing contingent of Sanmiguelenses began to push municipal authorities to bring more industries to the town during the 1960s. These individuals envisioned factories as more than just a way to combat unemployment. Manufacturing facilities would also be San Miguel's key to participating in Mexico's economic modernization miracle. Furthermore, proponents of industrialization portrayed it as the nationalist alternative to tourism. Through Mexican-owned industries, they argued, Sanmiguelenses could end their reliance on revenues from foreign tourists and better protect local culture and traditions. These mostly middle-class individuals saw national identity and economic development strategies as thoroughly intertwined.

The regional political economy shaped debates over development. The Mexican miracle had very specific consequences for the state of Guanajuato, as well as the Bajío region surrounding San Miguel. The city of León, long a center of domestic shoe manufacturing, witnessed the rise of a variety of new productive industries, including automobile assembly lines, beverage bottling plants, and paper mills.[64] Mexican and international companies such as Green Giant, Del Monte, Gamesa, and Bimbo consolidated and mechanized agricultural production in the central and southern parts of the state. Refineries for the national oil company PEMEX completed the new industrial landscapes in cities such as Salamanca and Celaya. However, although industrial production expanded throughout much of the state, communities in northeastern Guanajuato continued to rely on subsistence agriculture.[65] Moreover, small-scale farmers throughout the Bajío struggled to compete with the large corporations. Consequently unemployment and underemployment remained high across the region. Guanajuato, as well as the neighboring states of Jalisco and Michoacán, were the primary staging areas of migration to the

United States, whether through the official Bracero guest-worker program or undocumented channels.[66]

Residents of San Miguel, positioned between the industrializing southern part of the state and the poverty-stricken northeast, knew all too well the potential benefits and pitfalls of the Mexican miracle. For the majority of the twentieth century the Fábrica La Aurora was San Miguel's largest single employer. The Mexican textile industry benefited from ISI tariff and import-control regulations, and the Fábrica La Aurora was no exception.[67] At its peak in the 1960s it employed approximately 350 workers, almost all male, from San Miguel and the surrounding area. Most employees were the first generation in their families to transition from working in the fields to working in a factory, and Fábrica La Aurora jobs were associated with upward socioeconomic mobility.[68] These employment opportunities contrasted sharply with most tourism-oriented jobs, such as housekeeping, cooking, and gardening. Although service-industry employees often had access to higher wages or foreign currencies because of their contact with tourists and expatriates, they had less job security and fewer opportunities for advancement. Moreover, women occupied most of these tourism-related jobs, except for gardening, driving taxis, and doing odd jobs. Women working in tourism-affiliated roles were often augmenting existing family incomes, but some became the primary household wage earners. Chapter 5 examines the gendered implications of a service-based economy in greater detail.

Even as San Miguel's tourism industry and the Fábrica La Aurora enjoyed a period of growth during the 1950s and 1960s, local unemployment levels far outpaced job openings, revealing the gap between the promise of the economic miracle and the reality in San Miguel. Although in July 1951 Mayor Malo Sautto assured the governor of Guanajuato that Sanmiguelenses were not seeking Bracero guest-worker contracts (an indicator of unemployment or underemployment), he backtracked a month later, likely bowing to local public pressure. That August he submitted a list of more than 175 Sanmiguelenses, all men between the ages of twenty and forty, who hoped to obtain labor contracts in the United States. In the accompanying letter to the governor Malo Sautto attributed the number of aspiring migrants to drought and the resultant loss of the corn and bean harvests. "These individuals," he stated, "have absolutely nothing to do on their parcels of land until January when they will have to prepare the fields for the 1952 harvest season." Guest-worker contracts, he added, "would not only alleviate the financial situation of their families, but also the general economy of the entire district."[69] His request, and the rationale behind it, would have been quite typical for towns across Mexico during this time.

The list he compiled, however, suggests an economic problem far greater than drought. Fewer than ten of the men on the list came from the countryside. The rest provided addresses in the town center. While many of these individuals likely did work on ranches and land parcels, their desire to seek work abroad also implied a lack of economic opportunities in local businesses and trades outside of San Miguel's agricultural and tourism industries. Linguistic limitations would have curtailed some workers' opportunities to obtain service industry jobs, and thus work abroad would potentially provide short-term income and the long-term advantage of learning English. Furthermore, this example suggests that San Miguel's workforce likely reflected broader national trends in which nearly half of the men who sought Bracero contracts did not meet the program's requirements of having prior agricultural experience and being currently unemployed, even though the language in Malo Sautto's letter claims otherwise. In fact, as the historian Michael Snodgrass has argued, local officials frequently doled out these contracts to supporters as a form of political patronage.[70] Throughout the 1960s numerous Sanmiguelenses went abroad or to other cities in the region to find work, a trend replicated in towns across Mexico. For many residents this pattern of migration highlighted the need for other local economic development strategies.[71]

In 1967 Pepe Rodríguez Martínez, who wrote for *El Vocero* under the byline "Incrédulo," observed that a summer drought had forced an exodus of people from the countryside to Mexico City in search of better opportunities. He blamed local proponents of the tourism industry, which included some government officials as well as hotel owners and individuals with ties to the Instituto Allende. "They need to realize," he wrote, "that they are the only ones to benefit, not the community, and especially not the people in the countryside." He implored the *turisteros* to bring more "noble industries" so that their fellow Sanmiguelenses (*paisas*) would not have to leave in search of work.[72] The local artist and historian Donato Almanza concurred. He remarked that the lack of jobs, combined with tourism-related inflation, hurt families whose members were already struggling, especially those who were not homeowners. High rents forced many to live farther from the town center, and many more chose to emigrate. Almanza pointed to the example of Taxco, where many locals had to sell their property to foreigners and hotel owners, and he warned that the same was happening in San Miguel.[73]

Proponents of industrialization cited San Miguel's industrial past as well as its twentieth-century textile factory as examples of what they envisioned for the town's economic future. As chapter 1 has demonstrated, San Miguel had been producing textiles, leather goods, and metal supplies since the colonial period, and those industries had reached their apex during the mid-eighteenth century. A combination of global economic factors and regional competition had sent San Miguel's industries into decline by the late eighteenth century, and they never quite recovered.[74] Only the Fábrica La Aurora and a handful of smaller industrial enterprises still remained in operation in the twentieth century. Data collected in 1968 on the young adult male population in San Miguel reveal that most were employed in the agricultural sector as farmers and day laborers. Of the remaining individuals about a third worked in shops, businesses, or service-related industries, another third worked in factories or specific trades, and the final third claimed to be students. A very small percentage listed construction-related work as their primary source of employment. These records provide only a snapshot, but they suggest that while a significant portion of this generational cohort was taking advantage of educational opportunities, agriculture was still the primary source of employment for San Miguel's male population.[75]

The Fábrica La Aurora was the major local alternative to agricultural labor throughout much of the twentieth century. British investors first built the factory in 1902, likely selecting the site for its proximity to a rail line, a water source for power, and markets in the nearby cities of Querétaro and Guanajuato.[76] The factory operated throughout the early decades of the twentieth century, converting cotton produced across Mexico into *manta*, a coarse cloth used for bedding, clothing, and other purposes. Although the Fábrica La Aurora was a relatively small textile mill, it was easily the largest employer in San Miguel. The owners provided company housing across the street in what is now known as Colonia Aurora, San Miguel's oldest neighborhood outside of the historic center. Colonia Aurora has since been engulfed by the city, but the simple stone houses were once considered so far outside of town that there was no mail service.[77] Whereas textile mills in other parts of Latin America tended to hire mostly female workers during this period, such was not the case in Mexico. Locals recall that it was quite exceptional when women temporarily replaced the male workforce during the revolution.[78] Production languished in the 1920s, and in 1932 the Garay family, Spaniards with long-standing interests in the Mexican textile industry, acquired the factory. The Fábrica La Aurora likely benefited from tariff protections and low import rates of foreign textiles during the Great Depression. Indeed, as the historian Susan Gauss has argued, by the 1940s the textile industry was Mexico's largest manufacturing sector, which opened many opportunities for Sanmiguelenses.[79]

The Fábrica La Aurora served as a model for how industrialization could contribute to the larger community both economically and culturally. Most significantly, jobs at the factory provided a stepping stone into the middle class. Even though the Garay family initially brought many of the skilled laborers from other factories, about half of the employees were locals and many were working in a factory for the first time. Both the owners and the textile workers' union provided opportunities for employees to receive training and advance up the pay scale. Emigdio Ledesma, for example, was sent to textile factories in Guadalajara and Puebla to learn how to maintain the machinery, and this training resulted in a significant pay raise.[80] Factory workers also received various nonwage benefits, similar to those of unionized workers in other industries in Mexico and beyond. The factory had its own store, where workers could purchase food staples and other basic goods on credit, as well as a pharmacy and doctor. Although in some contexts, especially in more isolated company towns, these types of company-owned services have a reputation for exploiting a vulnerable workforce, former Fábrica La Aurora employees and their families look back on these institutions with nostalgia. The company store operated like a cooperative, with members of the employee community contributing to help cover the costs for everyone. Community members recall that when the factory closed the pharmacy and ended medical services in the 1970s in response to new federal programs that would provide those services, the quality of and access to medical care declined. Finally, workers were able to purchase their homes in Colonia Aurora through payroll deductions, and to this day relatives of former factory workers still own almost all of the original company homes.[81]

Employment in the factory and union membership offered other benefits as well. Fábrica La Aurora workers were eligible for credit at other local stores and received family discounts for local events. Workers also were eligible for paid vacations and annual bonuses, and the union leadership monitored employees to ensure that they did not squander their money. In some cases wives collected the money to prevent their husbands from spending it in a local cantina.[82] Through a combination of relatively high wages, access to credit, and financial self-policing, factory workers saved enough money to become homeowners and send their children to regional universities, and many Sanmiguelenses wanted to increase these types of employment opportunities.[83]

Beyond serving as an alternate model for local economic

development, the Fábrica La Aurora and the union also became the center of working-class social and cultural life in San Miguel. The Garay family had a reputation for looking after their workers outside the factory walls. On Sundays the workers and their families frequently gathered to listen to the factory band and participate in athletic competitions at the factory's sporting facilities. Like other industrial employers, the Fábrica La Aurora sponsored employee baseball and soccer teams that competed in regional leagues, as well as against other San Miguel teams. The local headquarters for the textile workers' union was prominently located just two blocks from the Jardín in the middle of town and served as a meeting place and venue for cultural events ranging from dances to poetry readings. Finally, the employees and their families initiated their own traditions and events, most of which revolved around religious holidays. This working-class religiosity was built on the traditions of San Miguel's artisan guilds and *cofradías*, or confraternities, in earlier centuries.[84] For example, they participated in an annual procession in which they carried an image of Jesus, the Señor de la Columna, from Atotonilco to San Miguel, and they celebrated the feast day of the Virgin of Guadalupe on December 12 with a special mass inside the factory. The employees also initiated the Alborada, an annual celebration in September that begins in the predawn hours in honor of San Miguel's patron saint, the archangel Michael. Workers and their families continue to take pride in the role they have played in developing and preserving these traditions.[85] They also served as examples for how an economic development strategy could reinforce rather than disrupt Catholic, patriarchal values.

By contrast, critics claim that other local traditions had been co-opted by the municipal government, which in turn compromised their authenticity. For example, Félix Luna, whose father worked in the Fábrica La Aurora and who dedicated himself to the preservation of San Miguel's indigenous traditions, argued that the 1942 celebrations of San Miguel's fourth centennial (see chapter 2) marked a turning point in the festivities in honor of the local patron saint. When local elites stepped in to help fund the celebrations in 1942, they marginalized the indigenous communities that had originated the traditions. Luna maintained that over time, as San Miguel's indigenous populations reintegrated themselves into the annual celebrations, the "traditions" had fundamentally changed.[86] Luna, Ledesma, and others who were in some way affiliated with the Fábrica La Aurora see themselves as guardians of local traditions that are at risk of being co-opted and changed by proponents of the tourism industry.

The Fábrica La Aurora thus formed an integral part of San Miguel's economic and cultural life. As Robert Potash has observed in the case of a nineteenth-century factory in Orizaba, "More money in the hands of the factory employees meant more business for the town as a whole, and even the makers of fireworks could profit."[87] Many would make the same case for San Miguel. The example of the Fábrica La Aurora and other industrial developments across the region provided fodder for several pro-industrialization *El Vocero* columnists. Incrédulo wrote about an invitation that the Guanajuato governor, Dr. J. Jesús Rodríguez Gaona, extended to executives from companies in the United States, Europe, and Japan to tour prime locations where they might invest and build factories. "I hope the Governor does not forget to bring these individuals to San Miguel," he exclaimed.[88] In another column Incrédulo described the municipality of Villagrán, located in the industrial corridor between Celaya and Irapuato, as "touched by the hand of God" after the Mexican operations of the Campbell's food company decided to build a factory there. The factory, which would produce the company's signature soups, was expected to hire a minimum of eight hundred employees. Incrédulo argued that the economic benefits would extend throughout the entire community.[89] The largest concentration of factories and other types of industrial investment was in the cities of León, Celaya, and Salvatierra, where industries as diverse as meat-packing plants, hat-making factories, and rock quarries brought a stream of new employment opportunities.[90]

Proponents of industrialization ardently disputed claims that factories would detract from San Miguel's colonial ambience and have a negative effect on the tourism industry. Incrédulo mocked the idea that San Miguel even had a colonial ambience. He challenged those who claimed it did to give up their radios, televisions, and telephones, trade their cars in for donkeys, and cook over small fires so that modern conveniences would not detract from the colonial atmosphere.[91] Following a similar logic, the historian Antonio Ruíz Valenzuela argued that if Sanmiguelenses really wanted to remain true to their colonial heritage, they would convert San Miguel back into the industrial and commercial center it had been during the seventeenth and eighteenth centuries.[92] Incrédulo summarized the pro-industrialization position best when he said he would rather see a "prosperous San Miguel surrounded by factories" than a colonial San Miguel "living off of memories alone."[93] While these references to San Miguel's colonial industries were mostly a rhetorical device to draw attention to the selective memories of historic preservationists, the pro-industrialists also engaged in selective remembering. San Miguel's eighteenth-century prosperity had often relied on the labor of slaves and other marginalized—and thus easily exploited—workers who bore the brunt of cost-cutting measures that kept local textile workshops and tanneries economically competitive.[94]

Arguments in favor of industrialization were closely intertwined with concerns about the cultural implications of a tourism industry that catered to foreigners, signaling that the 1949 boycott had not put the culture wars to rest. *El Vocero* columnists feared that San Miguel was becoming "gringo-ized." Ruíz Galindo complained that signs and advertisements in English were becoming ubiquitous in San Miguel, a phenomenon that he labeled *pochismo*, a derogatory term that usually referred to Mexicans who had lost their language or had been otherwise Americanized. "It is very nice, [as a] courtesy toward the numerous tourists who visit us daily, to have everything displayed in the English language," he somewhat sarcastically conceded. However, he explained, people "have to remember that we are in Mexico, where the official language is Spanish," and he insisted that every sign be in Spanish before bearing a translation in another language.[95] Incrédulo worried that tourism would affect local culinary traditions, and he recommended that the menus of every restaurant that catered to foreigners include traditional Mexican foods and beverages.[96] According to another columnist, a foreign tourist guide welcomed a group of Texans to San Miguel by stating, "Welcome to this Mexican land, whose people want to be like us, the admirable North American people." The columnist explained that the guide misrepresented Mexicans. "We [Mexicans] do not want to be like them," he asserted. He suggested that, instead of having foreigners serve as guides, there were plenty of "good Mexicans" who were well prepared to provide the service.[97]

These columnists urged Sanmiguelenses to reclaim their town for Mexicans, rather than let foreigners dictate its development and representation. However, the influence of local tourism officials and the whims of foreign and Mexican investors meant that only a few small-scale factories came to San Miguel, and other industries never successfully rivaled tourism. Instead another alternative emerged that temporarily placated the demands of the pro-industrialists and that promised to advance San Miguel's reputation as a center for Mexican culture.

El Centro Cultural Ignacio Ramírez

If municipal officials and business leaders remained committed to a San Miguel "without smokestacks," Sanmiguelenses insisted on other forms of job creation and investment in local youth. The most popular solution to surface was the establishment of a government-funded cultural center (*centro cultural*), modeled on similar centers throughout Mexico. This entity was potentially a way to preserve local cultural traditions while benefiting the economy. Under the jurisdiction of the National Institute of Fine Arts (INBA) and the Ministry of Public Education (SEP), these cultural centers provided instruction in dance, music, writing, fine arts, cooking, sewing, and folk arts (*artesanías*). The centers also served as venues for concerts, plays, conferences, and performances by students and outside groups.

The Centro Cultural Francisco Eduardo Tresguerras in Celaya, which opened in 1961, likely inspired calls from *El Vocero* columnists who demanded that INBA open a similar center in San Miguel.[98] One journalist argued that support for training in and production of arte-sanías would improve the economic situation of the entire town by supplying instructors with an income, supporting home workshops, teaching the Mexican youth marketable skills, and developing prod-ucts that artisans could sell to tourists or abroad.[99] An INBA center appeared to be an acceptable compromise between those interested in cultivating the arts in San Miguel and those who wanted other forms of economic development.

INBA officials announced in 1961 that they would convert Las Mon-jas, the former convent that housed Bellas Artes in the late 1930s and 1940s, into a cultural center, a move that Sanmiguelenses from both sides of the economic development debate initially praised.[100] INBA officials appointed Miguel Malo as director and named the center after nineteenth-century Liberal intellectual and San Miguel native Ignacio Ramírez, an ironic choice considering that the building was a former convent and he supported anticlerical policies. Sanmiguelenses eagerly anticipated the 1962 inauguration of the center. "Without a doubt," one journalist wrote, "we will soon have a magnificent opportunity for the youth of this city and the surrounding communities to learn skills that will provide secure sources of employment."[101] The inaugural celebration on August 17 brought a great deal of fanfare. Local radio station XESQ broadcast the proceedings live in their entirety. Many dignitaries attended, including Guanajuato governor Juan José Torres Landa, INBA director Celestino Gorostiza, and Armando Olivares Carrillo, rector of the University of Guanajuato.[102] Within a year San Miguel's Centro Cultural was enjoying an enrollment of more than 350 students. It was easily the highest enrollment per capita of the thirty-one similar cultural centers across the nation. The majority of students in San Miguel enrolled in dance and art, but music and theater courses were also quite popular.[103] In addition to classes the Centro Cultural sponsored numerous performances and exhibitions.

Reminiscent of the cultural programs José Mojica and the Friends of San Miguel had coordinated in the 1930s and 1940s, the events featured artists and performers from across Mexico and around the world.[104] On paper the new cultural center was a huge success.

Despite these apparent accomplishments several former proponents expressed frustration with the direction of the cultural center. Whereas the INBA cultural centers in other parts of the country aimed to meet the needs of a Mexican constituency, the majority of students and event attendees in San Miguel were foreigners. *El Vocero* columnist Erasto Cortés Juárez lamented the fact that so few Mexicans took advantage of the cultural opportunities offered at the Centro Cultural. "Why," he asked, "are so many Sanmiguelenses indifferent or perhaps forgetful, that they do not appreciate" the events? "There are many communities in the provinces," he continued, "that would like to have what the people of San Miguel" enjoy as a form of mental escape from the problems of daily life.[105] If the majority of the students at the Centro Cultural were foreigners, then the entire economic argument in favor of the cultural center in the first place—that it would train local youth and provide them with paths to future employment—collapsed.

Several factors explain why foreigners outnumbered Mexican participants at the Centro Cultural. The primary reason was purely economic. Unlike other federally funded cultural centers across Mexico, the San Miguel center was an experimental attempt to incorporate municipal, federal, and private funding. For example, Carmen Masip de Hawkins, a local cultural leader with strong ties to the foreign population, cosponsored many of the events through the Asociación Cultural San Miguel, A.C., or her Spanish-language school, Academia Hispano Americana (Masip assumed the directorship of the Centro Cultural following Malo's death in 1972). In fact INBA officials in Mexico City lauded this funding strategy and looked to San Miguel's Centro Cultural as a model for future cultural endeavors.[106] In some cases initiatives like the Institute for Adult Continuing Education held classes and events at the Centro Cultural specifically designed for foreigners, with the objective of raising money to subsidize other events aimed at a broader audience. For the most part, however, the combination of public and private resources meant that the Centro Cultural could not exist solely for the education and enjoyment of Mexicans. Cultural programs that targeted foreigners were also essential. Manuel Zavala Zavala commented that some people claimed the ticket prices for cultural events were too high for most Mexicans to afford, but he argued that the prices were not to blame. Instead, he speculated, the town had lost its affinity for the theater.[107] There likely was some truth behind the argument that Zavala dismissed. Foreigners in San Miguel generally had more time and disposable income for these courses and cultural events than did the local Mexican population.

Some of the Centro Cultural's programs did specifically target Mexicans. For example, Celestino Gorostiza, the INBA director, recruited the Canadian artist and World War II veteran Leonard Brooks, who had been training Mexican youths in classical violin and other string instruments out of his San Miguel home free of charge. Brooks continued to volunteer his time and offer free lessons from the Centro Cultural in exchange for instruments from INBA. He trained an entire generation of Sanmiguelense musicians, including the Aguascalientes brothers who eventually played professionally in their own group.[108] But these programs were the exception. Ultimately the private-public cooperation model increased local autonomy when compared to other INBA cultural centers but concentrated the decision-making power in the hands of those with close ties to the tourism industry. Despite the efforts of those who sought other ways to preserve San Miguel's Mexicanness, foreign tourism continued to drive local economic growth.

Tourism Trumps Factories

By the early 1970s the weaknesses of Mexico's ISI economic development plan had been fully exposed. Economic protectionism, corruption, and nepotism had weakened Mexican industries and made it difficult for them to compete in the global economy.[109] In San

Miguel the owners of the Fábrica La Aurora scaled back employment after introducing new technology, reducing the workforce by more than a third. The number of employees continued to dwindle into the 1980s. The owners also shifted from the production of tablecloths and other household textiles to making cotton panels for tennis shoe manufacturers in an attempt to keep the factory financially solvent.[110] Industrialization lost its appeal as an economic panacea, and tourism remained as the only locally viable, if not the most satisfactory, option for future economic development.

In the waning days of the Mexican miracle the federal government's renewed commitment to tourism development indicated that the industry would be vital to Mexico's new economic strategy. From the centralization of government control over museums to massive, government-led resort developments in places like Cancún, federal agencies inundated with oil revenues invested immense sums of money in the tourism industry.[111] Tourism was increasingly a priority for state governments as well, and San Miguel finally received government funding for a bus terminal and new roads.[112] The decades-long local effort to establish a museum in the independence hero's former home caught the attention of Governor Luis H. Ducoing in the late 1970s. Local business and cultural leaders drew him into a contentious dispute over Miguel Malo's collection of pre-Hispanic artifacts. A 1972 law empowered INAH to confiscate Malo's sizable collection, and he tragically chose to take his own life rather than part with his artifacts. Malo's widow and other community leaders fought federal officials to have his collection displayed locally, and Governor Ducoing helped negotiate the creation of the Museo Casa de Don Ignacio Allende y Unzaga as a compromise. When the museum opened, only a small sampling of Malo's artifacts was on display, with the majority of the exhibition space dedicated to the late colonial period and the 1810 independence movement.[113] In terms of local economic development the museum and infrastructure investments were small but clear signals that tourism would be the main priority.

Additionally, factory employees initiated a new "tradition" that ironically became one of the largest draws for domestic tourists: the Sanmiguelada, a local take on the famous running of the bulls in Pamplona, Spain. What began in the 1970s as a local, one-day festival in between the Mexican independence celebrations at the beginning of September and the Fábrica La Aurora–sponsored Alborada at the end of the month eventually became a multiday spectacle that attracted thousands of Mexicans from around the country, as well as some foreigners. The new tradition did harken back to late eighteenth-century bullfights in San Miguel's main plaza, but any historic precedents were lost as the event became more commercialized.[114] The Sanmiguelada was a boon to hotel and restaurant owners, but as it grew from year to year most residents—foreign and Mexican alike—came to dread the event. The throngs of inebriated attendees constituted a public safety threat, not to mention a sanitation problem.[115] The Sanmiguelada is an extreme example of the challenges that the tourism industry presented, but it illustrates the difficulty of balancing economic needs with local desires.

The economic benefits that tourism proponents predicted and the promise of the Mexican miracle remained elusive for most Sanmiguelenses. Nonetheless, by the 1970s it was clear that tourism would remain a fixture of the local economy, leaving residents to figure out how to adapt and make it work for them. The challenge was not only economic but social and cultural as well, as larger numbers of foreigners descended upon San Miguel every year. Many of those foreigners were tourists passing through, but a steadily growing number put down permanent roots in San Miguel. Locals struggled to navigate between the economic need for tourism and their fears about the growing foreign presence in San Miguel.

4 Containing Threats to Patriarchal Order and the Nation

On a typical San Miguel Sunday in the summer of 1969 foreign and Mexican tourists relaxed under the shady laurels in the Jardín after a morning of sightseeing. A gathering of about eighteen young, long-haired Americans caught the attention of the municipal police, who looked on from their post on the main square. The police rounded them up and hauled them off to jail, where other prisoners promptly shaved the new arrivals' heads. When the father of one man demanded his son's release, the police took him into custody and the prisoners shaved his head, too.

The father turned out to be Dr. Amnon Issacharoff, an American physician traveling with his family and that of his colleague, John Schimel, on their way to the International Forum of Psychoanalysis in Mexico City. Horrified by the haircutting incident, Issacharoff and Schimel immediately returned with their families to their Manhattan homes without attending the conference. They initiated a letter-writing campaign warning other Americans of Mexicans' penchant for violating individual rights, and they demanded that Mexican officials punish the police in San Miguel appropriately. Issacharoff and Schimel reported that the officers merely cited "disrespect for authority" when explaining the arrests, but the two men believed that the "brutal" acts were "gross violations of international decency."[1] Friends of the two men also wrote to Mexican foreign relations officials, asserting that the publicity from this incident would harm Mexico's tourism industry unless they remedied the situation. One letter labeled the head shavings a "crass violation of personal freedom and barbaric affront to human dignity"; another referred to the occurrence as a "scalping."[2] The language in these letters drew from a long American tradition of casting Mexicans as savage, racialized "others." Rather than shaming the *sanmiguelenses*, however, the incident—which occurred in the broader context of efforts to target undesirable foreign visitors in San Miguel—became a source of local pride. Not only did the episode become fodder for local humorists, but it also inspired numerous Americans and Canadians to send letters praising San Miguel's municipal officials for their strict policies against long-haired youth and expressing frustration with their own governments for not doing the same. Ultimately, by shaving the heads of American men, San Miguel's police symbolically restored patriarchal order at a time when many feared it was slipping out of reach.

San Miguel's head-shaving raid was emblematic of efforts the ruling elite was making across Mexico to contain deviant bodies in an attempt to preserve the future of the nation. Although these policies also targeted long-haired Mexicans, in San Miguel foreign long-haired hippies served as a convenient foil against which local political and religious leaders could articulate their visions for a Mexican national identity. They accused the foreign population of undermining traditional Mexican values and called for a return to patriarchal authority and order, a call that resonated with leaders across the Western world. In so doing these leaders conveyed an ideal for modern Mexicanness rooted in a nationalist masculinity. The Mexican governing class's perception that they were losing control over the nation's image and identity was more acute in places like San Miguel with increasingly pervasive foreign populations.[3]

Concerns about local economics were thoroughly intertwined with concerns about national identity and patriarchal authority. The most ardent critics of the foreign presence in San Miguel were often those with little to gain in a service-based economy: middle-class heads of households who envisioned industry, patriarchal order, and Catholicism as the foundations for Mexican progress. While some of San Miguel's Mexican residents were willing to compromise strict nationalist and patriarchal values to maintain their claims to power, others viewed patriarchal order as the only way they could claim relevance and power in a rapidly changing society. Scholars have documented the relationship between changing economic regimes and changing gender relations, demonstrating that these concerns were not necessarily without merit.[4] For these individuals, containing deviancy was both a cultural and an economic statement.

The strategies that Mexican officials adopted to contain foreign influences must be interpreted within the context of the broader Cold War. Consistent with anticommunist leaders in other parts of the world, Mexican politicians, religious leaders, and cultural producers frequently linked communist threats with foreignness and immorality.[5] Although this tendency was not unique to the Cold War period, the Cold War did offer a new lens through which they could interpret the level of the threat. Thus they explicitly connected the containment of foreigners with anticommunism. But these leaders—principally San Miguel's socially conservative religious leaders—were also concerned with containing domestic women and young people, whom they deemed particularly susceptible to negative foreign influences. Through the politicization of everyday life, from fashions to intimate relationships, figures such as the parish priest José Mercadillo Miranda and columnists for the local weekly newspaper *El Vocero* sought to equate patriarchal authority with the protection of the nation from external threats.

While sweeping rhetoric about national identity and patriarchal order united most religious, political, and economic interest groups in San Miguel, for some the underlying goal was much more concrete and specific. Local elites had to develop a more nuanced relationship with San Miguel's growing expatriate community and foreign tourists. As Sanmiguelenses first learned from the 1949 boycott (chapter 2), foreigners had become indispensable to the local economy and rejecting them altogether was not a viable option. Therefore many elites sought not only to welcome tourists and expats, who participated in the formal economy by frequenting hotels, shops, and restaurants, but also to minimize the presence of hippies and other transients who contributed little to the formal economy while potentially frightening away the more desirable sort. By othering objectionable outsiders through public spectacles like head shaving, local officials simultaneously allowed Sanmiguelenses to vent their frustrations over the influx of foreigners, reinforced patriarchal notions about appropriate gender roles, established a hierarchy between desirable and undesirable foreign influences, and protected their economic interests.

Both expatriates and Mexicans stood to gain from the head-shaving episode. It allowed expats to distance themselves from tourists and the conduct critics associated with a foreign threat to a Mexican national identity: gender-bending fashions, same-sex relations, drug use, transience, and exclusive use of the English language. To be sure, many of the expats exhibited these same behaviors. However, when Mexican officials enacted a series of policies, from head shaving to deportations, designed to rid the town of "bad" foreign influences, the implication was that those who remained were relatively acceptable. The distinction Mexicans made between desirable and undesirable foreign influences created a space in which expats could secure their position in San Miguel society by supporting efforts to protect the town from objectionable, and often more transient, foreigners. Furthermore it afforded certain Mexican politicians, journalists, and other local leaders the freedom to criticize the youth culture as foreign and undesirable, while at the same time heralding business and personal relationships with the expat community as positive and modern. This distinction amounted to a shift from the 1949 boycott examined in chapter 2. At that time the foreign community was smaller, more homogeneous, and less permanent, and it had been unclear whether foreigners would remain in San Miguel at all. In the two decades since the boycott the permanence of the expatriate community had gone largely unquestioned, not least because of the expats' economic contributions to the town. In San Miguel transnational discourses and Cold War politics shaped anxieties about deviance from patriarchal norms, but local economic realities limited the realm of possible responses.

Preoccupations with Youth, Gender, and the Future of the Nation

In 1948 José Mercadillo addressed to the nuns in charge of San Miguel's Catholic schools a letter in which he wrote of a "profound pain in his soul." The parish priest observed that with each passing day the town's youth were losing their "spirit of discipline" and no longer displayed proper submission to church authorities. Moreover he noted with despair that fewer children were participating in the Parroquia's weekly Catholic mass. Mercadillo called upon the sisters to require all of the children at their schools to attend a Saturday mass, and he urged them to provide enough supervision to ensure that the children behaved respectfully. He also expressed his concern that parents were not doing enough to raise their children as proper Catholics, thus threatening the future of Catholicism in Mexico.[6]

Mercadillo and other Sanmiguelenses, most notably several columnists for *El Vocero del Norte*, viewed the decline in religious participation among the youth as symptomatic of a larger problem. They expressed much anxiety over what they perceived to be very real threats to patriarchal authority, including the rise of youth culture and the rejection of traditional gender roles. Although they identified many dangers within Mexican society, their biggest concern was the growing foreign presence in San Miguel. Mercadillo frequently portrayed foreigners as prone to vices and determined to pervert the Mexican youth. In the eyes of these critics Mexico and San Miguel in particular faced an almost existential crisis, and the restoration of patriarchal authority was imperative.

As the historian Eric Zolov has argued, by the late 1950s and early 1960s Mexican authority figures considered youth culture to be one of the most significant threats to patriarchal order in the family and within the nation. This youth culture—including music, films, fashion, and political activism—and consumer culture more broadly linked Mexicans to cultural developments and political movements across the globe.[7] While Zolov's research focuses on the capital city, San Miguel's Mexican youth were also exposed to films, music, fashions, and drugs that patriarchs feared would lead to both moral and physical degeneration, rendering the youth useless as future citizens. The concentration of foreigners in San Miguel (not to mention the large numbers of workers from the region who had spent time in the United States) likely increased the availability and accessibility of music, clothes, consumer products, and films that were, for many, emblematic of the international youth culture. This was especially the case when the Mexican government used censorship and tariff barriers to limit access to foreign films and music.[8] For example, when Don Patterson, an American, moved to San Miguel, he claimed that among the few possessions he brought from the United States were an eight-track tape player, his favorite Bob Dylan and Steppenwolf albums, and a Ché Guevara poster.[9] While the absence of a university in San Miguel precluded a politicized student movement like the one that materialized in Mexico City in the 1960s, certain individuals in San Miguel nevertheless considered the emergent youth culture a direct threat to their vision for Mexico, if not to the entire Western world.

Anxieties over youth culture in San Miguel reflected broader, transnational lamentations over changing ways in the 1960s. As Victoria Langland has observed in her work on student movements in Brazil, "global" youth culture may have shared certain aesthetic commonalities, but it was certainly not homogeneous and emerged within very specific national contexts. For opponents who were often, but not always, on the political right wing, these commonalities were damning evidence of a global phenomenon or even of a conspiracy to undermine tradition and patriarchy.[10] In Mexico these anxieties had many precedents in the late nineteenth and early twentieth centuries, from anti-Chinese sentiment provoked by perceived drug use and deviant femininity to the religious conflicts in the 1920s and 1930s, which highlighted the alleged threats that socialist education—and especially sex education—posed to patriarchal Catholic authority.[11] The influences of the latter on Mercadillo's own thinking are clear. Far from being stereotypical provincials, Sanmiguelenses were deeply engaged with contemporary national and transnational debates.

The *El Vocero* columnist Armando Ruíz Galindo tirelessly criticized the youth culture, which he described as one of the gravest problems confronting Mexico. Likely taking his cues from the Mexican Catholic press, Ruíz expressed concerns about the influence of films on Mexico's youth, and he reproached the municipal government for permitting the screening of what he described as immoral films in the Angela Peralta Theater and the Cine los Aldama. Although he does not identify the films by name, he held foreign and Mexican films in equal contempt. Whereas Ruíz acknowledged that most Mexicans realized that foreign films contained adult themes and glorified "rebels without a cause," he warned that Mexican films engaged similarly immoral themes. In particular he criticized the popular genre of *charro* films for portraying drunkenness and adultery in a positive light, even though the films often were advertised as family friendly.[12] If parents and local officials did not reassert their authority, Ruíz reasoned, the youth would begin to imitate the lifestyles they saw in films and on television. The condemnation likely extended to the actual theaters as the locus of immoral behavior regardless of what was happening on the screen, especially when local police began reporting that men were molesting girls in theaters during the 1970s.[13] Ultimately Ruíz placed the blame for "juvenile delinquency" squarely on the shoulders of parents, whom he claimed had a moral obligation to raise their children to be hardworking citizens.[14]

Ruíz also expressed unease with women's changing roles, sentiments he shared with others in Mexico. He scolded upper- and middle-class mothers for abandoning their parental duties to attend social engagements, and he insisted that they sacrifice everything for the well-being of their children. Ruíz implied that these negligent mothers were just as much of a threat to the nation as the youth were.[15] His chastisement harkened back to a long tradition that idealized a Mexican femininity tied to virginity and selfless motherhood and that contrasted with the image of La Malinche, the woman who allegedly betrayed her people by serving as mistress and translator for the Spanish conquistador Hernán Cortés. This tradition reemerged as Mexicans debated the proper roles for women in postrevolutionary society, particularly in connection with the emerging concept of *desmadre*, a slang term that literally translates to the "un-mothering" of society. Women who did not play their proper roles in the patriarchal hierarchy as wives and mothers were often the first to be blamed for perceived social ills.[16]

In San Miguel, as in the rest of Mexico, many elite and middle-class Mexican families held conservative views about appropriate roles for women in the public sphere. For example, unmarried women in these families rarely left the home unchaperoned, and the traditional *paseo* (a courtship ritual dating to the colonial period that involved chaperoned youths walking around the main square, also known as *serenatas*) persisted in San Miguel at least into the 1960s.[17] Tourist guidebooks warned foreign women not to wear pants in provincial towns such as San Miguel, lest they be viewed as "loose."[18] San Miguel's patriarchal political structure relegated women's role in politics to concerns over the moral well-being of the community, expressed through petitions about the regulation of *cantinas* and the commercial sex trade.[19] Although the fact that female property owners were eligible to vote in Guanajuato state elections as early as 1934—decades before women gained suffrage in national elections—suggests that the state was relatively progressive on women's issues, there remained a disjuncture between the views and ideals of the party functionaries in the state capital and those held by the rest of the population.[20]

Critics frequently attributed disruptions in the Mexican patriarchal order to negative foreign influences that ranged from the relatively benign to criminal behavior. It was a widespread belief that women and adolescents were more easily seduced by these influences, as could be seen in the story of La Malinche on the one hand and the more contemporary spread of youth culture on the other. Foreign languages, foods, fashions, and music appeared to corrupt the imagined cultural ties that linked all Mexicans. In addition, scholars have noted that it was a common perception that Mexicans, and particularly Mexican women, who spent time in the United States were promiscuous and more likely to subvert patriarchal authority.[21] In the 1940s another stereotyped figure—the *pachuco*—emerged in Mexican popular culture to depict Mexican or Mexican American youth in the United States or along the border who supposedly had lost their Mexican roots. Moreover Mexicans frequently employed the term *malinchista* to describe those who had sold out or betrayed their Mexican heritage, whether in the United States or in Mexico. For example, an *El Vocero* editorial asserted that it was better to remain "poor Mexicans" than to be "malinchistas" and traitors by accepting "dirty dollars" from San Miguel's foreign population.[22] Another columnist condemned foreigners and "malinchistas mexicanos" for what he considered the exploitation of local artisans for the tourist trade.[23] The anxieties over pachucos and malinchistas were primarily due to their alleged ambivalence: it was not clear where their loyalties lay.[24]

While many Mexicans in San Miguel looked down upon supposed malinchistas or pachucos, they ultimately directed the brunt of their criticism toward foreigners. Mercadillo, long a critic of San Miguel's foreign population, wrote a letter to President Adolfo Ruiz Cortines in 1953 that implored him to curb the debauchery in town. He blamed foreigners for the proliferation of cantinas and for organizing high-stakes poker games and "unscrupulous" dances where women drank, smoked, and gambled alongside men. Mercadillo claimed that corrupt local officials were complicit in spreading indecency across San Miguel, and he asked the president to send undercover agents to monitor the town.[25] The president forwarded this letter to the Ministry of the Interior, which had jurisdiction over the Mexican intelligence agencies, but it is not clear whether anyone followed up on this unusual request. It is clear, however, that foreigners continued to arrive and that many in the town remained preoccupied with the spread of what they considered to be vice.

The columnists of *El Vocero* explicitly linked a perceived escalation of crime and vagrancy in San Miguel to foreign tourists. Drugs were a particular concern, and in the 1960s San Miguel received negative press in the capital after federal officials deported a number of alleged drug traffickers from the town and uncovered a drug-trafficking network supposedly led by an American.[26] Nonetheless, several columnists argued that it was not enough to rid San Miguel of drug addicts and dealers. Even the "legitimate" tourists frequented cantinas and nightclubs.[27] In his own newspaper column Mercadillo condemned miniskirts, bars, and nightclubs as dangerous, slippery slopes into moral depravity. When women dressed and acted immodestly, the priest argued, they not only sinned but also tempted others to sin. He described nightclubs as the site of pagan orgies and blamed those who paid for vice, as well as those who accepted money for their services.[28] Invoking the youth rebellion epitomized by James Dean's character in the 1955 film *Rebel without a Cause*, one *El Vocero* columnist urged the municipal government to crack down on *rebeldones sin motivo* and to protect the community from vagrants and other vice-prone individuals.[29] Critics cast youth rebellion as a foreign plague that was infecting young Mexicans.[30]

Much of the preoccupation with foreigners and youth culture revolved around the need to protect Mexican feminine virtue from tourists and expatriates. Local columnists lamented that San Miguel was losing its traditions and sense of decency because of young North Americans, who came to San Miguel in search of liberty and adventure outside the confines of marriage. They blamed tourism for the declining moral values that encouraged "automobile romances" on dark streets and contributed to the "scandalous" increase in unwed pregnancies. One commentator warned that even though parents might think their children angels, they were not taking the car out at night to pray a rosary but to commit indecent acts.[31] Moreover some journalists suggested that the mere presence of foreign women in San Miguel attracted unsavory Mexican men from surrounding towns and cities. One American writer referred to this phenomenon as *la gringisa*, or the hunting of the gringa.[32] Foreigners were not only prone to vice, then; they also attracted the worst elements in Mexican society.

Local journalists and religious figures did not singularly perceive connections between foreigners in San Miguel and immoral practices. The Mexican novelist Sergio Galindo's 1970 novel *Nudo*, partially set in San Miguel, explores themes of infidelity and sexual ambiguity through a love "knot" between five individuals. The novel's protagonists are Mexican, Canadian, and European, and Galindo subtly suggests that the foreigners are more comfortable with moral ambiguity. For example, when a conversation turns to pornography and whether or not it is obscene, the leading Mexican character, Daniel, insists that it is and wants to change the subject, whereas the other characters are more open to discussing and debating the topic.[33] While Galindo certainly did not intend to make the same moralizing arguments as the most vocal critics of San Miguel's foreign population, he recognized that his audience would find his association of San Miguel with foreigners and moral transgression quite plausible. As Allan, one of Galindo's foreign characters, quips, "Poor San Miguel de Allende, assaulted by so many motherfuckers. Us included."[34]

Indeed San Miguel was a destination for many individuals whom locals perceived as transgressive, including gay travelers and others who did not fit neatly into binary notions of appropriate gender roles. Local Catholic leaders denounced all of these supposed "deviants," whether they were young people engaged in public displays of affection, women having sex outside the bonds of marriage, or men in same-sex relationships. In their eyes homosexuality, which they considered both symptomatic of and responsible for overall moral decline, constituted a grave threat to the nation on par with communism and drug use. Mercadillo often conflated such perceived threats as communism, atheism, and unnamed "perversions." Mercadillo distributed a handbill in 1950 that called upon locals to pray for the removal of Protestants, Masons, communists, and others who were "perverting the youth" because their presence endangered the community. A letter to the mayor that same year warned of "unspeakable immoralities

[that] have placed San Miguel in the pillory of shameful mockery" and that had converted the town into a "center of communist propaganda, a den of card players, and a lair for repugnant homosexuals." Mercadillo also alerted President Ruiz Cortines that foreign communists were stealthily spreading propaganda throughout San Miguel, women were able to secure abortions easily, and youthful vagrants swarmed the streets and succumbed to the most abhorrent vices.[35] His voice became even shriller in the 1960s, as his *El Vocero* column, written under the pseudonym "Cornelio Plas," warned of numerous threats to the town. He maintained that several active communist cells operated in San Miguel and that although they had originally focused on converting other foreigners to their "exotic doctrines" (which included communism, liberalism, and Protestantism), they had turned their attention to converting Mexicans. Moreover he railed against the "semi-orgies" and other "sordid scenes of pagan debauchery" that permeated San Miguel's bars and nightclubs. Perhaps because politicians had ignored his earlier warnings, he suggested that this was part of the PRI's vision for San Miguel.[36]

Mercadillo's rhetoric drew on semantics of Mexico's Catholic Right that dated back at least to the 1920s and 1930s, as well as on international concerns about threats to Catholicism. Whereas Mercadillo focused on the local implications of what he perceived to be a communist threat, other *El Vocero* columns emphasized the global danger communism presented to Catholicism. *El Vocero* coverage of communism reached an apex in 1961, following the failed Bay of Pigs invasion in Cuba, but it continued throughout the 1960s. This trend highlighted a broader shift among Mexican Catholics from viewing communism as a problem within the nation specifically to viewing it as a threat to Christianity on a global scale. For example, the newspaper reprinted a series of articles by Ricardo Lombardi, an Italian evangelist known as the "microphone of God" (*micrófono de Dios*). Lombardi presented the problem of global communism as likely to have a domino effect, explaining that communism had spread from Europe into Asia and then into the Americas (a reference to Cuba);

therefore, Mexicans should remain vigilant against its spread to their country. Indeed Lombardi went to great lengths to reveal "the naked truth about atheist Communism" and why Catholics should oppose it. His explanations of communist principles were superficial and focused on how communism and Catholicism could not coexist. He based his main argument against communism on the 1931 papal encyclical *Quadragesimo Anno*, which held that communism was concerned only with material well-being and denied the individual's spiritual needs. Lombardi also frequently resorted to fear tactics, claiming at one point that communists would take children from their parents.[37] Such ominous warnings appeared in the Catholic press throughout Mexico, often in conjunction with celebrations of the seventieth anniversary of the 1891 papal encyclical *Rerum Novarum* at which speakers were interrupted with chants of "¡Cristianismo, sí, comunismo, no!"[38]

By linking anticommunism with *Rerum Novarum* Catholic leaders hoped to demonstrate that through adherence to Catholic principles society would overcome the challenges Christianity faced. The 1891 encyclical emphasized social issues, and within the context of the Cold War Catholic leaders returned to their earlier advocacy of the "third way" between the excesses of capitalist and communist societies. In May 1961 Pope John XXIII issued his own encyclical, *Mater et Magistra*, which updated *Rerum Novarum* to address the issues facing mid-twentieth-century Catholics. *El Vocero* reprinted the entire encyclical over several weeks. This alternate vision for society, much like the vision put forward by the National Synarchist Union (UNS, discussed in chapter 2), centered on the Catholic familial unit, which encompassed both the nuclear family and the larger family of Christians.[39] Although the pope did call on governments to ensure the welfare of all citizens, he emphasized that individuals had a responsibility to look out for the rest of the family. Accordingly the Catholic leadership urged people to help improve the lot of peasants and the urban poor, so that communist doctrines would not tempt them.[40] These Catholics considered individualism the root of all social ills.[41]

In turning to the global Catholic Church the Catholics in San Miguel learned that their situation was not unique. Families, communities, and nations across the world faced similar challenges to patriarchal authority and the perceived Catholic moral order. Rather than address these challenges on an individual basis Church leaders targeted what they believed to be the underlying cause: communism. The anticommunism of the global Catholic Church resonated particularly well in Mexico, especially in communities that, like San Miguel, largely had opposed the policies of President Cárdenas in the 1930s. Catholics simply transferred their attention from a perceived communist threat at the national level (posed by leftist government programs and policies) to a communist threat at an international level, where foreigners and their ideologies became the greatest danger.[42]

Although Mercadillo's extreme rants and the alarmism in the pages of *El Vocero* are not representative of the views of all Mexicans in San Miguel, they do highlight certain broadly shared anxieties. As Jeffrey Pilcher demonstrates through the case of the popular Mexican film character Cantinflas (portrayed by Mario Moreno), Mexicans tolerated the subversion of gender norms as humorous in the 1940s, but it became increasingly taboo in the 1950s and 1960s. While Cantinflas regularly transgressed heterosexual norms through cross-dressing and innuendos in his early career, the character later conformed to ideals of "middle-class respectability" and by the late 1960s had become a moralizing critic of the Mexican counterculture.[43] Although Cantinflas became more moderate over time, the foreigners in San Miguel did not. Catholic leaders often played the most prominent role in condemning all kinds of supposedly transgressive behaviors. Others became preoccupied with the perceived slippery slope from communism to homosexuality and juvenile delinquency, all of which, they believed, threatened the well-being of the nation.[44] These concerns typically were divorced from reality, but not always.

The Myths and Realities of Foreign Influences

The American writer Charles Allen Smart seemed to confirm Mercadillo's fears when he remarked, "There are thousands of Americans in

Mexico of our own volition, and I imagine that a fairly high proportion of us are eccentrics, drunks, neurotics, and so forth, apt to get into trouble."[45] While some foreigners traveled to Mexico for wholesome family vacations and educational experiences, others embraced an explicitly countercultural worldview. Beatniks, hippies, and other free spirits frequently traveled to Mexico during the 1950s and 1960s. Many claimed that they were seeking a more authentic existence, a counterpoint to the rat-race mentality in the United States. In the most iconic example of Beat literature, *On the Road*, Jack Kerouac wrote of a transformation that occurred once his protagonists crossed into Mexico. "Behind us," he wrote, "lay the whole of America and everything Dean and I had previously known about life and life on the road. We had finally found the magic land at the end of the road and we never dreamed of the extent of the magic."[46] The "magic" that Kerouac and others encountered was less about some kind of spiritual or metaphysical transformation and more about acting out certain behaviors that were more difficult to get away with at home. In their accounts alcohol, prostitutes, and marijuana were cheap and easy to come by in Mexico. For some travelers vice was entirely the point.

Myths and debates abound regarding famous countercultural figures visiting San Miguel during the 1950s and 1960s. Most of these stories probably emerged long after the fact, propagated by foreign residents of San Miguel eager to bolster their own claims about brushes with celebrity. There are still contentious debates in the comment sections of blogs and articles that mention the Beats in San Miguel.[47] Although it is unlikely that Kerouac ever spent time in San Miguel, Allen Ginsberg did pass through. Neal Cassady spent the most time in San Miguel, first during a quick stopover with fellow Merry Prankster George Walker in 1967 and then for a few short visits later that year. His final visit in February 1968 became legendary in Beat lore. Locals found him unconscious by the railroad track outside of town in the early morning hours. He had attended a wedding party the night before and likely passed out due to a toxic combination of drugs and alcohol. He was later declared dead, and one-time travel companion

Ken Kesey memorialized the episode in a fictional account published as "The Day after Superman Died."[48] Regardless of the specific details about famous countercultural writers, many like-minded travelers, beatniks, hippies, and wannabes did find their way to San Miguel and into its cantinas in the 1950s and 1960s.

It was also true that San Miguel was a destination for gay travelers during this period. The idea of Mexico as an exotic place to release inhibitions attracted gay travelers, but other stereotypes about culture and gender in Mexico increased its allure. For example, as the travel writer Douglas Dean indicated in the introduction to his 1973 book, *Douglas Dean's Gay Mexico*, many American gay men would have been familiar with the idea that Mexico's conservative Catholic culture made it more likely that Mexican men, gay and straight, would seek out sexual liaisons with foreign men. In theory, strict Catholic mores prevented Mexican men from fully acting upon their sexual desires within the confines of marriage, and thus they needed outlets such as prostitutes and gay sex.[49] Gay travel guidebooks like Dean's also portrayed Mexican men as exotic, primitive, and racialized, and they reproduced colonialist attitudes through the use of terms like "conquest." To paraphrase Lionel Cantú Jr., gay tourism in Mexico was often a combination of sexual colonization and sexual liberation.[50]

The reality was more complex than the guidebook stereotypes. As the historian Victor Macías-González has explained, fair-skinned foreign men were seen as objects of sexual desire, but they also carried certain benefits, such as potential access to travel abroad or protection from "low-ranking public safety officials" who were "unlikely to importune someone who could raise the alarm at an embassy."[51] The uneven power dynamics that often existed between American men and their Mexican partners meant that foreigners could find younger, more attractive partners who were looking for, in Dean's words, a "sugar daddy" to take them back to the United States.[52] Dean's book, which was based on his personal experiences and originally published as a series of articles in *The Advocate* and *California Scene*, depicts Mexico as a veritable gay paradise, as long as one followed the rules.

Dean dedicated a chapter of his book to San Miguel, "another of these quaint and picturesque little *pueblos* in Mexico which Gays find an enjoyable place to visit."[53] It is clear from his account that while Sanmiguelenses might not have embraced homosexual relationships, it was a place where gay men could more safely be open than they could in Mexico City, where middle- and upper-class gay men kept their personal lives confined to their homes.[54] In 1950 openly gay Americans filming *The Brave Bulls* in San Miguel attracted the negative attention of the Mexico City press, likely with the help of those sympathetic to Mercadillo's warnings.[55] Dean recommended the Jardín as a good place to cruise and mentioned that he and his lover stayed in the Posada La Ermita, owned by Mario Moreno and one of San Miguel's most desirable hotels at the time.[56]

While it seems that Dean did not need to hide his sexuality in San Miguel, he indicates that he still acted with discretion. In the privacy of Stirling Dickinson's orchid garden Dean and his lover finally found freedom, and he rhetorically asked, "Who was to prevent us from making out a little as we strolled through this sun-lit paradise?"[57] Indeed even though 1960s San Miguel seemed in many ways more permissive and accepting than Mexico City or mainstream America, it was still a small town in the middle of Mexico, with all of the limitations that entailed. Dean's account is one of the few published about gay travelers' experiences in San Miguel during this period. His book suggests that it was quite common for well-to-do gay American men to travel to Mexico, or at least to be curious about it, but the actual numbers are impossible to quantify given the scant evidence. Accounts by lesbian travelers in San Miguel for this period are essentially nonexistent. Speculation abounds about the sexual practices of prominent San Miguel residents, including José Mojica and Stirling Dickinson. One scholar situates Mojica within a transnational network of gay Mexicans linked to the Mexican writer Salvador Novo.[58] Anecdotes and rumors suggest that Dickinson engaged in same-sex relationships, but his biographer, John Virtue, described him as asexual, and beyond that we do not have Dickinson's own voice on the matter.[59] According to

Virtue, even Mercadillo "was known by many Sanmiguelenses to be gay," although he provides no evidence to support this allegation.[60] At best we can extrapolate from accounts like Dean's that Dickinson and others created an environment in San Miguel that was relatively hospitable to queer visitors.

Nevertheless, the Red Scare and the Lavender Scare in the United States exacerbated fears linking San Miguel's foreigners to what some locals perceived to be twin threats of communism and homosexuality. The 1949 art school boycott discussed in chapter 2 was also a powerful precedent. While it is difficult to ascertain the effectiveness of Alfredo Campanella's red-baiting campaign in the context of the boycott, the many letters and telegrams Campanella and his supporters sent did become part of an archive that a U.S. Senate committee revisited as concerns over the spread of communism in Latin America deepened. At first glance local anxieties seem to have provoked the accusations against San Miguel's foreign population, but these accusations can be completely understood only when interpreted within this broader international context. By the late 1950s U.S. officials had rediscovered the files on the San Miguel boycott, as well as Stirling Dickinson's FBI file, which alleged that he had "homosexual tendencies" and associated with known communists.[61] The U.S. State Department dismissed embassy official Dorsey Fisher (one of Dickinson's strongest allies during the boycott) from his post following accusations of homosexuality, and intelligence officials listed Dickinson among the top American communists in Mexico. Prominent U.S. newspapers ran a story alleging that Dickinson was a threat to national security (a veiled reference to suspected homosexuality at the time) and described San Miguel as one of the top communist havens in Mexico.[62]

Dickinson successfully fought to clear his name and San Miguel's reputation in the United States through efforts culminating in testimony before the Senate and in a *Washington Post* article that acknowledged that Dickinson and San Miguel had been falsely maligned. The Mexico City newspaper *El Universal* echoed these sentiments. Because Dickinson was a central figure in San Miguel's international tourism industry, political and business leaders from across the state of Guanajuato rallied in his defense, thus highlighting the limits of moral outrage when economic development strategies were at stake.[63] However, the available historical record provides few insights into how ordinary locals interpreted the accusations about Dickinson. The efforts and priorities of San Miguel's best-connected citizens certainly do not reflect broader local attitudes.

As the concerns of local religious figures and journalists described in the section above indicate, same-sex relationships were not the only perceived sexual threat in San Miguel. These individuals also worried that young Mexican women who took housekeeping jobs in foreigners' homes were especially at risk of seduction. Other studies have shown that it was in fact common for sex workers to earn additional income as domestic servants.[64] The accusations in San Miguel ultimately reveal more about the columnists' fears—that women working outside of the home posed a threat to patriarchal authority—than they do about the actual practices of domestic workers.

In a similar vein the frequently deployed term "malinchista" had an explicitly sexual connotation. Historically Mexicans compared compatriots who married foreigners to La Malinche, essentially viewing these marriages as a betrayal of their race and nation. Ample examples of such malinchistas abound in San Miguel. As the historian Jocelyn Olcott has observed, policymakers frequently debated whether women who married foreigners were still technically Mexican.[65] Even when families did not go as far as to accuse their daughters of betraying the nation, they frequently expressed discomfort with the idea that they were sacrificing their identities for a foreign man. Cossío del Pomar described how one San Miguel family was disheartened to discover that their Mexican daughter, after moving to the United States with her American husband, elected not to teach her children Spanish. He suggested that this was a common practice.[66] Lucha Maxwell's parents expressed concern about her marriage to an American for other reasons, mostly because she was abandoning her career as a physical therapist in Mexico City.[67] In San Miguel locals regularly questioned the motives of the foreign men as well. Numerous mixed couples sought letters from the mayor's office verifying that they were legally married and living upright, moral lives as a safeguard against accusations.[68] Cross-cultural sexual relationships occurred with increasing frequency in the 1950s and 1960s and particularly seemed to raise the ire of some locals, even when the relationships led to marriage.

All of the marriages between Mexicans and foreigners in San Miguel could have been viewed as unconventional and disruptive. But critics were more likely to accept them when the foreigner assimilated into Mexican life and thus did not pose an immediate threat to the nation. Even though Dotty Birk, for example, was a rather independent young woman who breached such male-dominated spheres as the cantina and the bullring upon her arrival in San Miguel, marriage domesticated and Mexicanized her. She converted to Catholicism before her wedding, spoke Spanish, lived with her husband in his parents' home before they moved into their own house, and raised a family. Her path certainly was not typical, and unlike most Mexican wives of her socioeconomic status, she worked outside the home after marriage.[69] Nevertheless, after marriage she ceased to pose a threat to the local status quo.

The idea of assimilating into Mexican culture was cause for concern among some foreigners. *Señorita Okay*, a 1956 young adult novel by Claire Willis Callahan (pseudonym Nancy Hartwell), highlights the potential threats that often went unspoken in nonfictional accounts. The novel relates the story of Patricia O'Kane, a young American woman who studies art for a summer in San Miguel. When O'Kane begins to pursue a relationship with a Mexican man, her friend describes the hardships for American women trying to integrate into that lifestyle: "Some of these marriages [between Americans and Mexicans] turn out fine. . . . But usually it's hard on the girl. The boy's family . . . wants him to marry someone else like himself. They also want him to marry a Catholic. And they don't want him to go to the States to live. So the girl lives here in the Mexican way in an old house often without conveniences as she knows them."[70] Another American friend warns O'Kane to "watch your step" because "lots of American girls" fall for Mexican men, "but it doesn't work out very well as a rule."[71] The novel clearly suggests that marriages between U.S. women and Mexican men cannot work, yet it is silent on the topic of relationships between American men and Mexican women. This gendered subtext ultimately reveals prevalent attitudes about appropriate gender roles in a marriage, with the woman necessarily conforming to the religion and lifestyle of the man. It also draws upon a longer tradition of gendering international relations and specifically relations between the United States and Mexico. Whereas a union between the docile Mexican *señorita* and the American male would presumably Americanize the female, a union between the Mexican male and the American female would threaten U.S. masculinity. When O'Kane rejects the Mexican man in the novel, she emasculates him. Conversely, when real American women like Ruth Hyba, Nell Harris, and Dotty Birk chose to marry Mexican men, they symbolically reinforced Mexican masculinity.[72]

Despite doubts and concerns about these marriages, over time a critical mass of cross-cultural couples occupied a pivotal position between San Miguel's foreign and Mexican populations. Whereas the couples had clear roles to play as cultural interlocutors in San Miguel, their children occupied a more ambiguous societal position. Born in Mexico, yet bilingual and often possessing foreign citizenship, these individuals had to navigate a more complicated terrain when it came to identity. The parents of this generation attempted to address this situation through a variety of approaches to cross-cultural childrearing, but some common trends appeared.[73] Collectively they demonstrated a desire for their children to learn about and participate in the cultures of both parents. Language played a central role in this process. Some families spoke only Spanish in the home, some focused on English-language education first, and in other cases one parent addressed the children only in Spanish and the other only in English. None of the families interviewed reported hostility toward their children's bilingualism, notwithstanding the fears of *El Vocero* columnists that the widespread use of English in San Miguel would corrupt the Spanish language. In fact most families considered bilingualism a highly desirable competitive advantage.[74] Although "Mexican culture" did not seem to be at risk, it is clear that the multicultural literacy that proved to be an advantage for some Sanmiguelenses put others at a disadvantage.

Access to educational opportunities also set the children of Mexican-foreign couples apart from average Sanmiguelenses. Options for quality education beyond primary school remained limited in San Miguel from the 1950s through the 1970s, reflecting the state of education across the country. According to one expert on Mexican education, between the 1920s and 1970s "the overwhelming majority of Mexican students sought merely to complete the six years of primary education," and secondary school (*secundaria*, the rough equivalent of middle school in the United States) was not compulsory in Mexico until 1993.[75] During the 1960s a New Yorker named Augusta Irving ran a small English-language private school out of her San Miguel home, attended by a handful of Mexican-born students and a number of foreign-born children whose families were living in San Miguel temporarily. The school did not have a formal accreditation, so students attended a Mexican school in the sixth grade in order to meet the mandated educational requirements.[76] Most of the cross-cultural families had the financial resources to send their children to private secondary and high schools outside of San Miguel, a luxury that ordinarily only elite Mexican families could afford. Several private schools located in the nearby city of Querétaro served expatriate families in the business sector and diplomatic communities. Other families sent their children to live with relatives in Mexico City so they could attend school there, and some even sent their children abroad to boarding schools. In 1974 a group of Mexican and foreign parents established San Miguel's first nonprofit bilingual school, the Escuela José Vasconcelos. The school's stated purpose was to help students become "acquainted with the customs of another culture and thereby establish greater communication and understanding." More than half of the children at José Vasconcelos were from Mexican families and another 25 percent had one Mexican parent. By 1980 the school had students whose families were from Austria, Canada, Czechoslovakia, Germany, Guatemala, Japan, Norway, the United States, and of course Mexico.[77] These educational experiences, whether in San Miguel or elsewhere, reinforced the ties between San Miguel's foreign and elite Mexican populations.[78]

To argue that children raised in cross-cultural families posed a threat to Mexican culture or identity oversimplifies the matter. As adults, many of these individuals spent time studying and working abroad, particularly in the United States and Europe but also in other Latin American countries. It is not surprising, however, that many of them returned to live, work, and start their own families in San Miguel. Like the generation of expatriates before them, they leveraged their multilingualism and cosmopolitan backgrounds to take on roles in the service industry and forge international connections, including navigating San Miguel through the UNESCO World Heritage Site application process (a process explored in the epilogue). Perhaps only places like San Miguel could truly feel like home to these multicultural, transnational citizens. One woman commented that the strong bond she felt with the other families she grew up with in San Miguel kept drawing her back.[79] Most individuals with an American parent are American citizens or dual citizens, a status that facilitates movement across borders, but there was no strong correlation between citizenship and identity. Informal conversations and formal interviews have revealed that among those who remained in or returned to San Miguel, most did not identify exclusively with a Mexican national identity or with the nationality of their other parent but somewhere in between. Some did identify strongly as Mexican, though, so it is impossible to generalize.[80] Although this is not a representative sample, their reflections on identity do help to highlight some of the major issues at stake. Observers have credited these generations of Sanmiguelenses for the relative harmony between Mexicans and foreigners in San Miguel, despite their varied upbringings and means of self-identification. Moreover several of these cross-cultural individuals, nostalgic for the San Miguel of their childhoods, have assumed roles as stewards of San Miguel's history and culture, whether through political channels, nonprofit work, or other advocacy.[81] In many ways their ambivalence helped to diminish hard and fast divisions between Mexicans and foreigners in San Miguel, but it was most pronounced among those Mexicans of a higher socioeconomic status who had access to similar educational opportunities. Cross-cultural families did not bring about the demise of Mexican national identity. They do help illustrate how economic concerns became deeply entangled with anxieties over foreignness and identity in San Miguel.

San Miguel's growing foreign presence did at times cause problems and contribute to local anxieties, but foreigners did not bring all problems and vice to San Miguel. Mercadillo and other local newspaper columnists idealized San Miguel's pretourism past as free of vice, but this was simply not the case. A major stop for centuries on the route between the Guanajuato and Zacatecas silver mines and Mexico City, San Miguel had long catered to the desires of male visitors and workers living far from their families. When San Miguel's foreign tourism industry picked up in earnest in the late 1930s, a small-scale "vice" industry already existed to provide for both visitors and local residents. Cantinas, dance halls, and brothels practically surrounded the city.[82]

Some Sanmiguelenses particularly feared the effects that cantinas and brothels might have on local residents' morality. *El Vocero* columnists were more critical of prostitution when they viewed foreigners as the primary culprits, thus reinforcing the notion that protecting Mexican women was the equivalent of protecting the nation.[83] Government officials propagated this perception by associating "hippies who vacation in San Miguel" with all manner of unsavory activities, including "white slavery."[84] It was the women of San Miguel, however, who had initially drawn attention to prostitution as a problem *within* the Mexican community decades earlier. In 1933 more than two hundred women petitioned the municipal government to close the dance halls and brothels in San Miguel or, if the local government did not have the power to do so, to tax them so heavily that they would be forced to close. The petitioners considered these establishments a threat to the morality of the community and an unnecessary temptation for men, who often spent their salaries on alcohol and women.[85] The municipal government responded by following the lead of other towns and cities in increasing regulation of the so-called vice industries and creating a "tolerance zone" within the city. However, unlike the petitioners, the officials considered the problem to be health related, and their efforts primarily sought to protect male residents from disease.[86] Municipal officials monitored the sex workers in San Miguel, just as their counterparts did in towns and cities throughout Mexico and across the world, by conducting invasive medical exams before issuing the workers licenses. As the historian Katherine Bliss has observed in the case of Mexico City, this mode of government intervention established male control over what previously had been a female-dominated industry.[87]

By the mid-1930s one of San Miguel's largest brothels was several blocks outside of the approved zone. Municipal government files on the women licensed to work there provide a rare glimpse into the local commercial sex trade during this period. Of the twenty-seven women newly licensed to work at this house in 1936 most were from neighboring cities and states, although some came from as far away as the state of Zacatecas and Mexico City. None were Sanmiguelenses, and nearly all of the women were from urban areas or at least areas that were more urban than San Miguel. According to these records, the average age of the women was twenty, with the oldest being thirty-five and the youngest fifteen. Two were married.[88] This brothel predated San Miguel's foreign tourism industry, and therefore the women who worked there served a primarily Mexican clientele.

The advent of San Miguel's tourism industry certainly expanded the local commercial sex trade.[89] Although most foreign residents and visitors have not openly discussed their role as patrons of these establishments, some have indicated in informal conversations and fictionalized accounts that it was a common practice.[90] One American writer and part-time San Miguel resident admitted that the word *puta*, Spanish slang for prostitute, was among the first he learned in Mexico.[91] State law permitted and regulated sex work in Guanajuato until 1962, after which sex workers continued operating illicitly (although many women working in the sex trade likely did so clandestinely before 1962 to avoid licensing fees and examinations).[92]

One of the best-known spots in San Miguel for foreigners as well as locals was the Casa de la Turca. Gloria León, more commonly known as La Turca, read tea leaves and told fortunes by day and ran a dance hall, brothel, and more upscale call-girl service at night. Within the so-called tolerance zone, the Casa de la Turca was at the time in the last row of residences bordering the fruit orchards on the outskirts of town (although the location now would be considered near the city center). La Turca allegedly continued operating her sex-related businesses after the state prohibited prostitution. This former brothel, now a guesthouse and art gallery, carries a stigma among many Sanmiguelenses. The bad reputation derives not only from the sex trade that once operated there but also from a history of violence linked to the trade. According to local lore, the spirits of aborted fetuses, sex workers who died from botched abortions, and men killed in barroom brawls continue to haunt the site. An American woman who converted the space into a modern guesthouse even had a shaman cleanse the building of negative spirits before completing renovations.[93] While the story of La Turca relegates prostitution to a sordid past, San Miguel's sex trade continues. Moreover the town has a reputation, at least among some in Mexico City, as a primary destination for the euphemistically labeled "infidelity tourists," a place where married Mexican men look for weekend flings with foreigners, whom they seem to conflate with prostitutes.[94]

Although political and business leaders did not necessarily share religious leaders' views on foreign threats to morality, they did increasingly acknowledge the need to contain certain negative influences. In the summer of 1969 business owners called upon the local government to clear foreign "hippies" and roving Mexican vendors from the Jardín. They viewed both groups as a menace because they did not participate in the formal tourism economy, and furthermore their presence detracted from the main square's ambience as the town prepared for the September 1969 patriotic festivals and jubilee celebration of Allende's birth (see chapter 3).[95] Here they found common ground with Mercadillo, who came around to the idea that some foreigners could change their ways and convert to Catholicism. Mercadillo enlisted Erika Schedel to reach out to San Miguel's English-speaking population. Schedel, a German woman who had spent time in the United States, wrote a regular column in *El Vocero* on religion and the arts. It was the only English-language column to appear in the newspaper, and it urged foreigners to attend Catholic mass at the Parroquia. Mercadillo initiated English-language religious services to reach out to foreigners, and Schedel led an English-language prayer group. She also ran an art gallery affiliated with the parish and often encouraged expatriates to attend gallery events as another way to get them involved with the Church.[96] Their motivations were quite different, but the concerns of religious, economic, and political leaders seemingly converged. It was unrealistic to expel all foreign influences from San Miguel. Head shaving, adopted widely across Latin America during this period, played a very specific role locally by targeting foreigners that all constituencies agreed were undesirable.

Shaving Heads and Deporting Undesirables

On Saturday, August 2, 1969, the day before the incident described at the beginning of this chapter, San Miguel's municipal police received complaints from business owners about American "hippies" smoking and "raising a fuss" (*armando un gran alboroto*) in the Jardín. They dispersed the group, only to discover the next day that the foreigners had once again congregated in the plaza. This time the police detained eighteen of them in the municipal jail, where other prisoners shaved the new arrivals' heads. The police released the detainees a few hours later on the orders of Mayor Antonio Gil Vega.[97] The time-line is telling. While Sanmiguelenses had long registered grievances against foreigners, complaints from the business community elicited an immediate response.

The specific details about the incident vary widely depending on the account. According to a Mexican intelligence report compiled two weeks after the arrests, Gil denied having any prior knowledge of the plan to detain the foreigners and shave their heads. The police, too, denied any involvement in the outcome and instead blamed unruly prisoners for the head shavings. In this same account Gil suppos-edly castigated the police chief for not forcing the other prisoners to respect the foreigners. The official police reports for that month contain no reference to the incident at all, allegedly because the arrested individuals refused to disclose their names. Although the intelligence report does not name informants, the insistence that Gil had nothing to do with the incident other than to demand the release of the foreigners in custody suggests that at least one source was very close to the mayor. Indeed the claim that it took the police chief nearly three hours to locate and inform Gil of the arrests seems implausible given the small size of the town in 1969.[98]

Accounts from some of the foreigners involved contradict the nar-rative in the August 15 intelligence report. Amnon Issacharoff, for one, insisted that he and his teenage son were innocent bystanders and that the police accosted them for the benefit of the crowd that had gathered in the plaza. In a report submitted to the Mexican ambassador to the United States five days after the episode Issacharoff claimed that he did not see any "hippies" in San Miguel, only "typical American youths," and he described himself as a "scholarly and balding American physician." While the report states that other presumably Mexican prisoners were responsible for cutting the Americans' hair with sheep shears, it presented the police as complicit. Moreover Issacharoff claimed that upon his release about an hour after being taken into custody someone led him to Gil's office, just upstairs from the jail, where the mayor apologized and denied any knowledge of the event.

Issacharoff did not seem convinced that Gil could have been unaware of the spectacle that had occurred outside his office. He described the overall climate surrounding the arrests as "pandemonium" that wrought "terror among the Americans, particularly the mothers."[99]

Two other Americans filed complaints on August 4 that corroborate Issacharoff and John Schimel's report. One of the men, Martin D. Kriegel, was a twenty-something New Yorker studying Mayan civilization in Mexico. Kriegel explained that on the day of the incident he was leaving Los Dragones, a restaurant next to the police station, when police officers approached him and claimed that one of his friends was in trouble. They rushed him into the jail, where about twenty men, whom he identified as prisoners, were gathered around a table with a pair of scissors and shaving razors. Kriegel alleged that the men insisted that they had to cut his hair on the mayor's orders. He claimed that he and the other Americans whose heads were shaved were permitted to leave without any further statements or explanations. James Glenn Meyer, another New Yorker, filed the other complaint. He stated that he was waiting to get his shoes shined in the main plaza when police officers approached him and escorted him to the jail. Meyer explained that they said something to him in Spanish, but he did not understand them. Once inside the jail, he reported, men in civilian attire forced him into a chair and cut his hair while a group looked on, laughing and enjoying the spectacle. He, too, alleged that the man who cut his hair said it was on the order of the mayor. Afterward Meyer was detained with several other Americans, and he claimed that no one asked for their names or other forms of identification before the police released them about an hour and a half later. Both of these complaints appeared in an intelligence report compiled on August 16 and riddled with errors. The author of the report cast doubt on the veracity of the claims, citing the Americans' affiliation with Dr. Felipe Dobarganes, whose family had close ties to the Instituto Allende and who allegedly had had a falling out (enemistado) with Antonio Gil Vega.[100]

More than anything, it seems that Gil's denial of involvement in the head shavings was an attempt to provide cover against reprisals from national officials. Locally his participation had already entered popular lore. A columnist for *El Vocero* remarked that it was common knowledge that the municipal government authorized the local police to shave the heads of long-haired men and that they had already targeted approximately twenty Mexicans and foreigners prior to the August 3 event.[101] According to one account, Gil occasionally wielded scissors himself.[102] At the time of the 1969 head shavings in San Miguel police across Mexico were conducting similar haircutting raids.[103] Mexican authorities were not the first to utilize head shaving as a form of repression and domination; the practice has long been equated with symbolic castration or forcibly restrained sexuality.[104] Haircutting has played a particularly pertinent role in the history of U.S.-Mexican relations, from violent head-shaving incidents at the border in the 1930s to the 1943 Zoot Suit Riots in Los Angeles, during which U.S. servicemen cut the hair of Mexican American youths.[105] Police officials in other countries across the political spectrum, from right-wing military regimes to Cuba's revolutionary government, also targeted long-haired males throughout the 1960s and into the 1970s.[106] It is not surprising then that Mexican authorities turned to head shaving as a form of repression and a way to mark supposedly deviant male bodies. A few weeks before the head-shaving incident in San Miguel became an international story, a journalist for a newspaper in the nearby city of Celaya joked that, upon hearing that Mexican officials were forcing hippies to bathe and get haircuts before crossing the U.S.-Mexico border, the astronauts of Apollo 11 remarked that they wanted to cut their hair too so they could go to Mexico to escape the hippies.[107]

If Gil feared reprisals, he was quite mistaken. Americans and Mexicans in San Miguel and beyond wrote letters praising the conduct of the police officers. One American, Norman Pearl, mused, "If our government would do the same we would reduce our troubles many fold."[108] Others reportedly sent checks to buy the police officers beer. Expatriates also seemed to embrace the head-shaving policy because it created an "other" that made them look desirable by comparison. Some expatriate men intentionally maintained clean-shaven faces and wore crew cuts to distinguish themselves from the hippies.[109] Rather than cause an international uproar, the head-shaving incident became a punch line for local humorists. A columnist for *El Vocero* commended the municipal authorities, claiming it was their only real accomplishment.[110] *El Fisgón* printed a phony letter from the local barbers' union that accused the police of undercutting their business by providing free haircuts, as well as a telegram from a fictional Cuban who applauded San Miguel's restrictions against long hair and beards but requested that the town suspend the restrictions if Fidel Castro ever visited.[111] The physical containment of deviant bodies through forced head shavings built consensus among many Mexicans and foreigners in San Miguel that long-haired men and others who subverted traditional gender roles were an acceptable target. This consensus, as *El Fisgón* editor Manuel Zavala Zavala demonstrated with his joke about Castro, was part of an emerging transnational framework for addressing the hippie problem.

Consequently Mexican foreign relations officials did not express concern about the potentially negative impact of the San Miguel head-shaving episode on Mexico's image abroad. The response that the Mexican ambassador to the United States sent to Issacharoff, Schimel, and their families was revealing. Ambassador Hugo Margáin expressed regret about their "unfortunate experience" with San Miguel's "overzealous police" but insisted that Americans ultimately were to blame. He explained that police in many parts of Mexico had been overwhelmed by the large number of drug-seeking American youth and that it was difficult to "distinguish students and other bona fide young Americans from the so-called 'hippies.'"[112] For Mexican officials the incident was a source of national pride more than anything else. Foreigners were quick to praise the Mexican government for containing what they perceived to be negative aspects of youth culture, rather than allowing the counterculturalists to run amok. A 1965 survey in the United States provides context for this praise, revealing that 80 percent of those polled "believed that schools should prohibit boys from wearing their hair long."[113] The head shavings symbolically inverted the international roles that Americans and Mexicans played (as imagined in the United States), with the United States portrayed as disorderly and chaotic, while Mexico was hailed as a place where law and order prevailed. The Mexicans were policing the Americans, rather than the other way around. While these episodes did little to invert the actual power dynamic between the United States and Mexico, they did create an "other" against which Mexican leaders could define a modern Mexican identity.

As Margáin's comments suggest, the head-shaving incidents across Mexico took place within the context of a growing preoccupation with hippies and other deviant types. The strident crackdown on hippies and other undesirable foreigners in 1969 represented a significant departure from Mexican policy only a year earlier. In the years leading up to the 1968 Olympic Games in Mexico City government officials were preoccupied with presenting a positive image of Mexico to the world. They focused on tourism promotion, including the production of films and brochures for Mexican consulates worldwide to distribute.[114] Even residents of San Miguel understood that the Olympics could bring additional revenue through tourism and urged local officials to clean up the trash in the streets and repaint buildings to make the town more attractive to visitors.[115] Beyond superficial attempts to polish Mexico's image, some commentators advised Mexicans to improve their personal behavior to accommodate foreign guests during the Olympics. Specific suggestions included respecting other teams during athletic competitions, allowing foreign visitors to take open seats on the bus, providing accurate directions to venues and tourist destinations, and showing courtesy to visitors from the moment of their arrival to their departure.[116] Police did round up and deport some foreign "hippies" before the Olympics, mostly from the tourist areas of Mexico City and the Huautla area, where mushrooms with hallucinogenic properties attracted visitors from North America and Europe. Immigration officials also had instructions to keep dirty, long-haired foreigners from entering the country.[117] In April 1968, however, Mexican president Gustavo Díaz Ordaz (1964–70) defended the rights of an individual to "let his beard, hair, or sideburns grow if he wants to," in an attempt to portray Mexico as a tolerant, democratic society.[118]

Mexican officials viewed the escalating student movement in Mexico City as the main threat to a successful 1968 Olympic Games. Government anxieties about the movement related to concerns about communism. Officials feared linkages between foreign hippies, the student movement, and the more violent armed struggles across Latin America, but young Mexicans were the primary targets of repression. The government crackdown on this movement—culminating with the massacre of hundreds of protesters in the Plaza of Three Cultures at Tlatelolco on October 2—provoked negligible foreign protest.[119] In fact many foreign governments and individuals praised the Mexican administration's handling of the protests, effectively emboldening officials.[120] As Eric Zolov has argued, the massacre and fear of repression drove more individuals to express opposition to the government through countercultural means rather than through protests or more violent guerrilla movements.[121]

Accordingly government officials became less tolerant of hippies, countercultural travelers, and any others who might instigate or encourage another oppositional movement. In the 1960s Americans increasingly crossed the border in search of pleasure and vice, but by the 1970s border officials had tightened restrictions against the entrance of suspicious foreigners, and local police, like those in San Miguel, increased vigilance against dubious visitors and turned more frequently to deportations.[122] Officials used words such as "penetration" and "invasion" to describe the threat foreign hippies posed to national territory, yet they also increasingly grouped Mexican hippies into their reports, implying that these nationals were simply symptomatic of a foreign contagion. As Mexican national security officials observed, the threat that hippies posed was not violent but rooted in their lack of both hygiene and *buenas costumbres*, or good manners. Above all they set a bad example for Mexican youth. So although Mexican officials recognized hippies as a national problem, they offered no concerted response. Ultimately they left it up to local authorities to figure out how best to contain the threat.[123] Confident that the tourism industry was strong, Mexican officials could afford more restrictive policies. The San Miguel case demonstrated that these attempts to control foreigners successfully reinforced a patriarchal vision for Mexican society and enabled a more nuanced relationship with the town's expatriates and other desirable foreign visitors.

Limits of the Patriarchal Ideal in San Miguel

The priorities of local business, political, and religious leaders temporarily converged when it came to dealing with undesirable foreigners. While head shaving may have taken on many meanings across Mexico and the rest of the world in the 1960s, in San Miguel it occurred within a very specific set of circumstances. There, many perceived the foreign threat as tangible and immediate. The head-shaving raid established the parameters of appropriate behavior and appearance for Mexicans and foreigners alike. Moreover it created a space in which Mexicans could forge acceptable alliances with foreigners who were desirable because of their contributions to the local economy, while also allowing San Miguel's foreign residents to separate themselves from unsavory compatriots. Above all the policy allowed male Mexican leaders to assert their authority and their vision for Mexico. By containing deviant women through marriage and familial duties and undesirable men through violence, Mexican officials believed that they could preserve the patriarchal foundations of the nation.

Opponents of San Miguel's foreign presence lost their most committed advocate in 1969 when Mercadillo left his post as parish priest. Rumors and speculation about the reasons for his departure abound. As one resident recalled, Mercadillo lost his power and influence overnight.[124] Although he maintained a circle of devoted followers until his death in 1984, it appears that a combination of economic scandals involving his operations at the Sanctuary of Atotonilco, conflicts over the mysterious disappearance of sacred artifacts from numerous local churches and chapels, and changing winds in the Latin American Catholic Church all likely contributed to his diminished role in San Miguel.[125]

Ultimately the head shavings in San Miguel were symbolic. They did not end undesirable foreign influences, nor did they advance an alternate economic model that would reinforce traditional patriarchal values. Despite these attempts to defend an ideal of nationalist Mexican masculinity, dramatic economic changes across the nation accelerated San Miguel's shift to a feminine, service-based economy and forced many Mexican residents to become reliant upon the charity of foreign-run philanthropic organizations, further diminishing the role of family patriarchs. The following chapter examines why the town became a model for economic development in this climate.

5 San Miguel's Two
Service Economies

In 1974 Margaret Cecilia Galloway, a British expatriate, first visited
San Miguel, the final stop of a two-month trip to Mexico. The town
kept drawing her back, and just south of San Miguel Galloway eventually built a house with a view of the reservoir, a lake known as Presa
Allende. Like many other expatriates she quickly immersed herself
in the town's vibrant social life, participating in an equestrian club,
amateur theater performances, and a local orchestra. Galloway also
became quite involved in charitable work. News that five elderly
Mexicans died of exposure one winter prompted her to help organize the group Knit for the Needy, which gathered foreign women
to make sweaters, hats, scarves, and gloves for poor elderly Mexicans. The group soon discovered, however, that the objects of their
charity were more adept with yarn and needles, and they decided to
rename the group Knit *with* the Needy. Galloway was quick to learn
from this experience and went on to lead other, more collaborative,
charitable organizations, including a project called ALMA, which
opened a home for elderly Mexicans in 1996. She took pride in the
fact that Mexicans took over the entire leadership of ALMA only a
few years later. Galloway explained in a memoir that her specific
concern for the elderly stemmed from her observation that many
families in San Miguel "lost their men to look for higher paid work

in the U.S. and could not afford to look after their grandparents."[1] Her efforts and those of hundreds of other foreigners who joined her in philanthropic work help illustrate why San Miguel emerged as a model for economic development in Mexico and why that model was fundamentally flawed.

The proliferation of foreign-led philanthropic efforts in San Miguel in the 1980s and 1990s illuminates the primary dilemma created by the combination of neoliberal economic policies and the growing expatriate population. The foreign population formed many charitable organizations to fill the vacuum left by steep cuts to Mexico's social services in the wake of the 1982 debt crisis; I refer to these philanthropic efforts collectively as San Miguel's other "service" economy. However, they often failed to identify the precise causes of the suffering they sought to alleviate and did not critically examine the economic implications of their presence in San Miguel. Expatriates like Galloway frequently mistook the symptoms of rural poverty—female-headed families resulting from the emigration of male workers—for the cause. The subtle shift in the name and mission of Galloway's knitting group highlighted a common misperception: contrary to the beliefs of some expatriates, it was not necessarily the absence of skill or ambition, or of charitable giving in Mexican culture, but rather a lack of access to resources that affected many Mexicans who lived in poverty. While Mexico has long been plagued with endemic poverty, government austerity measures and the expansion of San Miguel's service-oriented industry accelerated processes that forced families into precarious living conditions and resulted in many workers leaving to find employment elsewhere. San Miguel's service-based economy became a model in the neoliberal era because it continued to expand while most of the Mexican economy was in a state of crisis. However, the model was flawed in that it reproduced the very structural conditions that exacerbated poverty.

This chapter examines tensions that emerged as the result of San Miguel's two service-based economies in the neoliberal context. Many of San Miguel's most pressing public concerns, from historic preservation to water management, and from the prevalence of bars to the proper role of foreign philanthropy, revolved around a central problem: given limited government resources, how could municipal officials provide essential services such as water, garbage collection, and road improvements while also investing in the tourism industry? Although some of the issues at stake, such as road improvements and the construction of a bus station, would theoretically benefit both local residents and tourists, other subjects, such as water, were more sensitive. How would municipal officials explain why expats spent hours watering their gardens or golfing on carefully manicured fairways when entire neighborhoods had no water supply at all? The exponential growth of San Miguel's population further complicated these discussions. Between the 1930s and the 1970s San Miguel's urban population tripled, to more than thirty thousand, and the total population, including the rural communities, exceeded seventy-five thousand.[2] These statistics likely did not include many of the expats, whose numbers neared one thousand by 1980.[3]

As more foreigners moved to San Miguel, they demanded a say in local decision-making processes. It is no small coincidence that *Atención*, a bilingual newspaper founded by expatriates in 1975, was San Miguel's only local weekly newspaper after *El Vocero* ceased publication in 1974. *Atención*'s rise to prominence as the primary local print news organ paralleled expatriates' insertion of themselves into debates over civic improvement.[4] Expatriates did not simply voice their opinions in weekly newspaper columns. They also increased their involvement in San Miguel through a number of philanthropic organizations. Many of these organizations funded initiatives beyond the reach of the limited municipal budgets, including school construction, meals for the elderly, and medical care. While these organizations supplied essential services, they also fueled local controversies over who provided for the *sanmiguelenses* most in need.

The debt crisis that engulfed Mexico in the 1980s sent shockwaves throughout the economy and meant a steep reduction in resources dedicated to tourism development. Although the weaknesses of Mexico's import substitution industrialization (ISI) model were evident by the 1970s, the discovery of new oil fields, combined with the high price of oil, enabled the government to secure international loans, also known as "petrodollars," that funded everything from basic social services to investments in resort destinations such as Cancún. However, a 1982 international oil glut led to the collapse of petroleum prices, and Mexico's foreign lenders hiked interest rates on the nation's debt. Desperate to secure more loans, the Mexican government turned to lending institutions such as the International Monetary Fund (IMF), which lent money on the condition that Mexico and other indebted developing nations restructure their economies to conform to neoliberal economic principles. These principles included the privatization of the public sector, trade liberalization, and the implementation of austerity measures to reduce social services and other government costs—essentially a reversal of Mexico's economic policies for most of the twentieth century. As a result, the government slashed salaries or cut jobs altogether, eliminated or significantly reduced housing and food subsidies, and began to repeal tariffs and other protectionist policies that insulated Mexican businesses from foreign competition. People across Mexico, particularly the middle classes, suffered tremendous hardships.[5]

Mexico's shift to a neoliberal economic model was part of a broader global trend. Certain changes, however, were specific to the Mexican experience, particularly the revision of Article 27 of the Mexican Constitution of 1917 and the promulgation of the North American Free Trade Agreement (NAFTA, or TCLN, as it is called in Mexico) in the early 1990s. The revision of Article 27 permitted and encouraged the privatization of *ejidos*, the communally held land parcels that were the centerpiece of postrevolutionary agrarian reform. NAFTA formalized efforts to eliminate trade barriers between Mexico, the United States, and Canada. The agreement had different implications depending on the region of Mexico. Cities along the U.S.-Mexican border saw a dramatic increase in the number of factories and assembly plants (*maquiladoras*), as well as a corresponding influx of migrants seeking work in those factories. People in towns and cities across Mexico had unprecedented access to American products and foodstuffs. However, small-scale farmers, particularly in the Bajío and in southern Mexico, struggled to compete with heavily subsidized corn and other staples from the United States. Unable to support their families, these farmers often had to sell their land and turn to wage labor or migrate. In San Miguel these policies further intensified a workforce hierarchy that privileged bilingual employees and service-industry jobs frequently occupied by women, thus destabilizing the patriarchal hierarchy built on manufacturing and agricultural work that local men had sought to reinforce over the years. While these changes brought benefits to some Mexicans, they threatened the livelihoods of many others.[6]

It is within this context that the national government finally recognized San Miguel's historic center as a Zone of Historic Monuments (Zona de Monumentos Históricos) in 1982, a designation that was in many ways a tacit acknowledgment of the successes and failures of Mexican economic development strategies since the Mexican Revolution of the 1910s. The Mexican economic miracle of the forties, fifties, and sixties seemed like a distant memory, and massive state investment in luxury tourist destinations like Cancún was unsustainable under the neoliberal economic regime. Even the communal lands distributed to fulfill the promises of the revolutionary government failed to meet the needs of Mexico's exponentially growing and increasingly urbanized population. But at a moment when Mexico's future appeared bleak San Miguel served as a beacon of possibilities under a neoliberal economic order. As previous chapters have demonstrated, San Miguel was peripheral to most of these development strategies. Although several ejidos existed in the rural areas around San Miguel, most Sanmiguelenses had opposed revolutionary land reform. Sanmiguelenses failed to industrialize their town. Finally, while San Miguel did reap some benefits from federal and state investment in tourism, local tourism development was primarily the result of municipal and private spending. This municipal and private investment in a service-oriented economy enabled the town to survive the economic crisis and Mexico's transition to neoliberal economic models. Even though the financial crisis forced the Instituto Allende to close temporarily in 1982, it quickly rebounded, and 1983 was a record-breaking year.[7] In spite of—or perhaps, more accurately, because of—the economic downturn, the local tourism industry and the expatriate community continued to grow. After decades of cultivating a national image centered on the capital's urban modernity, economic crisis and a devastating earthquake in 1985 literally left Mexico City in ruins. San Miguel offered the comfort of nostalgia for another time, as well as the advantage of an established tradition of private investment in the tourism infrastructure, and thus became a model. The creation of Mexico's Pueblos Mágicos tourism development strategy, explored at the end of this chapter, reaffirmed this shift.

As the Mexican government struggled to redirect its economic strategies and salvage its credibility among its citizens and the global community, the public-private collaboration in San Miguel became a model for future Mexican tourism development. However, disputes over resources and planning and the shifting social hierarchies in San Miguel reveal that its successes had costs. The national government's official recognition of San Miguel as a special historic site in 1982 yielded few concrete dividends, revealing the limits of an economic development strategy linked to national identity.

The Cultural Politics of Civic Improvement

By the late 1970s few people in San Miguel were discussing whether the local economy would depend on tourism. Instead the conversation revolved around the extent to which the local government should allocate resources for tourism promotion at the expense of other municipal services. If tourism was supposed to be a boon to the local economy, residents expected to see tangible results in their daily lives. Mexicans, foreigners, and government officials engaged in lively debates about the nature of civic improvement, revealing visions for San Miguel that at times overlapped but also frequently diverged. Foreigners advocated for investments that would minimize the burdens and idiosyncrasies of life in Mexico, Mexicans hoped for some of the same conveniences that their foreign neighbors enjoyed, and local officials tried to address their constituents' concerns while also expanding the tourism infrastructure.

Although government resources were scarce following the 1982 debt crisis, efforts to obtain state and federal support for San Miguel's tourism industry in the years immediately prior had been quite successful. From the creation of the Allende museum to San Miguel's inclusion in national promotional materials, local officials raised their town's profile as a destination for national and international tourism. Two major shifts explain these successes. First, as industrial production and profits lagged and inflation soared, petroleum and tourism became vital to Mexican economic development. The high price of petroleum from 1977 to 1981 allowed the Mexican government to secure large amounts of credit that, in turn, enabled government agencies to invest in tourism. Officials prioritized investments in new resort cities such as Cancún, but San Miguel was also a beneficiary.[8] Second, a number of politicians and businesspeople from San Miguel obtained posts in state tourism agencies. For example, Dr. José Luis Bribiesca became the director of tourism in northern Guanajuato in the late 1970s following his term as mayor of San Miguel. Meetings between state tourism officials and representatives of hotels, restaurants, art and language schools, taxi drivers' associations, artisan groups, and other tourism-related industries often took place in San Miguel. While these developments did not guarantee ample funding for San Miguel's tourism industry, they did increase the amount of money available and San Miguel's access to that money.[9]

In the late 1970s and early 1980s San Miguel's tourism officials anticipated a significant increase in tourist volume. Data compiled between 1975 and 1982 indicate that San Miguel's hotel occupancy steadily increased at an average of 22 percent each year.[10] The municipal government continued to expand services and events to accommodate these new visitors. Barbara Dobarganes, who had helped her mother, Nell Fernández, run the Instituto Allende and the hotel on the school grounds after her stepfather's death in 1968, became San Miguel's head tourism official. Under Dobarganes's direction the tourism department prepared a new bilingual guidebook and relocated the municipal tourism office so that it was next to the Parroquia.[11] During the late 1970s the September patriotic festivals continued to expand, attracting numerous regional visitors as well as international tourists. There was a full schedule of parades, bullfights, musical performances, artisan fairs, sporting competitions, and fireworks, and Luis Bribiesca, the Guanajuato tourism official and former San Miguel mayor, estimated that approximately fifteen thousand visitors came to San Miguel each day of the festivities.[12] He likely inflated the numbers to demonstrate the successes of tourism marketing efforts. Nevertheless it was clear that officials at the state and local levels were attempting to transform San Miguel into a premier destination to celebrate Mexican independence. Finally, plans were under way to inaugurate an air taxi service to connect San Miguel to the capital and other Mexican tourist destinations by plane. A similar venture existed in the 1960s, but it was short-lived due to lack of business. Municipal officials believed that the growing tourism industry would sustain the five-passenger plane service this time around.[13]

These developments did not have a substantial impact on the majority of San Miguel's residents, though. According to local estimates, unemployment loomed around 50 percent in San Miguel and the surrounding countryside, and even for those who had jobs San Miguel was located in the administrative zone with the lowest wages in the state of Guanajuato.[14] More often than not the municipal and state governments spent their scant resources on superficial renovations and commemorative plaques in San Miguel rather than on social services or infrastructure. The symbolic gestures and inaugural ceremonies made good photo opportunities and public spectacles, but they did little to placate the residents, Mexican and foreign alike, who were forced to endure streets filled with garbage, frequent power outages (if they had electricity at all), and an unpredictable water supply.

Radio XESQ and *Atención* were two of the primary local forums for the dissemination of information and public debate about these issues. The first issue of *Atención*, on May 30, 1975, featured an interview with Mayor Silvestre Bautista López that focused on water and electricity shortages.[15] The radio station frequently alerted residents when a power blackout was imminent, and people reported to the radio station when they unexpectedly lost water pressure or electrical power.[16] The editors of *Atención* also used a Saturday-morning radio program to solicit residents' thoughts on pressing issues of the day for publication in the weekly newspaper. Through these media, residents with access to radio programming or the newspaper were thoroughly informed about the challenges people faced across San Miguel and the government's efforts, or lack thereof, to address those needs.

Inadequate urban planning remained a pressing problem. Water and electrical distribution and road maintenance were difficult enough in the center blocks of San Miguel. Despite superficial changes to the buildings and façades, the town center remained laid out according to the logic of colonial times—when electricity did not exist, when there were no cars, and when springwater from up the hill supplied the entire town and surrounding fruit orchards via a series of fountains and channels in the streets.[17] As the urban population expanded, most new *colonias*, or neighborhoods, emerged haphazardly. The poorest residents lived in shanties along ravines filled with garbage and sewage.[18] On the other end of the spectrum the primarily foreign residents of large housing developments, or *fraccionamientos*, on the outskirts of town expected regular water and garbage service, even though the town's scant resources were already extended beyond capacity. People began to dig deeper wells to access subterranean aquifers, and as a result the natural springs that had long supplied local water went dry. The depletion of the aquifers also accelerated the migration of rural populations into the city. Runoff and sewage polluted the nearby reservoir, Presa Allende, limiting its function as a source of potable water for the town.[19]

When the mayor gave his annual address in January 1978, he tackled many concerns that the residents of San Miguel shared, from water

157

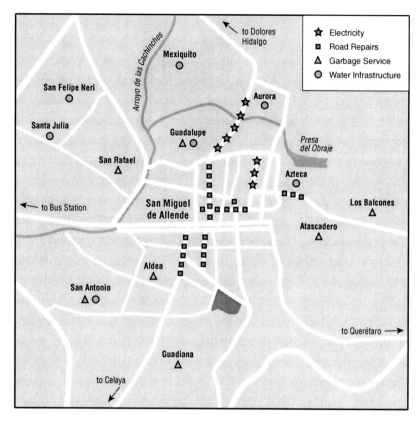

Map 4. Infrastructure projects, circa 1978. Map by Erin Greb.

to the market and from garbage to public safety. He reported that the municipal and state governments had initiated efforts to provide water to wells in several of the neighborhoods on the outskirts of the city to help compensate for several years of drought. Additionally, Guanajuato governor Luis Ducoing personally donated the materials and funding for improving the water service in Colonia San Antonio, and residents of other neighborhoods contributed materials and money to improve their own drainage systems. The mayor also announced that the municipal government had extended electricity to two streets, Calzada de Aurora and Calle de las Animas, and had repaired a number of roads, including Calle de Jesús, Calzada de la Prensa, Cuesta de San

José, Zacateros, Hidalgo, Mesones, and Pepe Llanos. The municipal government had also initiated garbage collection services in Villa de los Frailes and Barrio de la Aldea and had extended previous services in the following colonias: San Antonio, Los Balcones, San Rafael, Guadalupe, Atascadero, and Guadiana. Finally, the mayor informed the public of several smaller projects the municipal government had completed in 1977, including the promotion of local sports leagues, repairs to several benches in the Jardín, and even the addition of rooms for conjugal visits in the municipal prison.[20]

The mayor's extensive claims about public works projects did not match public perceptions. Mexican and foreign residents of San Miguel mostly agreed that these measures barely had begun to address the town's numerous problems and that some were completely super-fluous. They insisted that the government adopt a more transparent method of prioritizing these projects. For example, in the spring of 1979 an article in *Atención* reported that a group of representatives from San Miguel advised the governor that the "majority of important San Miguel citizens" agreed that the state should allocate funding for renovating the Jardín. The editor of *Atención* expressed indignation over the entire process. "Who," the editor probed, "is considered an important citizen?" and "How many spoke for the 'majority' of San Miguel's citizens?" The editor suggested that the government use these funds instead to address San Miguel's water problem. Other *Atención* readers echoed these sentiments.[21] A subsequent *Atención* editorial argued that, without a sufficient water supply, no tourists would want to visit the renovated Jardín. "Anyone who comes to see San Miguel," the editor commented, "will eventually want a bath, but may not get one."[22] These examples reveal that the *Atención* staff often challenged local officials and in this way followed in the footsteps of *El Vocero* writers.

That summer a debate raged in the newspaper and over the radio waves about how the municipal government should spend state funding. Although *Atención*'s readers seemed to concur that a more democratic process for allocating resources was necessary, opinions on what to prioritize diverged widely. These suggestions for improvements highlight the different experiences of the Mexican and foreign populations in San Miguel. Most Mexicans and foreigners agreed that water and a sewage system were the most pressing issues. Yet, for many Mexican families, the problem was access to any source of potable water, whereas most expats were concerned with a more reliable supply of water. Similarly several Mexicans noted the need for electricity in their neighborhoods, but no expats made comparable requests. In an extreme example of the different priorities of Mexicans and foreigners, one expat even recommended that the government repave San Miguel's cobblestone streets so that she would not sprain her ankles. Several expats foregrounded their status as homeowners and taxpayers as they called for the construction of a bus terminal, expansion of the garbage collection system, and a more sanitary public market. They implied that as permanent residents they had a right to make such demands. This style contrasted sharply with the more indirect, deferential Mexican tradition of petitioning government officials. Other expats offered their technical expertise in urban planning. One individual even provided step-by-step recommendations for developing a new sewage system, in a manner that suggests he believed that as a foreigner he had greater access to certain knowledge than Mexicans did.[23] Another foreigner argued that angry letters from expats would do little to persuade Mexican government officials. He proposed instead that San Miguel send a truckload of "handsome [Mexican] kids with big grins on their well-scrubbed faces" to make the case to the governor.[24] This statement captured the sentiment that state officials would be more sympathetic toward Mexican families with pressing needs than they would be toward expatriates experiencing the common trials and frustrations of life in Mexico.

Even when residents agreed on the necessity of a specific improvement, the plethora of ideas on how best to go about it demonstrated why municipal officials were reluctant to solicit public opinion in the first place. A petty debate among foreigners over the most suitable materials for repaving San Miguel's streets illustrates this problem.

In 1977 local officials selected decorative cement paving stones called *adocreto* to replace cobblestones on several streets in the town center. Adocreto is flatter than cobblestones, less expensive, and more durable. However, a number of residents petitioned the local government to use cobblestones instead because the adocreto was neither aesthetically appealing nor did it conform to San Miguel's colonial style.[25] Several expats voiced their opinions in *Atención*. Some objected because the adocreto made it easier for the "tourist hordes" to drive automobiles onto roads originally designed for pedestrians and burros.[26] Other foreigners supported the change for exactly the same reason: it would make San Miguel more accessible to automobile traffic, potentially increasing the town's tourism revenues. Those in favor of adocreto claimed it was easier to clean and therefore more hygienic than cobblestones. Finally, supporters challenged the authenticity of San Miguel's colonial ambience in the first place, suggesting that people in San Miguel used the term "colonial" quite loosely. Adocreto, they reasoned, would hardly make a difference.[27] The energy that foreigners dedicated to this trivial debate highlights the degree to which they felt entitled to participate in the town's decision-making process. It also demonstrates the cacophony of voices with which the municipal government had to contend.

Due to the combination of increased government resources and public outcry, the new municipal administration under Mayor Pedro Gerez made substantial progress toward satisfying many of the residents' demands. In July 1980 the municipal government announced plans to build a bus terminal in San Miguel. That fall the federal government hired a team of consultants, engineers, architects, and lawyers to discuss San Miguel's future together with local officials. They developed strategies for improved urban planning to accommodate the rapidly growing population, including better systems for water distribution and drainage; the completion of roads to divert traffic from San Miguel's historic center; the extension of electricity to the outlying communities; the recruitment of more doctors and nurses; and the creation of additional secondary and preparatory schools. The consultants pressed local officials to specify who would be responsible for enforcing the preservation of San Miguel's historic buildings according to the 1939 typical town designation and for assessing the town's gravest social problems. The mayor's annual report in January 1981 revealed that the municipal government had taken concrete steps to address numerous concerns that had preoccupied the population in previous years, from improvements to the water distribution and drainage systems to the expansion of garbage collection services.[28]

The local government's ability to balance tourism development with urban planning priorities and the provision of social services in 1980 and early 1981 corresponded with increased interest in tourism development at the state and federal levels. In 1981 Guadalupe Rivera de Iturbe, the local representative to the national legislature, presented the municipal government with a five-point plan for San Miguel. Her proposals included establishing a branch of the University of Guanajuato in San Miguel that would be dedicated to archaeological research, government designation of the town's environs as a protected archaeological zone, and the creation of an "independence route" that would lead tourists to various sites throughout the town that were related to the independence movement.[29] INAH officials were working to restore the former home of Ignacio Allende and finally inaugurated the museum in 1985.[30] In addition the new federal Ministry of Human Settlements and Public Works (Secretaría de Asentamientos Humanos de Obras Públicas) enlisted architects and local artisans to lead extensive restoration efforts at the Sanctuary of Atotonilco, updating and repairing the work that Mercadillo had completed decades before.[31]

When representatives from the National Institute of Fine Arts (INBA) announced in October 1981 that the government was going to declare San Miguel a Zone of Historic Monuments, the local reaction was mixed. Mayor Gerez insisted that he had not sought out this designation, and he expressed concern over the implications of the rules and regulations that it would entail. Many locals still blamed INAH for Miguel Malo's death (see chapter 3) and believed that the agency's handling of his collection of pre-Hispanic artifacts demonstrated that federal officials could not be trusted to act in San Miguel's best interest.[32] Carmen Masip de Hawkins, who became director of San Miguel's INBA center following Miguel Malo's death, was more enthusiastic about the decision. She reported that the idea came out of a seminar in which Mexican architects and historians discussed the preservation of Mexico's historic monuments and towns. Echoing debates that had occurred in San Miguel since the 1950s, the seminar's participants determined that such a designation was necessary to protect San Miguel from industrial "spillover" from the neighboring cities of Celaya and Querétaro.[33] This time, however, locals were mostly excluded from the conversation. While local businesspeople, government, and tourism officials had long sought federal recognition of San Miguel's historic architecture and contributions to Mexican history, by 1982 they had many questions about the practical benefits this designation would bring.

Regardless of the local sentiments, in 1982 President José López Portillo (1976–82) officially declared the center blocks of San Miguel de Allende a Zone of Historic Monuments. The designation characterized the architecture within this zone to be of "exceptional value for the political, social, and economic history of art in Mexico." The decree also celebrated San Miguel as a "testimony to the civic and human trajectory of its inhabitants, linked fundamentally to [Mexico's] right of self-determination," marking it as a primary setting for events that led to Mexican independence. Rather than claim that San Miguel was somehow a timeless representation of the past, the declaration instead acknowledged that the town "was a faithful reflection of an important cultural tradition and of the historic evolution of the town since its foundation."[34] The national government finally reaffirmed San Miguel's place in the nation, but this gesture was too little, too late. The truth is that we will never know whether San Miguel's new status would have inaugurated a new era of federal investment in the local tourism industry. The formal designation by presidential decree coincided with one of the largest economic crises in Mexican history.

Overnight the lavish spending on tourism development financed by petrodollars became unsustainable. San Miguel's brief flirtation with increased federal attention and funding came to an end, and once again the town had to seek out other remedies to keep its economy afloat. The philanthropic exploits of the growing expatriate community provided one solution.

San Miguel's Other Service Economy

San Miguel's foreign population grew steadily and became more diverse in the 1970s and 1980s. Despite their differences, one thing most San Miguel expats seemed to have in common—at least in their public rhetoric—was their belief that they could somehow benefit their Mexican neighbors, whether through their contributions to the local economy, the knowledge they had acquired abroad, or their volunteerism. Indeed many of the expats who arrived in the 1970s and 1980s fancied themselves modern good neighbors, private emissaries of goodwill from abroad. One historian has referred to San Miguel's expatriate community as "the most earnest and self-righteous of the American colonies [in Mexico]," and as one contributor to a newsletter for expatriates in Mexico claimed, "Some are turned off by what they see as an excessively artsy-craftsy do-gooder emphasis."[35] These descriptions create a caricature of San Miguel's foreigners that oversimplifies the diversity within the foreign population and the complicated nature of their philanthropic work.

Over the years San Miguel's expatriate population underwent many changes that directly influenced the forms and terms of their interactions with Mexicans. While the town remained a destination for artists, hippies, and other bohemian types who came in the forties, fifties, and sixties, during the seventies and eighties San Miguel attracted numerous professionals and retirees. This shift partially stemmed from restrictive immigration policies introduced in the 1970s that made it more difficult for foreign residents to legally work in Mexico.[36] As a result the expatriate community became even more economically stratified and culturally divided. The earlier generations of expats came to San Miguel because it was off the beaten path, artsy, and relatively inexpensive. They were frequently single, and, as previous chapters explore in greater detail, friendships and marriages between Mexicans and expats were fairly common. Above all the earlier generations had been more inclined to adjust to life in Mexico rather than to reproduce the comforts of their home countries. By contrast the new wave of expats, and especially retirees, arrived with a different mind-set. Eager to enjoy an active, comfortable, and relatively affordable retirement, they came to San Miguel precisely because it had an established foreign community. They were typically already married and therefore less prone to enter into romantic relationships with Mexicans. They were also less likely to learn Spanish, which inhibited their interactions with San Miguel's Mexican population. The majority of this new wave of expatriates still hailed from the United States and Canada, but growing numbers came from Europe and Asia as well.[37]

Although San Miguel's new expatriates may have seemed more insular compared to the previous generations, several of them had spent much of their very transnational lives as public servants or representatives of major multinational corporations. In fact even though the overwhelming majority of the expatriates claimed U.S. citizenship, life abroad was the norm for many of San Miguel's newest residents. For example, the expat community included an executive who worked for major food-processing companies in the Bajío, including Del Monte, the former director of market research for the foreign division of Sears, Roebuck and Co., and a retired U.S. Navy admiral who had lived in Brazil and various Asian cities.[38] Other former U.S. military officials followed in the footsteps of the GIs who had settled in San Miguel in the 1940s, including William J. Fox, a Marine, and Phil Roettinger, who spent time as a diplomat in Mexico after his involvement in what he referred to as a "paramilitary operation" in 1954 (likely the overthrow of Jacobo Arbenz Guzmán's government in Guatemala).[39] Their corporate and military backgrounds meant that they frequently held worldviews that contradicted those of San

Miguel's hippie-artist expats and in many ways reinforced the imperial mind-set evident in their philanthropic work.[40]

The new American expats repeatedly pressed for formal linkages with representatives of the U.S. government. Unlike the GIs in San Miguel who had struggled to get the attention and support of U.S. government officials during the 1949 boycott debacle, in the 1970s and 1980s American expats received frequent visits from the U.S. consul general in Guadalajara. Legal and bureaucratic challenges associated with living abroad, specifically troubles with visas and property laws, constantly preoccupied expats, and the primary purpose of the diplomat's visits was to address these specific concerns and needs. During his visits to the town the consul general also met with Mexicans who sought immigrant visas.[41] In the mid-1980s the American expat Philip Maher volunteered to serve as a U.S. consular agent in San Miguel, and the U.S. government eventually formalized the diplomatic post.[42]

During the 1970s, a decade characterized by high inflation across the globe, many retirees went to Mexico because their pensions and retirement funds could be stretched further. A number of Vietnam veterans also chose to move to Mexico, particularly those who needed inexpensive home health care.[43] This trend increased in the wake of Mexico's 1982 debt crisis and the subsequent peso devaluation, which made Mexico even more affordable for foreign pensioners. Despite Mexico's relative affordability, many foreigners still struggled to adapt to life on a fixed income and they shared strategies for doing so. One couple, for instance, encouraged other retirees to abandon the "traditional American supermarket philosophy of life" because imported store-bought foods were more expensive than fresh foods in the Mexican public markets. They also recommended learning Spanish so that one could negotiate the best prices.[44] Many of San Miguel's foreigners had a difficult time navigating Mexico's rapidly changing financial landscape and were confused about the implications of inflation, currency devaluations, and exchange rates for their personal savings. During the 1980s the pages of Atención often functioned as a crash course on personal finance and global economics.[45]

Despite the challenges, most retirees were happy in San Miguel because of the large expatriate community and the plethora of activities available in the town. In response to an *Atención* survey of local retirees in 1980 one person commented, "Where else can one easily explore the pleasures of welding, painting, pottery, and weaving?"[46] Retirees and other expats took advantage of the courses and cultural programs at the Instituto Allende and the Centro Cultural, but they also created their own theater troupes, lecture series, music festivals, and writing workshops.[47] While some expats opted for a quiet lifestyle of painting and writing, others golfed, organized bridge tournaments, played tennis, and made the rounds on the cocktail party circuit. In short San Miguel offered a wide variety of social, athletic, and cultural activities that attracted expatriates, and especially retirees, in search of an active lifestyle abroad.

Many expats also volunteered their time and services. This practice dates back to the first Americans to settle in San Miguel in the 1930s, with Stirling Dickinson serving as a model for expatriate involvement in community life. He contributed time and money to countless local causes, from the Red Cross to schools, and even a baseball league.[48] Some expats worked on an individual, case-by-case basis without much recognition or fanfare. Among these were Sylvia Samuelson, a former registered nurse who helped give neighborhood children shots and kept track of their medical records, and Leonard Brooks, who provided Mexican children with free music lessons in his home before the Centro Cultural invited him to head its music program.[49] Certain occasions inspired groups to mobilize, such as a 1958 flood in nearby Salamanca, which prompted San Miguel's foreign residents to organize a relief fund.[50] In general the foreign residents had both the financial resources and the free time to dedicate to these causes.[51]

More systematic philanthropic efforts emerged during the 1950s, as exemplified by the foundation of the Biblioteca Pública (Public Library) in 1954. Like many other charitable organizations in San Miguel, the Biblioteca Pública began as the private, informal effort of one woman. Helen Wale invited Mexican children into her San

Miguel home to look at her collection of books and magazines. Several members of the community, foreign and Mexican, helped translate the books into Spanish. Others donated books, supplies, and time, and the collection quickly outgrew the available space. In 1958 a committee formed to locate a larger, more permanent space for the library. The state government granted the city of San Miguel possession of an abandoned building, a former convent turned slaughterhouse, and the city allowed the library committee to use part of the building as long as they helped pay for its restoration.[52] It became the largest bilingual library in Mexico outside of the capital. The Biblioteca Pública quickly expanded beyond a simple children's library and still offers classes, raises funds to support scholarships for local children and other local causes, and houses the *Atención* staff. A diverse group of Mexican schoolchildren and expatriates fills the central courtyard each day. Over the years the Biblioteca Pública has become one of the central cultural institutions in San Miguel life.

The Biblioteca Pública's combination of philanthropic activities and social events set the standard for San Miguel's charitable organizations. Since the library's early days its biggest fundraiser has been the weekly home and garden tour. On Sundays foreign tourists and some expatriates would pile into buses to visit some of the town's nicest homes, many of which also happened to be for sale or rent. The Biblioteca Pública also offered both film and speaker series, musical performances, events celebrating all of the major Mexican holidays, a restaurant, and a gift shop.[53] Benefits, galas, and other fundraising events organized by San Miguel's numerous philanthropic groups became a central aspect of expatriate social circles. One San Miguel expat explained that where you volunteered reflected your standing in the local social hierarchy, confirming the historian Ann Blum's observation (albeit in another context) that "conspicuous consumption and conspicuous benevolence went hand in hand."[54]

Foreigners' charitable activities in San Miguel emerged out of the conditions of their interactions with the broader community. Unlike multinational NGOs or groups on short-term service trips, expatriates have a lasting impact on surrounding communities whether or not they participate in charitable causes. In this case expatriates' Mexican neighbors also affected them in profound ways. The presence of expats demanded an expansion of the service economy beyond the tourism industry and often involved the development of long-term, intimate relationships with locals who worked in their homes and businesses.[55] Indeed these close personal relationships typically functioned as the gateway to participation in charitable causes because their employees offered a window into the often harsh realities of Mexican life. Many expatriates took up the "white man's burden," often propelled by guilt for the low wages they paid. Beyond that, foreigners' depictions of their San Miguel neighbors in photography, artwork, and writings reveal an acute awareness of the poverty and inequality that surrounded them. As Jason Ruiz has remarked about foreign portrayals of Porfirian Mexico, these representations reinforced the idea that Mexico, "though rapidly modernizing, still required rescue from a more advanced, progressive nation."[56] Charitable work provided an entrée into the work of rescuing Mexico.

But expatriate philanthropy was not simply a personal decision. It was and continues to be a central part of the expatriate social milieu. Peer pressure and the desire to fit in also drove the economy of patronage and benevolence in San Miguel, where for many foreigners care of the Mexican community became a hobby. In this way foreigners in San Miguel were not much different from expats and foreign enclaves in other places during other historical periods. Collectively their charitable activities were inspired by a sentiment not unlike what scholars have described as the "benevolent colonialism" of the nineteenth century or the "imperial progressivism" of the early twentieth: because of what they consider to be their superior expertise and ingenuity, these outsiders inject themselves into the everyday lives of those they deem both needy and worthy.[57] Like their counterparts from different eras, San Miguel's rapidly expanding expatriate community founded philanthropic organizations that met numerous important social needs in San Miguel, but not without a cost. In tandem with Mexico's 1982 economic crisis these organizations created a new kind of "service" economy, one dependent on private funding and generosity that were often as fickle as the global economy.

The number of philanthropic associations in San Miguel increased dramatically in the 1980s and 1990s as more retirees and other individuals with time to spare arrived. Some of these groups had religious affiliations; Feed the Hungry, for example, was a school lunch program that the local St. Paul's Episcopal Church founded in 1984.[58] Most did not, however, and their origins are as diverse as their causes. Committees, clubs, cooperatives, and formal nonprofits dedicated resources to local children, animals, rural women, the environment, and the elderly, to name a few. Foreign press coverage portrayed San Miguel's expatriates as munificent benefactors, providing food, clothes, shelter, education, and jobs for a poor Mexican community.[59] The town's expatriates even established a chapter of the International Good Neighbor Council, founded "on the belief that ordinary people working together can promote and increase international understanding and good will."[60] The expatriates involved in charitable work considered themselves good neighbors, and the Mexican government formally recognized them as such. Among the most celebrated foreign residents was Stirling Dickinson, whom the municipal government honored as San Miguel's "Adopted Son" as early as 1942, just a few years after he first arrived in the town. On multiple subsequent occasions local and national government officials acknowledged Dickinson's tireless efforts to serve the Mexican community. In 1999 the Mexican government featured Dickinson posthumously in a book dedicated to foreigners who lived in and served Mexico.[61] Mexican officials also honored other expats, including Jaime Morris and Margaret Galloway, for their service and for "furthering the good relations between Mexicans and foreigners."[62]

These tributes to foreigners reveal the extent to which various levels of the Mexican government valued the expatriate community's efforts. Even when tension existed at the national level between NGOs and the state, in San Miguel there was a better relationship.[63]

Mexican officials had long appreciated and defended the expatriates' contributions to San Miguel, but during the 1980s and 1990s their philanthropy took on a new meaning. Officials recognized that the expatriates' organizations were providing services that the government could not due to Mexico's precarious economic condition. When banks and organizations such as the IMF imposed harsh austerity measures on the Mexican government in the 1980s, social safety nets such as food and housing subsidies were among the first items cut from the budget. Over the course of the 1980s the Mexican government cut social spending by approximately 53 percent.[64] Thus the service groups, nonprofits, and other charitable organizations in San Miguel functioned as a sort of informal foreign aid, a different kind of service economy based on patronage and benevolence.[65] And because foreign currencies had a favorable exchange rate in Mexico, the money coming into these organizations could be stretched further and potentially accomplish more. These stark economic realities highlighted the growing power imbalance in San Miguel: more than ever before the local government relied on the goodwill of the expatriate population.

The image of the benevolent foreigner, which both the municipal government and the expatriates themselves cultivated, did not go unchallenged in San Miguel. As previous chapters have demonstrated, many Sanmiguelenses believed that the expatriates had a negative influence on the town. Others had long argued that the foreigners' charitable impulses were misdirected or self-serving or that they did not adequately meet Sanmiguelenses' needs. For example, one newspaper columnist criticized the Biblioteca Pública because it contained too many books and signs in English, thus revealing local tensions over language and culture.[66] Some expatriates worried too that San Miguel's foreigners were meddling too much in local affairs. One woman cautioned her fellow foreigners not to interfere with the charitable works that the Catholic Church historically carried out in Mexican society.[67] Foreigners and Mexicans alike questioned whether the economic benefits of expatriate philanthropy outweighed other potential social costs.

There were also Mexicans who seemed to accept the premise that foreigners benefited the town in many ways but sought equal recognition for their own contributions and charitable activities. Most notable among these individuals was Manuel Zavala Zavala. A long-time member of several local service groups, including San Miguel's Lions Club, Zavala frequently used his weekly newsletter and later his program on Radio XESQ to publicize Mexican charitable works. Columnists for *El Vocero* also drew attention to Mexican civic and religious organizations that gave back to the community until that newspaper ceased publication in 1974.[68] However, as foreigners came to dominate the local print media with *Atención*, Mexicans received less and less recognition for their contributions. This shift often strained foreign-Mexican relations in San Miguel. It is also likely that the foreigners' charitable work and economic contributions disrupted the roles that Mexican immigrants traditionally played through remittances, gifts, and financial contributions in other communities.[69] Many Mexicans resented the implication that foreigners had to get involved in charity because Mexicans did not do enough to take care of their own.

A dispute over the origins of a knitting program at the local jail highlighted these tensions. In 1976 Melissa Cannon reported in the pages of *Atención* that individuals in search of "fashion bargains" could find them at San Miguel's jail, where the prisoners "work like beavers, knitting sweaters and coats, spinning their own woolen yarn, weaving rugs and making baskets." The prisoners sold the items at the jail and kept the money they earned. They even accepted special orders for custom-made products. Cannon acknowledged that there were several stories about how this tradition had begun, but she shared only her favorite: that an American man arrested for drug dealing taught the other prisoners how to knit and subsequently opened a retail outlet to sell the finished goods. Several images printed alongside the article depict smiling male prisoners displaying their finished products through the bars of their jail cells or working on a loom donated by the local American Legion. Cannon exclaimed that this project exemplified "typical Yankee ingenuity," and some of *Atención's*

Mexican readers took offense. Several prisoners wrote to Manuel Zavala Zavala, denying that a foreigner had taught them to knit. Zavala submitted their letter, as well as his own recollections of the origins of the knitting program, to *Atención* as a corrective. He recalled that the knitting program dated back at least forty years and that Mexican women had taught the prisoners how to craft sweaters. Zavala also claimed partial credit for the success of the program because he had sold some of the sweaters in a store he ran until 1962. While he acknowledged that the members of the American Legion did provide some support, he insisted that "in no way was it an American who began all this."[70] These letters reveal that Mexicans in San Miguel, from prisoners to media personalities, objected to their portrayal as passive recipients of foreign charity.

In fact Sanmiguelenses had a long tradition of philanthropy and service independent of the expatriates, and others played an integral role in the foreigners' organizations. Even though the Mexican government had attempted to centralize control over private charitable organizations since the beginning of the twentieth century, in provincial towns such as San Miguel many private organizations still operated with more autonomy to meet needs the state did not. Public-private collaboration had long been the norm.[71] For instance, the local Mexican Rotary Club, founded in 1955, participated in numerous projects, such as doing renovations at a local orphanage, providing rural schools with books, and funding scholarship exchange programs.[72] The local Lions Club helped fund a kindergarten and provided medical aid to local children.[73] In 1978 Pedro Hernández Ramírez became the first Mexican to preside over the Biblioteca Pública, and other Mexicans volunteered their services there.[74] Mexicans also took charge of other charitable causes started by foreigners, including ALMA, the home for the elderly that Margaret Galloway had established.[75] Ultimately charity and philanthropy in San Miguel were a largely collaborative effort.

Foreigners and Mexicans had different motivations for claiming credit for their charitable activities. Foreigners presented their charitable efforts as evidence that they contributed to San Miguel in a positive manner. Mexicans, on the other hand, sought to demonstrate that they did not need to rely on foreign philanthropy and that they were capable of tending to their own needs. Regardless of who took the credit, these collective efforts—the new service economy—came to provide an invaluable safety net in San Miguel at a time when the government, faced with an unprecedented economic crisis, scaled back its social services. But at the same time, the expatriates' very presence irrevocably altered the local economy and upended local power and gender hierarchies.

New Hierarchies in San Miguel's Traditional Service Economy

If philanthropic activities converted San Miguel's economy into one partially based on benevolence, the expatriates' presence also sped the town's transition to a service economy in a more traditional sense. The growing number of tourists and expatriates in San Miguel during the 1980s and early 1990s meant that in San Miguel, unlike many other parts of Mexico, employment opportunities were expanding. The majority of these jobs were in the service sector and traditionally women's work with limited prospects for advancement. In white-collar service industries such as banking, where a person could move up the pay scale or the corporate ladder, bilingual workers were in greatest demand. A service economy did not emerge in San Miguel overnight. As previous chapters have demonstrated, this gradual transition began in the 1930s. The failures of Mexico's import substitution industrialization model and the turn toward neoliberal economic principles in the 1980s accelerated these processes throughout the nation, especially in places like San Miguel that had largely eschewed industrialization in favor of tourism. Consequently San Miguel's labor market increasingly gave preference to female and bilingual workers and offered fewer opportunities for males and those who spoke only Spanish.

Trade liberalization policies drove Mexican workers into San Miguel's service economy. For example, when the Mexican Congress changed Article 27 of the constitution to permit the privatization of ejidos and amended laws to lift restrictions on foreign property ownership, developers bought the majority of these communal plots surrounding San Miguel. These developers, both foreign and Mexican, converted the land into residential complexes that served as homes for expatriates and wealthy Mexicans or as tourist rentals. In most cases the families that formerly had cultivated that land either migrated to the United States or sought work in San Miguel's service industry.[76] San Miguel's only remaining large-scale factory, Fábrica La Aurora, closed its doors on March 11, 1991, another casualty of neoliberal policies. The textile factory could no longer compete with manufacturers from Asia after free trade agreements guaranteed their access to Mexican markets.[77] Long a pathway to the middle classes for its unionized workforce, the factory's closure was ominous. In such an economic environment San Miguel's only redeeming quality was the inherent territorialization of its tourism industry. Whereas factories could come and go and plots of land would be bought and sold, tourism was firmly rooted in the idea of San Miguel as a place, developed over several decades by Mexicans and foreigners alike. As long as the town continued to attract visitors and new residents, the local service economy could stay afloat.[78]

The federal government recognized that tourism could provide a glimmer of hope in an otherwise bleak economic landscape following the 1982 economic crisis. In a February 1983 address before Mexico's Chamber of Deputies, Mexico's secretary of tourism, Antonio Enríquez Savignac, made the case that tourism was an important way to attract much-needed foreign currency, and he argued that large numbers of service-industry jobs could be created with minimal investment. He claimed that every occupied hotel room generated approximately three and a half jobs and provided an indirect economic benefit to an additional twelve to twenty Mexicans. Rather than expend resources on new tourist destinations, he recommended improving extant destinations.[79] In another speech to elected officials in Oaxaca later that week he proposed "decentralizing" the national economy, by which he meant that state and municipal governments would have more control over programs that had previously been under the purview of federal bureaucracies.[80] "Decentralizing" was essentially a euphemism for placing a greater burden on already strained local budgets. For towns like San Miguel that were already accustomed to receiving little assistance from federal tourism agencies, the decentralization policy was more of a continuation than a departure, and San Miguel was poised to bring in even more foreign visitors.

San Miguel lured tourists and foreign residents in part because of the idea that they would not have to pay a great deal to have domestic help. Even though the cost of living in the town had steadily increased over the decades, the favorable exchange rates for foreign currencies meant that in Mexico foreign individuals and families could actually live the lifestyles to which they aspired—or as one Missourian described it, could "live graciously":

> And graciously is the key word. In my view, living in Ladue and doing your own dishes is not gracious living. A dinner party with the hostess leaving the table between courses is not gracious living. This is not to criticize St. Louis hostesses—it is simply that the cost of help is prohibitive. Gracious living in San Miguel means literally not lifting a finger! From the moment you arrive at your front door with your luggage until the moment you depart, you are not allowed to do anything for yourself. The American housewife, who has pretty well learned to wait on herself and everyone else in the family, is suddenly in a tropical heaven. No grocery shopping, no cooking, no dishes, no cleaning, no washing or ironing—no work whatever![81]

For this individual, and countless others, the idyllic lifestyle was one free from the drudgery and toil associated with household labor. In San Miguel foreigners and wealthy Mexicans could easily afford to have a cook, a maid, a gardener, and a handyman on staff. What this American did not seem to consider, however, was that if his wife was able to live graciously in San Miguel, it was only because others did not. Someone had to do the shopping, cooking, cleaning, and other household labor so that his wife could enjoy her "tropical heaven."

This predicament is part of a process that the sociologist Saskia Sassen has called "high-income gentrification," or the concentration of high-income urban residences reliant upon a supply of low-wage labor.[82] While the level of gentrification in San Miguel does not compare to the scale that Sassen describes in her study of Manhattan, the structural changes to the economy and the social geography are similar, especially concerning the spatialization of class and the expansion of the informal economy and casual labor. Accordingly, as more foreigners and wealthy Mexicans moved to San Miguel, they renovated old homes in the center of town or constructed sprawling new estates, driving up property values. As the federal bureaucrats correctly predicted, the presence of these better-off outsiders, from their arrival in San Miguel to their construction projects and eventually their daily needs as household managers and consumers, created numerous jobs. Unlike the union jobs at the Fábrica La Aurora, most of these were low-paying jobs and provided few prospects for advancement into the middle classes.[83] Moreover the low wages made the newly inflated property and rental rates in the center of town prohibitively expensive for locals, forcing workers to move to the outskirts of San Miguel into neighborhoods where access to water, sewage systems, garbage collection services, and electricity was unreliable at best. Although this process was not new to San Miguel in the 1980s and 1990s, Mexico's unprecedented economic crisis and the presence of a large expatriate population hastened the polarization of the haves and have-nots.

San Miguel's casualized, service-oriented economy not only restructured the town's social geography but also financially disrupted the patriarchal order, based as it was on a nationalist masculinity that had long been under siege. While men held short-term jobs on construction sites, women typically held the relatively long-term jobs as domestic servants. The gendered division of labor was the consequence of long-held beliefs about men and women—not only beliefs about the types of work of which each gender is capable but also the idea that women workers were less expensive because traditionally they were not the breadwinners of a household. In other words employers justified lower wages for women and thus preferred female employees, based on the underlying assumption that women provided a secondary household income. This trend, coupled with the decreasing number of local "masculine" jobs in manufacturing and agriculture, effectively feminized San Miguel's economy.[84]

The feminization of the local economy extended beyond gendered divisions of labor to the expatriates' expectations for employee behavior. Foreign employers regularly used the classified section of *Atención* to request recommendations for a "good" housekeeper, which usually implied one who was subservient, who could follow directions in English, and who would not steal. When foreigners did employ Mexican men, they frequently spoke of them in infantilizing terms, referring to them as "boys" rather than adults.[85] The expectation that employees should be deferential and that they needed to be policed and disciplined like children reinforced patriarchal hierarchies but placed foreign employers, rather than Mexican fathers, at the top.

Mexican workers did not passively accept the roles that foreigners expected them to play. The scant archival sources on the matter suggest that domestic workers took advantage of legal channels to file formal grievances about wages and dismissals without cause.[86] Most cases went before the municipal labor inspector (*inspector del trabajo municipal*), but some complainants requested that the municipal inspector forward their case to an arbitration committee (the Junta Local de Conciliación y Arbitraje) that convened in Celaya. The most common grievance against foreign employers was that they failed to pay the federally mandated minimum wage, and in almost every case the inspector or the committee decided in the complainants' favor. In some cases, such as the dispute between retired New Yorker Albert Levy Selinger and his domestic servant Isidra Gómez Chávez, the foreigners pled ignorance about Mexican labor laws and accepted the decision without much resistance. Most employees filed their grievances with the help of an experienced representative and included detailed citations of Mexican labor codes. The foreigners also typically relied on a Mexican intermediary for representation and certainly found themselves at a disadvantage when navigating these procedures due to the language barrier and a general lack of knowledge about Mexican laws. These legal channels opened small spaces for Mexicans to challenge the conditions of their labor.[87]

The termination cases were more complex and offer valuable insights into the different expectations held by foreigners and their employees. They also demonstrate how foreigners could use their transnational mobility to skirt obligations to their employees. For instance, a woman by the name of Imelda Juárez Ramírez filed a complaint against her employer, Katherine Maas, for back pay. She alleged that Maas, who frequently traveled abroad, had unreasonable expectations about the amount of time that Juárez would spend watching the house during these trips. Maas's San Miguel home had been burglarized during one trip, and Juárez alleged that when she subsequently claimed she was afraid to stay in the house alone Maas fired her. Juárez's complaint reveals that she first approached Lucretia Sautto, a Mexican with a higher social status and more connections with the foreign community, to intervene on her behalf. When that strategy failed, Juárez filed a formal complaint and urged the local labor inspector to act quickly because she feared Maas would leave the country again soon. Maas claimed that she had fired Juárez because she suspected that she was involved in the burglary. Ultimately the municipal official awarded Juárez a portion of the back pay she claimed she was owed. The case illustrates the types of demands that foreigners' transnational lives placed on their employees, the assumptions that employers sometimes made about their workers, and the avenues that workers pursued for recourse when they felt their rights had been violated.[88]

Another dispute, between Margaret Nevin and her former employee, María de Jesus Mendoza Vargas, also highlights the disjuncture between foreigners' and employees' expectations. In this case Mendoza had worked for Nevin for almost eight years, and she alleged that Nevin had wrongfully dismissed her when she participated in the annual religious pilgrimage to San Juan de los Lagos. According to Mendoza, she went on the pilgrimage in 1976 and asked her sister to cover her responsibilities, as she had done in previous years, but this time Nevin informed the sister that her services were not necessary and that Mendoza was no longer her employee. Nevin had met with a lawyer to file the appropriate paperwork to terminate Mendoza's employment, and upon Mendoza's return the lawyer offered her a small settlement. Mendoza, who believed that the amount of the settlement did not approach the amount to which she was legally entitled, made a claim against Nevin for back pay to bring her wages to the corresponding minimum wage rate and three months' severance pay for unjustified termination. Her claim totaled more than four times the amount the lawyer offered. Nevin's defense was revealing. She explained that although she had allowed Mendoza to make the pilgrimage in previous years, this time she did not give permission because she was suffering from a medical condition that severely limited her mobility. Nevin felt that it was reasonable to expect that Mendoza not take any days off because she urgently needed her. Mendoza made a special request that her case be presented before the Junta Local de Conciliación y Arbitraje in Celaya, which proved to be an effective strategy because it awarded her the entire claim. The San Miguel labor inspector, by contrast, typically awarded only a portion of the claims. It appears that while Mendoza viewed her connection to Nevin as strictly a work relationship, Nevin believed that Mendoza would act with the degree of loyalty that one would show a family member or friend, an assumption many foreigners made about their employees. The Junta Local de Conciliación y Arbitraje agreed with Mendoza that these expectations were extraordinary.[89]

Together these labor disputes provide insights into the complicated dynamics that emerged in San Miguel's service industry. While some employees were aware of their rights and took legal actions to protect themselves, the different expectations each party brought to the work relationship created vulnerabilities for the mostly female domestic workers. The public nature of the grievance process meant that most workers likely did not seek recourse until after they had been fired, and even then they were taking a risk that by speaking out they might jeopardize future employment opportunities. Foreign employers also recognized that they needed to protect themselves. Expatriates frequently wrote letters and op-ed pieces to express their interest in learning the intricacies of Mexican labor law, from the minimum wage requirements to hiring and firing policies, ostensibly so that their employees would not cheat them. To satisfy this demand, the Biblioteca Pública even commissioned a local lawyer to create a Mexican labor law manual.[90] Unlike the more established industries of the traditional economy, the service economy's associated expectations and terms created an environment of uncertainty and risk for the most vulnerable workers.

The shift toward a feminized workforce at the lower rungs of the pay scale coincided with an increase in the number of Mexican women employed in white-collar jobs. Foreign women in San Miguel had worked outside the home as secretaries and in their own businesses for decades, but in the early 1980s Mexican women in white-collar jobs were still a rarity. One *Atención* article underscored this point by describing a young Mexican woman "who knows about such things as time deposits, interest rates, investments, loans, savings, and other mysterious (to most of us) banking secrets." The writer paused to directly address the readers: "'Whew!' you're probably thinking, 'She's unique!'" In fact the woman was not unique at all, and the article went on to tell the story of three Mexican sisters—Patricia, Eugenia, and Carina García—all of whom fit this description and worked in local banks.[91]

The example of the García sisters exemplified the growing hierarchy among monolingual and multilingual workers, regardless of gender. While the beginning of the *Atención* article focused on the novelty of three young Mexican women in the banking industry, the writer later revealed the privileged circumstances that enabled the women to procure their banking jobs: their aunt, an American woman married to Sanmiguelense Cosme Sánchez, taught the sisters English at a young age. Carina was the only employee at San Miguel's Banamex who spoke English, and, as the article acknowledged, "Her skills [we]re much in demand."[92] As bilingual employees, the García sisters were indispensable, especially in industries that had a large foreign clientele, such as banking, real estate, and legal services, making it difficult for even the most qualified monolingual job applicants to compete. This was equally true for lower-paying jobs, such as gardeners, construction workers, and taxi drivers. One San Miguel resident observed that many expats preferred to hire cooks who had previous experience working for other foreigners because they would be more familiar with foreign tastes and more experienced in communicating with someone who did not speak Spanish.[93] Bilingual workers, whether they had grown up in a multicultural family, had the resources to study at one of San Miguel's bilingual schools, or had spent time working in the United States, had a highly valued advantage.

All of these forces—Mexico's shift to a neoliberal economic model, the feminization of the local service economy, and the competitive advantage of bilingual workers—contributed to an exodus of male workers from San Miguel. Wages decreased so much due to the 1982 economic crisis that even men with relatively good jobs had to find other work in the service sector or leave San Miguel. One foreigner who worked for the government agency INAH recalled that after the crisis his salary dropped to 6 percent of what it had been before, forcing him to resign his post and open a travel agency.[94] Most did not have the same options he did. Whereas male workers had long left San Miguel in search of higher wages, the wave of migration this time around was different. First, since wages plummeted across Mexico, finding work in a neighboring city was no longer a viable option. Second, the United States did not continue the Bracero program—the formal guest worker agreement with Mexico—after 1964. This meant that Mexican workers increasingly went to the United States through undocumented channels. State officials estimated in 2000 that at any given moment approximately 30 percent of Guanajuato's total population was in the United States.[95] Although some took advantage of connections they made with expatriates in San Miguel to find work in the United States, the journey was nonetheless perilous.[96] Due to the militarization of the U.S.-Mexico border during roughly this same period, they frequently had to pay *coyotes* (human traffickers) to help them navigate the dangerous border zone, making the journey more costly.[97] It also deterred workers from making regular return trips to visit their families. Consequently men traveled farther from San Miguel to find work and returned less frequently, if at all, and although most sent money back to their families in Mexico, some neglected to do even that.[98] Even though San Miguel's tourism industry did keep the local economy afloat, it exacerbated the nationwide trends that restructured Mexican families.

Many families in San Miguel thus became female-headed households and were frequent objects of expatriates' charity. In a move that calls to mind Margaret Galloway's concern for rural female-headed households, an organization called Mujeres en Cambio set out to provide women in the rural community Agustín González with a way to supplement their incomes. A majority of the community's adult males spent most of the year working in the United States. Ironically, as chapter 1 has explained, the state government of Guanajuato originally established Agustín González in the 1930s as a settlement for Mexicans repatriated from the United States. Mujeres en Cambio taught the women of Agustín González the art of rug-hooking, donated supplies, and helped them sell their finished pieces in Mexico and abroad.[99] Several other groups, cooperatives, and organizations in San Miguel did similar work so that female heads of household could afford school supplies, medical care, and food for their families.[100] When charity "relied on the spirit of the giver," the more sympathetic women and children were the most likely beneficiaries.[101]

Here we see the nexus between San Miguel's two service economies. These philanthropic programs certainly improved the quality of many lives, but they did not challenge the systemic problems that placed Mexican families in these situations. Instead the charitable organizations more often than not reinforced San Miguel's socioeconomic hierarchies. The emphasis on teaching women to produce and sell handicrafts—also a gendered skill set—did help some rural women become more self-sufficient, but it did not provide local employment alternatives for their male family members. Moreover the sale of arts and crafts in San Miguel relied upon the tourism industry, rather than being independent of it, thus continuing the local economic dependency on visitors and foreigners. To be sure this problem was not a new phenomenon introduced by foreign philanthropists. Government welfare programs also tended to focus on women and children, whom reformers considered more vulnerable and more deserving. Whereas during the early to mid-twentieth century the state stepped in to fill the patriarchal role for families in need, now that role was filled by foreigners.[102]

Critical analysis of charity is complicated terrain, and not all philanthropic efforts fit neatly into this mold. Children should not go hungry simply because efforts to feed them do not challenge structural causes of poverty. Indeed some of San Miguel's philanthropic organizations have successfully bucked the trends by empowering local residents to make decisions and by creating pathways out of traditional service industry labor. One of the most successful examples is CASA, an organization founded in 1981 by Nadine Goodman, a social worker from New York, and her husband, San Miguel native Alejandro González. What began as an effort to provide family planning education to local women and youth evolved into a maternity hospital and the first professional midwifery school in Mexico.[103] Other efforts have achieved a degree of success—with some unintended consequences. For example, when some organizations have focused on creating employment opportunities for male residents, women are often relegated once again to a supporting role. Furthermore, as one Mexican involved in local nonprofits explained, gender conflicts often posed the greatest threat to the success of initiatives ranging from health clinics to entrepreneurship workshops to environmental efforts because Mexican men who returned from living abroad often discouraged their wives and daughters from participating. This stance might partially stem from the perception among male immigrants that their patriarchal authority declines while they are abroad, and therefore it must be reasserted upon their return.[104] Scholarships and opportunities for young people frequently result in them leaving San Miguel altogether, sometimes for nearby Mexican cities such as Querétaro and sometimes for opportunities abroad. In some cases the recipients of scholarships and various charitable donations faced resentment from other Mexicans who did not have access to the same resources.[105] The broader point is not to condemn this other service economy but to examine and understand its implications, especially because the forces that have propelled it—the expansion of expatriate populations and the retreat of state-provided services—show no signs of slowing.

These challenges were symptomatic of the larger problems facing Mexico in the neoliberal era. Philanthropy and private investment provide only a temporary bandage or salve for the human consequences of broad social and economic restructuring. When the main benefactor behind a charitable organization dies, when the executive committee decides to shift the focus of their giving from one school to another, when the funds dry up because of global economic downturns, or when the flow of tourists, expats, and private investors slows due to fears of infectious diseases or drug-related violence, the new service economy, despite the good intentions of benefactors, ceases to provide a reliable safety net for society's most vulnerable. As Ann Blum's study of Porfirian Mexico demonstrates, government expansion into welfare originated in part to address this very issue, "the recurrent problem that individual commitment to charity tended to wane."[106] Rather than address these underlying structural problems, however, leaders in San Miguel and elsewhere in Mexico have doubled down on the twin service economies.

Indeed San Miguel's local economy expanded in the 1980s and 1990s, but the dilemma of a service-oriented economy remained. It exacerbated existing hierarchies among the local workforce and further increased the town's dependence on foreigners. By the turn of the twenty-first century the Mexican government would embrace this economic model—a service economy based on private, rather than public, investment—and attempt to replicate it in towns across the country.

A Model for the Neoliberal Order

In 2001 the Mexican government initiated a new tourism promotional campaign known as Pueblos Mágicos. The Mexican Ministry of Tourism (SECTUR) designated certain towns as "magical towns" because over time they "preserved, valued, and defended their historical and cultural inheritance." In short, SECTUR proclaimed, a "Pueblo Mágico is a reflection of Mexico." The Pueblos Mágicos initiative promoted tourism in smaller towns and cities across Mexico (a total of thirty-two at the time of a 2008 report). The program aimed to use tourism to elevate standards of living, offer new sources of employment, and provide a model for sustainable local development in the selected towns. San Miguel de Allende received Pueblo Mágico status in 2002, as well as the government funding that accompanied it.[107]

The Pueblos Mágicos program was the counterpoint to another government tourism initiative unveiled in 2001: the Escalera Náutica (Nautical Ladder). This program aimed to develop the coastlines along the Gulf of California in order to attract high-income tourists. The budget and scale of the proposal were enormous and the planned resorts did not overtly embrace Mexican themes and culture, only the idea of luxury that could be anywhere.[108] This focus contrasted sharply with the centrality of Mexican history and culture in the more modest Pueblos Mágicos program.

The outcomes of these initiatives signaled a shift in Mexico's tourist development strategies. The Escalera Náutica program represented a continuation of government interest in large coastal resort destinations such as Acapulco, Cancún, and later Ixtapa and Huatulco. However, the resort development schemes along the Pacific coast and the Gulf of California never achieved the success of Cancún. Indeed the government drastically scaled back the Escalera Náutica program in 2004.[109] In an era when private investment was central to development the government could no longer effectively manage such massive initiatives. The government's 1989 decision to relax laws that limited foreign investment in resort areas was an important precedent for this private-public collaboration.[110] On the other hand, seven years after the Pueblos Mágicos program commenced, SECTUR declared it an overwhelming success.[111]

Pueblos Mágicos also sought to coordinate public and private efforts to develop local tourism industries. This strategy revealed that neoliberal reforms did not completely eliminate government involvement in the economy, but they did limit the scope of government ambitions. The plan attempted to synchronize the goals and resources of an unprecedented number of institutions and delineated the specific objectives and responsibilities of fourteen federal offices, ministries, and commissions, from SECTUR and INAH to the National Water Commission (CAN) and the Ministry of Public Education (SEP). This comprehensive strategy demonstrates that the Mexican government learned from previous tourism development projects. In Acapulco, for instance, failure to adequately plan for population growth led to serious problems with the city's infrastructure for water distribution and drainage.[112] Despite the unparalleled coordination of federal resources, the full implementation of the Pueblos Mágicos program still relied heavily on private funding. In San Miguel more than 75 percent of Pueblos Mágicos funding between 2002 and 2006 came from unnamed nongovernmental sources.[113] San Miguel was not alone. Every town in the Pueblos Mágicos program received a significant amount of private funding. It is notable, however, that San Miguel received the second highest amount of funding overall after Pátzcuaro, Michoacán, and the highest percentage of private money. The government plan still relied on San Miguel's long local tradition of public-private collaboration.

In many ways then the Pueblos Mágicos initiative mirrored the efforts made by municipal officials and entrepreneurs in San Miguel since the 1930s. For the smaller cities and towns on the periphery of

Mexico's economic strategies, San Miguel has long served as a model for how to utilize private, and specifically foreign, investments.[114] Several of the expatriate communities emerging across Mexico also explicitly attempt to replicate the "San Miguel model," from the establishment of cultural institutions such as the library to the idea that the corresponding service industry could help drive economic growth more broadly. As one study of Mérida optimistically pointed out, despite the potential drawbacks, the city's growing foreign population meant that Mexicans could "benefit from North American prosperity without having to cross the border."[115] Indeed by balancing a growing foreign population with the distinction of being a typical Mexican town San Miguel has charted a course for economic development under a neoliberal regime. And if San Miguel's present economic model is any indication—the dramatic growth in the tourism industry and the service sector, the feminization and bilingualization of the labor force, the accelerated migration into and out of the town, and above all a dependency on a large foreign population—Mexico's development strategy is wrought with contradictions. Above all it suggests that the preservation of San Miguel's imagined past relies on its antithesis: contemporary transnational flows of people, ideas, and capital. In this way San Miguel is indeed a reflection of Mexico, but not in the way the framers of the Pueblos Mágicos program intended.

Epilogue

From Typical Town to World Heritage Site

In July 2008 UNESCO designated the historic center blocks of San Miguel de Allende and the Sanctuary of Atotonilco as World Heritage Sites. The municipal government spent several years (and a substantial amount of money) compiling a nearly five-hundred-page nomination dossier prepared by a team of lawyers, archeologists, urban planners, historians, tourism officials, and local politicians. The Statement of Outstanding Universal Value, which explained the grounds for the World Heritage Committee's decision to award San Miguel World Heritage Site status, cited San Miguel as an "exceptional example of the interchange of human values" because it "acted as a melting pot where Spaniards, Creoles, and Amerindians exchanged cultural influences." The statement referred to exchanges of cultural influences during the colonial period and neglected to address those that occurred into the twenty-first century. The committee also noted that San Miguel and the sanctuary "played a significant role in the process of Mexican independence" and that they have "been subject to few alterations over time." Ultimately the UNESCO World Heritage Site designation marked San Miguel as globally—rather than nationally—significant and reaffirmed the sanitized version of local history advanced by José Mojica, Francisco de la Maza, and others who followed.[1]

San Miguel's most recent designation culminates decades of local efforts to bring resources and recognition to the town. Beginning in the 1930s with the Friends of San Miguel, these attempts involved situating San Miguel within an official narrative of national history, tradition, and progress, and later, for UNESCO, within a global historical narrative. In both cases politicians, businesspeople, intellectuals, and tourism promoters sought to demonstrate that San Miguel was central to Mexico's struggle for independence and that it maintained a historic appearance worthy of preserving for future generations. The number of hotel, restaurant, vacation rental, and other travel-related websites that mention San Miguel's UNESCO designation testifies to the perceived linkages between these labels and potential financial dividends.

In the years leading up to 2008 local officials worked to make San Miguel more appealing to the UNESCO committee. Part of this effort included canceling the Sanmiguelada, the bull-running event discussed in chapter 3. The Sanmiguelada had become quite unpopular with local residents because of the enormous, inebriated crowds (estimated at twenty thousand in 2006) that often became violent. Several injuries occurred during the actual bull running, but it was usually fellow runners who caused the injuries and not the bulls. For locals the growing number of injuries after the event, including two shooting deaths in 2006, was more disturbing. Even though the Sanmiguelada generated significant revenue, many local business owners elected to close shop for the weekend rather than contend with the drunken hordes. Most residents would not venture out of their homes if they could avoid it. Some locals speculated that public outcry did not lead to the cancellation. They believed instead that municipal officials were concerned with the liability issues and the fact that the Sanmiguelada would put the UNESCO efforts in jeopardy.[2] Another strategy to position San Miguel for UNESCO status involved repainting the buildings in the historic center. José Guadalupe Ramírez, who was born in the 1930s, recalled that during his childhood the buildings were pastel colors and not the bold ocher, salmon, and marigold hues that now dominate. During our conversation Ramírez

Fig. 9. A newly painted house next to a whitewashed house in San Miguel's historic center, 2007. Photograph by the author.

took me out to the street and proudly gestured to his own house's crumbling, whitewashed walls. He claimed that local officials had been pressuring him to paint his house to conform to the predominant local aesthetic, but he refused to allow them. Ramírez insisted that his house was the only one on his street in the historic center that still reflected San Miguel's true historic appearance, while the other buildings reflected a generic aesthetic that appealed to outsiders. At the time Ramírez predicted that the UNESCO committee would see through the local officials' superficial efforts because San Miguel had not been truly preserved.[3] But he was wrong.

Rather than minimize the changes that San Miguel had undergone in the previous decades, the UNESCO nomination dossier embraced them as essential.[4] For example, the local committee sought to demonstrate that San Miguel's sizable expatriate population did not detract from its historical significance or authenticity. Indeed throughout the twentieth century transnational actors such as Stirling Dickinson were central to efforts at defining San Miguel's Mexican identity. At times these artists, writers, intellectuals, and businesspeople played an integral role in the promotion of San Miguel as a typical Mexican town and in the preservation of its supposedly historic characteristics. This identity helped legitimize the individuals' own reasons for traveling to and living in the town, but it also meant that more foreigners would likely follow in their footsteps, with important economic consequences for those invested in the tourism industry. Additionally, some *sanmiguelenses* have argued that the town's foreign population contributed to a desirable juxtaposition of colonial architecture with a sophisticated cosmopolitanism. By cultivating a local identity rooted in national history and transnational culture, these Mexicans and foreigners also expressed their vision for Mexico's future. The UNESCO committee's decision validated this vision.

As this study has revealed, these efforts did not go unchallenged. Some Sanmiguelenses articulated alternate visions for San Miguel rooted in religious nationalism, modern industrial productivity, and adherence to patriarchal values. Although local elites often rejected their ideas, the service economy has failed to address the majority of Sanmiguelenses' needs in a satisfactory way, allowing these critiques to bubble beneath the surface. Locals continue to seek other forms of economic development, better infrastructure, access to clean water, and ways to protect and promote their culture.

When Dickinson died suddenly and unexpectedly in a 1998 car accident, several observers noted that hundreds of Mexicans of humble origins easily made up the largest number of mourners at his funeral—a testament to his long-standing commitment to the broader community.[5] It is impossible to know how he interpreted his own role in the town, but his tireless work to help those less fortunate suggests that he felt a great deal of responsibility toward the people of the town who had adopted him as their own decades before. Dickinson helped set the wheels of change in motion back in the 1930s, but I suspect that the San Miguel of the twenty-first century is far beyond what he ever envisioned. In fact, aside from the spires of the Parroquia, he probably would not recognize modern San Miguel at all.

Despite all of the changes, in some ways twenty-first-century San Miguel has come full circle. As I write these final pages, plans are under way to develop an industrial corridor around San Miguel, inspired by the nearby city of Querétaro, which has one of the fastest growing manufacturing sectors in Mexico. While some residents welcome this attempt to diversify the economy, others fear the potential for environmental degradation and express concern that these jobs will not offer the same social contract that inspires so much nostalgia for the Fábrica La Aurora. In addition, domestic rather than foreign tourism represents the sector with the biggest growth potential in San Miguel. It took international recognition, whether through UNESCO, international film, food, and wine festivals, or international luxury hotel chains, to validate San Miguel as a destination for elite Mexican travelers. This trend of growing Mexican tourism, particularly weekenders from Mexico City, coincides with a slow but steady decline in the number of visitors from the United States. A number of factors have contributed to this decline, including the 2008 economic recession and persistent concerns about drug-related violence in Mexico. The challenge for Sanmiguelenses is that foreign tourists have tended to stay longer and therefore have had a greater economic impact. Now locals tend to grumble about the weekend chilango invasion, and there is a bit of longing for the days when San Miguel was primarily a gringo paradise.

A visit to the Fábrica La Aurora also underscores how everything old is new again in San Miguel. The factory once again buzzes with activity, but in its current manifestation it houses art studios, galleries, interior design shops, and restaurants. The Garay family modernized some parts of the grounds while maintaining some vestiges of the factory's past, such as machines and turbines, in line with the broader trend of repurposing postindustrial spaces.[6] The artists and store owners intend for these paintings, antiques, and objets d'art to appeal to a market outside of San Miguel, like the textiles that factory

Fig. 10. Fábrica La Aurora sign, 2008. Photograph by the author.

workers once produced there. Now, however, the production for an outside market is because the items are prohibitively expensive for all but the wealthiest local residents. Most of the retail locations advertise that they will facilitate domestic or international shipping. The Fábrica La Aurora building remains a center for cultural life, but this iteration caters to the champagne crowd.

The juxtaposition of the high-end Art and Design Center in the building with the company houses in Colonia Aurora across the street, still occupied by working- and middle-class families, speaks to the degree to which San Miguel's identity and reputation have shifted to appeal to international tastes. It also explains why Emigdio Ledesma was so eager to share his story with me in 2015. When a colleague and I met with Ledesma (who, like many former workers, lives a stone's throw from the old factory), he led us to some metal folding

chairs in a shed behind his home. As we sat surrounded by a warren
of dusty tools, props for San Miguel's many religious festivals, and
piles of documents he had collected over the years, it was clear that
he worried the histories and contributions of working-class Sanmiguelenses might one day be forgotten.[7] Félix Luna shared similar
sentiments in his oral history of San Miguel's traditions, published in
1999. He expressed concern that commercial interests were compro-
mising local religious and indigenous practices and customs. In one
enlightening anecdote he explained that the municipal government
tried to co-opt the annual tradition of decorating altars to honor the
Virgen Dolorosa by converting it into a contest. "Las tradiciones
deben guardarse por lo que se siente, no por interés," he cautioned.[8]
It is poignant and ironic that the working-class families that once
exemplified an economic alternative to tourism now provide a festive
backdrop for the industry.

The case of San Miguel de Allende illustrates that it is not just a
coincidence or a correlation that debates about economic development
strategies and national identity were intertwined. By linking ideas
about national identity to different economic development strategies,
Sanmiguelenses reveal their values, hopes, and fears. But more than
that they also help trace a change in Mexico a century in the making.
Whereas in the wake of the Mexican Revolution Sanmiguelenses
attached a significance and value to staking a claim as a typically
Mexican place, by the twenty-first century that value and significance
had diminished. This decline occurred in part because of widespread
disillusionment with postrevolutionary narratives about the nation,
but, more important, it is the result of economic restructuring that
has diminished the role of the state in distributing resources. The
most symbolic evidence of this transition in San Miguel occurred in
2009, when the fact that the World Heritage designation superseded
San Miguel's Pueblo Mágico status led officials to withdraw the town
from the program. Even though the Mexican government still plays a
role in helping San Miguel maintain its World Heritage designation,

that role is clearly secondary to UNESCO's international consultants and tastemakers. San Miguel de Allende has proven to be fluid and malleable rather than static and timeless, and its history offers many lessons and cautionary tales for other towns as they confront economic and cultural change.

Introduction

1. Emigdio Ledesma Pérez, interview by author and Fredy González, San Miguel de Allende, May 5, 2015; Virtue, *Model American Abroad*, 52.
2. Ledesma Pérez interview.
3. For the total population see the 2010 census data in México en Cifras, INEGI, last accessed August 23, 2016, http://www3.inegi.org.mx/sistemas /mexicocifras/default.aspx?src=487&e=11. The census number includes all surveyed residents of San Miguel de Allende, both Mexican and foreign, and the estimated number of foreigners includes permanent and seasonal residents. Precise numbers of permanent foreign residents are notoriously difficult to compile. On the unreliability of population estimates for foreigners in Mexico see Topmiller, Conway, and Gerber, "US Migration to Mexico"; Dixon, Murray, and Gelatt, *America's Emigrants*, 23–24; Croucher, *Other Side of the Fence*, 43–52; and Bantman-Masum, "'You Need to Come Here,'" 8–9.
4. "Best Cities in the World, 2013," *Condé Nast Traveler*, last accessed September 29, 2015, http://www.cntraveler.com/galleries/2013-10-15/best -cities-world/25. For other examples see "Best Places to Visit in Mexico and Central and South America," *Travel + Leisure*, last accessed August 8, 2016, http://www.travelandleisure.com/worlds-best/cities-in-mexico -south-central-america#intro; "Best Places to Visit in Mexico," *U.S. News and World Report*, last accessed April 29, 2016, http://travel.usnews.com /Rankings/Best_Mexico_Vacations/; "Top 10 Destinations—Mexico," TripAdvisor Travelers' Choice 2016, last accessed April 29, 2016, https:// www.tripadvisor.com/TravelersChoice-Destinations-cTop-g150768; and Stacy Suaya, "Weekend Escape: San Miguel de Allende, Mexico, Is a Vibrant

Weekend Getaway," *Los Angeles Times*, last accessed April 29, 2016, http://www.latimes.com/travel/la-tr-d-escape-san-miguel-20160207-story.html.

5. Yuhl, *Golden Haze of Memory*, 12.

6. For example, see the contributions to Joseph, Rubenstein, and Zolov, *Fragments of a Golden Age*; Walker, *Waking from the Dream*; Gauss, *Made in Mexico*; Bachelor, "Miracle on Ice"; Clancy, *Exporting Paradise*; Gillingham and Smith, "Introduction"; Snodgrass, "Golden Age of Charrismo"; and Moreno, *Yankee Don't Go Home!*

7. Studies of communities in other parts of the world that have influenced this analysis include Adams, *Art as Politics*; Lipman, *Guantánamo*; Yuhl, *Golden Haze of Memory*; Pessar, *From Fanatics to Folk*; Rothman, *Devil's Bargains*; and Merrill, *Negotiating Paradise*.

8. Claudio Lomnitz has led this field of inquiry with *Deep Mexico, Silent Mexico, Death and the Idea of Mexico*, and "Narrating the Neoliberal Moment." Historians of tourism in Mexico also have been among the small group of scholars to extend analyses of national identity and state formation beyond the 1970s. For example, see Clancy, *Exporting Paradise*; Covert, "Political Economy of Mexico's Independence Heroes"; and chapters in Berger and Wood, *Holiday in Mexico*: Castellanos, "Cancún and the Campo"; Coffey, "Marketing Mexico's Great Masters"; and Saragoza, "Golfing in the Desert."

9. On the shifting meanings of the term "expatriation" see N. Green, "Expatriation, Expatriates, and Expats." The reflections on the challenges of labeling San Miguel's foreign population as described in Croucher, *Other Side of the Fence*, 17–24, also helped me think through the pros and cons of different terms.

10. This study builds on a number of prior studies that examine foreigners in Mexico, including Buchenau, "Small Numbers, Great Impact"; and Palma Mora, *De tierras extrañas*. For other studies on Americans in Mexico see W. Schell, *Integral Outsiders*; Hart, *Empire and Revolution*; Schreiber, *Cold War Exiles in Mexico*; Anhalt, *Gathering of Fugitives*; Palma Mora, *Veteranos de guerra norteamericanos en Guadalajara*; Banks, "Identity Narratives by American and Canadian Retirees in Mexico"; Otero, "U.S. Retired Persons in Mexico"; Bantman-Masum, "'You Need to Come Here'"; and several of the essays in Bloom, *Adventures into Mexico*.

11. See, for example, the essays in Hernández and Patterson, *Memorias*; Bloom, "To Be Served and Loved"; Croucher, *Other Side of the Fence*; Hernández, *La soledad del silencio*; Virtue, *Leonard and Reva Brooks*; and Virtue, *Model American Abroad*.

12. This is a vast literature, but the works that have most influenced this study include González y González, *San José de Gracia*; Lomnitz, *Deep Mexico, Silent Mexico*; López, *Crafting Mexico*; Overmyer-Velázquez, *Visions of the Emerald City*; Gillingham, *Cuauhtémoc's Bones*; and Wright-Rios, *Revolutions in Mexican Catholicism*.

13. My approach has been influenced by some of the now foundational studies on empire and power, especially Stoler, *Carnal Knowledge and Imperial Power*; Joseph, LeGrand, and Salvatore, *Close Encounters of Empire*; Pratt, *Imperial Eyes*; and Fein, "Culture across Borders in the Americas," but also by scholarship on the "new borderlands" history, including Hämäläinen and Truett, "On Borderlands"; Cadava, *Standing on Common Ground*; and Adams, "Hipsters and jipitecas."

14. González y González, *San José de Gracia*, xxi.

15. Manuel Zavala Zavala, "Sucesos, sucedidos, o qué van a suceder," Radio XESQ transcript, August 5, 1962.

16. The following sources helped me situate these periodicals within the broader historical context of Mexican journalism: Piccato, *Tyranny of Opinion*, esp. chap. 1; and Mraz, "Today, Tomorrow, and Always." Trouillot, *Silencing the Past*, influenced my approach to archives and their absences.

1. Making a Typical Mexican Town

1. Mojica, *I, a Sinner*, 330.

2. Wright Carr, *La conquista del Bajío y los orígenes de San Miguel de Allende*, 11; Tutino, *Making a New World*, 32. For more on the history of pre-Hispanic settlements in the area around modern-day San Miguel see Nieto Gamiño, "Los asentamientos prehispánicos de la cuenca central del río Laja." For examples of scholarship that emphasizes the idea that the Bajío is "Hispanized" see Brading, *Miners and Merchants in Bourbon Mexico*; Knight, *Mexican Revolution*, vol. 2; Meyer, *Cristero Rebellion*; Serrano Álvarez, *La batalla del espíritu*, vols. 1 and 2; Valencia García, *Guanajuato*; and Newcomer, *Reconciling Modernity*. Tutino also took this approach in his earlier work, *From Insurrection to Revolution in Mexico*.

3. Tutino, *Making a New World*, 6. He develops this formulation in the book's introduction.

4. Brading, *Church and State in Bourbon Mexico*, 157–59.

5. On the emergence of the Bajío as the richest region in the Americas and the rise and fall of the mining industries see Tutino, *Making a New World*, esp. chaps. 3 and 6; and Brading, *Miners and Merchants in Bourbon Mexico*.

For perspectives on twentieth- and twenty-first-century industrialization in the Bajío see Newcomer, *Reconciling Modernity*; and Byrnes, *Driving the State*. Informal conversations during May 2015 (in San Miguel and at the international airports in Querétaro and León) with managers and consultants for several foreign corporations confirmed this view that the region is considered cheaper and safer.

6. For example, see Durand, *Braceros*; and "State of Origin of Migratory Agricultural Workers Entering the U.S., 1942–1968," Perry-Castañeda Library Map Collection, University of Texas at Austin, last accessed May 2, 2016, http://www.lib.utexas.edu/maps/atlas_mexico/migrations_1942 _68.jpg. According to this map Guanajuato ranked first among all Mexican states in terms of the numbers of persons who left for the United States.

7. Wright Carr, *La conquista del Bajío y los orígenes de San Miguel de Allende*, 42.

8. For a helpful exploration of the meaning of "Chichimeca" see Tutino, *Making a New World*, 70–71.

9. For a detailed history of San Miguel before and immediately following the Conquest see Wright Carr, *La conquista del Bajío y los orígenes de San Miguel de Allende*. Also see Tutino, *Making a New World*, chap. 1, which draws heavily from Wright Carr on San Miguel but also situates it in the context of the entire Bajío and reflects new analysis and research that improves upon the discussion of the Bajío in Tutino, *From Insurrection to Revolution*, chap. 2.

10. Tutino, *Making a New World*, 185.

11. On San Miguel's colonial economic development see Tutino, *Making a New World*, chap. 3; Chowning, *Rebellious Nuns*, chap. 1; Salvucci, "Aspectos de un conflicto empresarial"; and Cruz López, "Vínculos omnipotentes."

12. On the concentration of power in San Miguel see Tutino, *Making a New World*, chap. 6. On intra-elite conflict in eighteenth-century San Miguel see Salvucci, "Aspectos de un conflicto empresarial." On the Canal family see Chowning, *Rebellious Nuns*, chap. 1. On the role of marginal elites in the 1810 insurrection see Tutino, *From Insurrection to Revolution*, chap. 3. Sauto appears to be an alternate spelling for Sautto, which was the more commonly used spelling in the nineteenth and twentieth centuries.

13. Chowning's *Rebellious Nuns* focuses on the establishment of and conflicts within the Conceptionist convent in San Miguel. On the Canal family and the influence of Father Alfaro see Chowning, *Rebellious Nuns*, 21–27. For

more on the history of the sanctuary and Alfaro and on the artisan guilds and confraternities see Santiago Silva, *Atotonilco*, chaps. 3 and 38, respectively. For more on religious life in eighteenth-century San Miguel see Brading, *Church and State in Bourbon Mexico*, chap. 3; and López Espinoza, *Estampas sanmiguelenses*. On the history of the Sanctuary of Atotonilco see Hernández, *La soledad del silencio*.

14. On the broader history of textile manufacturing in New Spain and the relationship between its decline and the independence movements see Salvucci, *Textiles and Capitalism in Mexico*. On the origins of the insurgency and the role played by "marginal elites" see Tutino, *From Insurrection to Revolution*, esp. chap. 3; and Jiménez Codinach, "Memorias de una villa rebelde."

15. Chowning, *Rebellious Nuns*, 267.

16. On the revitalization of manufacturing in San Miguel see chap. 3.

17. Correa, "Sharecropping and Agrarian Reform," 159.

18. Tutino, *From Insurrection to Revolution*, 342–45.

19. Blanco, *Revolución y contienda política en Guanajuato*, chap. 3; Sánchez Rangel, "La transición revolucionaria en San Miguel de Allende." For another interpretation of the riot see Knight, *Mexican Revolution*, 1:211–12.

20. See the very brief account of San Miguel's experience of the revolution in the history by local *cronista* López Espinoza, *Estampas sanmiguelenses*, 76–77. On some of the negative effects of the revolution and other natural events in the region during this period see Knight, *Mexican Revolution*, 2:200–201, 415. According to the 1921 census San Miguel's population was 8,199, almost 2,000 fewer than in 1900. Marco Geoestadístico Nacional, Descarga de información correspondiente a la localidad geoestadística: 110030001 INEGI, last accessed August 23, 2016, http://www .inegi.org.mx/geo/contenidos/geoestadistica/introduccio.aspx.

21. Genaro Almanza Ríos, interview by author, San Miguel de Allende, November 8–13, 2007.

22. For examples of where these anticlerical polices were implemented earlier see Bantjes, "Regional Dynamics of Anticlericalism and Defanaticization in Revolutionary Mexico," 112–13; and Curley, "'First Encounter,'" 131–48.

23. "Calles Will Seize Catholic Churches When Priests Quit," *New York Times*, July 28, 1926, 1.

24. For an overview of the church-state conflict see Meyer, *Cristero Rebellion*; and Fallaw, *Religion and State Formation in Postrevolutionary Mexico*.

25. On supporters of the Cristiada in San Miguel see Almanza Ríos interview; and Sánchez Díaz, *La guerra cristera en Guanajuato*, 19, 43–44. For the 1921 census see Marco Geoestadístico Nacional, Descarga de información correspondiente a la localidad geoestadística: 110030001 INEGI, last accessed August 23, 2016, http://www.inegi.org.mx/geo/contenidos/geoest adistica/introduccio.aspx.

26. César Arias de la Canal, interview by author, San Miguel de Allende, January 17, 2008. For an overview of the experience of non-Catholics in Mexico during this period see Bastian, "Protestants, Freemasons, and Spiritists."

27. Correa, "Sharecropping and Agrarian Reform," 156.

28. Sánchez Díaz, *La guerra cristera en Guanajuato*, 136n13; Félix Luna Romero, interview by Morton Stith and Katherine Walch, May 16, 2001, SMHA; Susan Beere, "Spotlight on People: Celia Hoyos de Téllez," *Atención*, October 31, 1978, 5.

29. Almanza Ríos interview.

30. Benito Tegas Vasques, interview by Leonardo Rosen, September 24, 2002, SMHA.

31. Luna Romero interview; Sánchez Díaz, *La guerra cristera en Guanajuato*, 21; Bonifacio López Herrera y Ortega, interview by Elena Shoemaker and Katherine Walch, May 11, 2003, SMHA. Don Bonifacio claimed he fought with the Cristeros "sin comer, sin agua, sin pagar."

32. Countless tourist guidebooks, newspaper and magazine articles, travel accounts, oral histories, and websites have propagated the myth of a 1926 designation. For example, see Virtue, *Model American Abroad*, 55.

33. Secretaría General del Gobierno de Guanajuato, circular issued November 26, 1926, 1.03.68, Exp. 68, Fondo: Secretaría del Gobierno, Primer Departamento, AGGEG.

34. Presidente Municipal to Secretaría General del Gobierno of Guanajuato, July 7, 1927, Fondo: Gobernación, AGMSMA.

35. Jefe de la Oficina Federal de Hacienda, notice issued November 22, 1926, Exp. 10/422.1/244, Legajo 132, Caja 125, PGR, AGN; correspondence regarding the nationalization of property on Canal and Mesones Streets, 1929–43, Exp. 10/422.1/356, Legajo 391, Caja 340; correspondence regarding the former *beaterio* Santo Domingo, 1941–44, Exp. 10/422.1/355, Legajo 339, Caja 300bis; correspondence regarding the Hospital Civil, annex of Templo San Juan de Dios, 1941–61, Exp. 10/422.1/245, Legajo 391, Caja 340; correspondence regarding the Capilla del Calvario, 1958–72, Exp. 10/422.1/17229, Legajo 237, Caja 216, all in PGR, AGN.

36. The guide for the PGR archives at the AGN listed a file for the Parroquia, but the archivists were unable to locate it. The year 1957 for the completed nationalization is speculation based on the record in the guide. The guide usually, with few exceptions, listed other PGR files under the year of the last correspondence, the file for the San Francisco church being one of them. Correspondence regarding the Templo de la Tercera Orden, 1957–62, Exp. 10/422.1/17095, Legajo 489, Caja 438, PGR, AGN.

37. La Secretaría de Hacienda, circular, October 17, 1930, No. 93, Exp. 3.08.30; Subsecretary, La Secretaría de Hacienda, circular, May 7, 1930, No. 87, Exp. 3.07.30, both in Serie: Gobierno Estatal, Sección: Circulares, Fondo: Gobernación, AGMSMA.

38. Luis Caballero V., "La H. Colonia Española de S. Miguel," El Vocero del Norte, February 18, 1962, 3, 6. A 1936 survey listed twenty professionals in San Miguel: four lawyers, two accountants, three employees of the mail service, one dentist, two nurses, four pharmacists, two engineers, and two doctors. Approximately half of these persons were either Spaniards or Mexicans who had recently migrated to San Miguel. Survey, PNR Instituto de Estudios Sociales, Políticos y Económicos, December 23, 1936, Serie: Partido Nacional Revolucionario, Sección: Correspondencia, Fondo: Gobernación, AGMSMA.

39. Secretaría General del Gobierno of Guanajuato to Presidente Municipal, November 29, 1933, No. 421, Exp. 340.29, Serie: Asuntos Varios, Sección: Gobernación, Fondo: C. P. Miguel Herrera A., AGMSMA.

40. San Miguel Chamber of Commerce to Presidente Municipal, August 25, 1936, Septiembre-Octubre, Exp. 407-5-6, Sección: Asuntos Varios, Fondo: Gobernación, AGMSMA.

41. Correa, "Sharecropping and Agrarian Reform," 156.

42. Governor Melchor Ortega, "Informe de Gobierno, 1933," in Aveleyra Santos et al., Guanajuato en la voz de sus gobernadores. On the challenges of reintegrating repatriated Mexicans and their Mexican American children across Mexico see Balderrama and Rodríguez, Decade of Betrayal, chap. 8.

43. Fallaw, Religion and State Formation in Postrevolutionary Mexico, chap. 5. On the Segunda also see Blancarte, "Intransigence, Anticommunism, and Reconciliation."

44. See Correa, "Sharecropping and Agrarian Reform," 158. Another analysis of agrarian reform in the municipality of San Miguel does not specify who the beneficiaries of agrarian reform were and uses the more general terms campesinos or agraristas instead; see Sepúlveda Garza, "Historias rancheras," 243–60.

45. For example see Maria del Carmen Malo to the Governor, June 27, 1936, 1.54.(3).4, Allende, Fondo: Secretaría del Gobierno, Primer Departamento, AGGEG. For an analysis of why some parts of communities became agraristas and others Cristeros, see Purnell, *Popular Movements and State Formation in Revolutionary Mexico.* On conflicts over agrarian reform in other parts of Guanajuato see Uzeta Iturbide, "Ejidatarios y Chichimecas"; Guerrero Tarquín, *Memorias de un agrarista*; and Sepúlveda Garza, *Políticas agrarias y luchas sociales.*

46. The newly created ejidos were Agustín González, Atotonilco, Bocas, Calderón, Cerritos, Cruz del Palmar, Landeta, and La Petaca. Secretaría de la Economía Nacional, Dirección General de Estadística, Adjustments to 1930 Census Records, March 27, 1937, Sección: Datos del Municipio, Fondo: Gobernación, AGMSMA.

47. Correspondence regarding Atotonilco, 1935, Exp. 547.3/67, LCR, AGN; Gobernación to the Governor, January 23, 1936, 1.54.(3).2, Allende; Maria del Carmen Malo to the Governor, June 27, 1936, 1.54.(3).4, Allende; correspondence regarding hacienda Puente del Carmen, 1936, Exp. 1.54.(3).5, all in Fondo: Secretaría del Gobierno, Primer Departamento, AGGEG.

48. José López L. to President Cárdenas, September 23, 1936, copy in 1.52. (3).4, Allende, Fondo: Secretaría del Gobierno, Primer Departamento, AGGEG.

49. Correa, "Sharecropping and Agrarian Reform," 160–61.

50. Correspondence regarding the former Convento de San Felipe Neri, 1932, Exp. 163/7, ALR, AGN.

51. Presidente Municipal to the Secretaría de Comunicaciones y Obras Públicas, March 9, 1932, Sección: Caminos y Carreteras, Fondo: Gobernación, AGMSMA.

52. Correspondence between the Presidente Municipal and Airways Investment Company, 1931, Exp. 1.07.31, Sección: Asuntos Varios, Fondo: Gobernación, AGMSMA.

53. For more on the Fábrica La Aurora, see chap. 3.

54. Mojica's autobiography proved to be the most useful account of his life before his arrival in San Miguel, although his timeline occasionally conflicts with that of other, better documented sources. See Mojica, *I, a Sinner.* Some other useful sources are Usabel, *High Noon of American Films in Latin America*, 91, 96; Max Arthur, "The Padre Who Was Mojica," *Chicago Daily Tribune*, April 18, 1948, E5; and a series by Katherine Walch, "Remembering José Mojica," *El Independiente*, BD.

55. For example, López Herrera y Ortega interview; Luna Romero interview; and Raquel Mojica and Maria Herrera D. Williams, interview by Katherine Walch, December 2002, SMHA. Mojica's own autobiographical account, *I, a Sinner,* downplays his role in San Miguel social life, likely because of his subsequent religious conversion.
56. Walch, "Remembering José Mojica."
57. Toussaint, *Tasco.* Tasco is an alternate spelling for Taxco.
58. On the development of Taxco as a tourist destination see Oles, "Walls to Paint On," chap. 1. Many other towns throughout Latin America adopted similar strategies. Perhaps the most analogous example is the former mining town of Ouro Preto in Brazil. For example, see the following guidebooks: Bandeira, *Guia de Ouro Preto*; and Ruas, *Ouro Preto.*
59. Toussaint, *Tasco,* 211–15.
60. Oles, "Walls to Paint On," 80.
61. Toussaint, *Tasco,* 102.
62. Mabel Dodge Luhan, "Mexico in 1930," 65–66, Folder 1421, Box 56, Mabel Dodge Luhan Papers, Yale Collection of American Literature, Beinecke Rare Book and Manuscript Library, New Haven CT.
63. Dodge, "Mexico in 1930," 82.
64. On antimodernism see Lears, *No Place of Grace.* For the counterargument that Lears's antimodernists were actually modernists see Smith, *Reimagining Indians*; Stansell, *American Moderns*; Burke, *From Greenwich Village to Taos*; and Yuhl, *Golden Haze of Memory.*
65. Rick López makes this argument for Mexico more broadly. See López, *Crafting Mexico,* esp. chap. 3.
66. On the case of New Mexico see Montgomery, *Spanish Redemption.* For other examples of the economic and political underpinnings of heritage revival movements see Gillingham, *Cuauhtémoc's Bones*; Briggs, *Wood Carvers of Córdova, New Mexico*; Clarke, *Mapping Yoruba Networks*; Pessar, *From Fanatics to Folk*; Schwartz, *Pleasure Island*; and López, *Crafting Mexico.*
67. La Junta Patriótica de San Miguel de Allende to the Governor, August 7, 1936, 1.45.(3).1, Allende, Fondo: Secretaría del Gobierno, Primer Departamento, AGGEG.
68. Summary of Projects planned for 1934, December 13, 1933, Caja 5326, Serie: Monumentos Artísticos e Históricos, 1931–40, Sección: Departamento de Bellas Artes, SEP. On the incorporation of Miguel Hidalgo and the town of Dolores Hidalgo into the national historical narrative

see Vázquez Soriano, *Signos de identidad*; Covert, "Political Economy of Mexico's Independence Heroes"; and Archer, "Death's Patriots."

69. La Junta Patriótica de San Miguel de Allende to the Governor, August 7, 1936, 1.45.(3).1, Allende, Fondo: Secretaría del Gobierno, Primer Departamento, AGGEG.

70. The Zavala family first came to San Miguel in 1899, whereas the "old" families traced their roots in San Miguel to the colonial period. On the Zavalas' arrival in San Miguel see Manuel Zavala Zavala, interview by Leonardo Rosen, October 9, 2002, SMHA.

71. Ley sobre protección y conservación de monumentos arqueológicos e históricos, poblaciones típicas y lugares de belleza natural, y su reglamento, January 19, 1934, Departamento de Monumentos Artísticos, Arqueologícos e Históricos, SEP. For an analysis of the DMAAH's efforts at historic preservation during the 1930s see López, *Crafting Mexico*, chap. 4.

72. de la Maza, *San Miguel de Allende*, 134. The majority of the text in the second edition is identical to that of the first, with the exception of the introductions and the appendices.

73. For an example in the state of Guanajuato see Newcomer, *Reconciling Modernity*.

74. Secretaría de Educación Pública to Presidente Municipal, June 9, 1936, Sección: Asuntos Varios, Enero-Junio, Fondo: Gobernación, AGMSMA.

75. On the valorization of indigenous cultures and the ethnicization of the Mexican national identity see López, *Crafting Mexico*.

76. Oles argues that the twentieth-century interest in colonial architecture developed from a sense of nostalgia. By contrast this chapter argues that, in the context of church-state conflicts and the ethnicization of the national identity, popular interest in San Miguel's colonial architecture had origins that are more complex. See Oles, "Walls to Paint On," 52.

77. de la Maza, *San Miguel de Allende*, 9–10. The second edition offers a corrective to this version of history by including an appendix, written by Miguel Malo, on the pre-Hispanic peoples who populated the region.

78. I was unable to locate documentation explaining why SEP did not approve San Miguel. This is perhaps because from 1938 to 1939 the Cárdenas administration dissolved DMAAH and created a new agency in its place, the Instituto Nacional de Antropología e Historia (INAH). See López, *Crafting Mexico*, 232–35.

79. Zavala, *Tradiciones y leyendas sanmiguelenses*, 143–44.

80. Correspondence regarding Decree 292, 1939, 1.24.-3, Fondo: Secretaría del Gobierno, Primer Departamento, AGGEG.

81. Correspondence regarding Decree 292, 1939, 1.24.-3, Fondo: Secretaría del Gobierno, Primer Departamento, AGGEG.

82. Mojica's autobiography, *I, a Sinner*, reveals his long-standing interest in the history of the Franciscans in California. On the California Mission Revival see Kropp, *California Vieja*, esp. chap. 2.

83. Cossío del Pomar, *Cossío del Pomar en San Miguel de Allende*, 26. There are two editions of this book; the second is titled *Iridiscencia: Crónica de un centro de arte*.

84. On the history of the Parroquia and its renovations see López Espinoza, *Estampas sanmiguelenses*, 57–61.

85. Throughout *Cossío del Pomar en San Miguel de Allende* the author boasts about people he encountered over the course of his travels and in San Miguel.

86. Cossío del Pomar, *Cossío del Pomar en San Miguel de Allende*, 38–41; *Diario Oficial*, April 22, 1939, AGN.

87. Bowman, *Death Is Incidental*.

88. On Dickinson's first encounter with Mojica see Virtue, *Model American Abroad*, 37. On promotional efforts for the school see Cossío del Pomar, *Cossío del Pomar en San Miguel de Allende*, 46–47.

89. Note San Miguel's exclusion from the maps in Toor, *Frances Toor's Motorist Guide to Mexico*, 19–20.

90. Brenner, *Your Mexican Holiday*, 166–67.

91. Mexican National Railroad, *Mexico: Tropical Tours to Toltec Towns*, 14.

92. Missouri Pacific Lines, *Mexico: A Foreign Land a Step Away*, 21. For an analysis of debates over the aesthetics and authenticity of the new façade see López Espinoza, *Estampas sanmiguelenses*, 57–61.

93. Mexican Tourism Board, "México: Beyond Your Expectations" ad, printed in, e.g., *New Yorker*, April 18, 2005, 112.

94. Frederic Babcock, "Detour," *Chicago Daily Tribune*, October 17, 1937, E6.

95. On the appeal of places like Santa Fe and Taos to avant-garde artists see Burke, *From Greenwich Village to Taos*. On Santa Fe's transition to a middle-class tourist destination see Montgomery, *Spanish Redemption*, esp. the conclusion.

96. Judith Cass, "The South Gets Full Share of Summer Trips," *Chicago Daily Tribune*, July 6, 1938, 13.

97. Frederic Babcock, "Another Taxco Discovered in North Mexico," *Chicago Daily Tribune*, March 31, 1940, F7.

98. Frederic Babcock, "Tourists in a Hurry Pass Up These Oases," *Chicago Daily Tribune*, April 7, 1940, J9.

99. Cossío del Pomar, *Cossío del Pomar en San Miguel de Allende*, 51, 117–21.

100. Secretaría de Gobernación to the Governor, April 7, 1938, 1.19.-14; Secretaría de Gobernación to the Governor, October 4, 1938, 1.19.-6, both in Fondo: Secretaría del Gobierno, Primer Departamento, AGGEG.

101. On the failures of agrarian and educational reforms and the overall violence in this region see Fallaw, *Religion and State Formation in Postrevolutionary Mexico*, 182–92. On the repression of Catholics see Valencia García, *Guanajuato*, 39. See also Zermeño P. and Aguilar V., "Dos razones para el estudio y la investigación de la Unión Nacional Sinarquista-Partido Demócrata Mexicano en Guanajuato"; and Meyer, "Idea of Mexico." On Cárdenas's retreat from his more radical policies see Blancarte, "Intransigence, Anticommunism, and Reconciliation," 73–74.

102. On the appeal of postrevolutionary Mexico to foreign modernist and radical intellectuals see Tenorio-Trillo, "Cosmopolitan Mexican Summer, 1920–1949." On Dickinson's anticlerical sentiments see Virtue, *Model American Abroad*, 32, 63.

103. One article of the Constitution of 1917 claimed for Mexico the rights to all subsoil commodities. This article threatened foreign oil companies, but the inability of the Mexican government to enforce the constitution allowed the companies to retain their holdings for two decades, until the 1938 expropriations.

104. Secretaría de Gobernación, Report on the Mexican Tourism Industry, 1940, Exp. 606.3/35, LCR, AGN; Berger, *Development of Mexico's Tourism Industry*, 66–67.

105. Circular announcing the Mexican Tourism Biennial, January 29, 1940, 1.03.24, Fondo: Secretaría del Gobierno, Primer Departamento, AGGEG.

2. Good Neighbors, Good Catholics

1. See Zolov, "Discovering a Land 'Mysterious and Obvious,'" 234; Saragoza, "Selling of Mexico," 104; Fein, "Producing the Cold War in Mexico," 177; Berger, *Development of Mexico's Tourism Industry*, esp. chap. 5; and Moreno, *Yankee Don't Go Home!*, chap. 1.

2. For example, see the analysis of foreign representations of Mexico during the Porfiriato in Ruiz, *Americans in the Treasure House*.

3. On foreign travelers in Mexico in the 1920s and 1930s see Delpar, *Enormous Vogue of Things Mexican*; López, *Crafting Mexico*; Oles, "Walls to Paint On"; and Britton, *Revolution and Ideology*.

4. The 1940 Mexican census counted 9,030 residents in San Miguel. Marco Geoestadístico Nacional, Descarga de información correspondiente a

la localidad geoestadística: 110030001 INEGI, last accessed August 23, 2016, http://www.inegi.org.mx/geo/contenidos/geoestadistica/introduccio.aspx.

5. "The Voice of the Traveler," *Chicago Daily Tribune*, November 3, 1940, E4. Maps produced by the Mexican government in the 1940s supported the description provided in the article, indicating that all of the roads leading to San Miguel were unpaved. See Map of Road Projects in Guanajuato, 1945, Exp. 609/815–2, MAC, AGN; and Mapa de la República Mexicana mostrando el estado de los caminos federales, estatales y vecinales, 1944, Sterling Memorial Library Map Collection, Yale University, New Haven CT.

6. Amigos de San Miguel de Allende, *Guía de San Miguel de Allende*, 70–72. For a more detailed discussion of the significance of the Pan-American Highway (originally the Nuevo Laredo–Monterrey Highway) to the Mexican tourism industry see Berger, *Development of the Mexican Tourism Industry*, chap. 3.

7. Strode, *Now in Mexico*, 304.

8. This imaginative recreation of the arrival experience is drawn from a compilation of the accounts of many visitors to San Miguel during this era, as well as my own first experience of San Miguel: arriving by car at daybreak in August 2002. For examples, see a version of Dickinson's account in Virtue, *Model American Abroad*, 15; and Cossío del Pomar, *Cossío del Pomar en San Miguel de Allende*, 20–22.

9. Stirling Dickinson, Escuela Universitaria de Bellas Artes catalog, 1940, Exp. 1940–72, CCIR.

10. On her biographical details see the finding aid for Katharine Kuh Papers, Yale Collection of American Literature, Beinecke Rare Book and Manuscript Library, New Haven CT. Also see letters she received from Carlos Mérida in Folder 21, Box 2, Kuh Papers.

11. A survey of the Proquest databases of the *New York Times*, the *Los Angeles Times*, and the *Chicago Daily Tribune* revealed that a total of six articles about San Miguel appeared in these newspapers in the 1930s, whereas in 1940 there were five stories and a total of fifty-one in the 1940s.

12. "New Art Colony in Mexico Draws Many Americans," *Chicago Daily Tribune*, January 15, 1941, 15.

13. Amigos de San Miguel de Allende, *Guía de San Miguel de Allende*, 4.

14. Amigos de San Miguel de Allende, *Guía de San Miguel de Allende*, 59.

15. Amigos de San Miguel de Allende, *Guía de San Miguel de Allende*, 60.

16. Virtue, *Leonard and Reva Brooks*, 99–109.

17. Frederic Babcock, "Tourists in a Hurry Pass Up These Oases," *Chicago Daily Tribune*, April 7, 1940, J9.

18. "Gay, Romantic Art Colony Develops South of the Border," *Los Angeles Times*, February 2, 1941, C8; Frederic Babcock, "Tourists in a Hurry Pass Up These Oases," *Chicago Daily Tribune*, April 7, 1940, J9; and Ruth Dickinson, "San Miguel Is the Mexico of Your Dreams," *Chicago Daily Tribune*, January 2, 1944, N6. On the narrative developed by the Friends of San Miguel see chap. 1.

19. Strode, *Now in Mexico*, 311; Brenner, *Your Mexican Holiday*, 166.

20. On the history of the village panorama see Corbin, *Village Bells*, 296–97; and Avery, "Movies for Manifest Destiny." Banvard was best known for his "moving panoramas" of the American West, but he also created a series of panoramas depicting Europe and Jerusalem in response to a growing interest in travel to the Old World, giving the panorama a central role in the nascent tourism industries. See also McAlister, *Epic Encounters*, 16. On Fernández see Tuñón, "Femininity, 'Indigenismo,' and Nation," 81–96.

21. On the linkages between representations of a place and the expansion of empire, both formal and informal, see Pratt, *Imperial Eyes*; Salvatore, "Enterprise of Knowledge," 69–104; and Poole, "Landscape and the Imperial Subject," 106–38. Pratt wrote, "It is América's purported backwardness that legitimates the capitalist vanguard's interventions in the first place. Ideologically, the vanguard's task is to reinvent América as backward and neglected, to encode its non-capitalist landscapes and societies as manifestly in need of the rationalized exploitation the Europeans bring." Pratt, *Imperial Eyes*, 152.

22. This image has been reproduced countless times and attributed to different photographers. I first saw this particular version published in Hugh M. Hamill, "Experiments in International Living: American College Students, Mexicans for a Summer, Become Members of Households in Colonial Guanajuato," *National Geographic*, March 1953, 322, where it is attributed to Cecil B. Atwater.

23. Also see the photograph by Peter Olwyler on the cover of Virtue, *Leonard and Reva Brooks*; and the photograph titled "The domes and towers of San Miquel [sic] de Allende" in Strode, *Now in Mexico*, facing 112.

24. "New Art Colony in Mexico Draws Many Americans," *Chicago Daily Tribune*, January 15, 1941, 15.

25. On the efforts of the Mexican government to promote American travel in Mexico on the eve of World War II see Berger, *Development of Mexico's Tourism Industry*, chap. 4.

26. Whitaker, *Western Hemisphere Idea*, 1–2. On the history and development of the Good Neighbor policy see Schoultz, *Beneath the United States*; Gellman, *Good Neighbor Diplomacy*; Pike, *FDR's Good Neighbor Policy*; and Roorda, *Dictator Next Door*.

27. On the origins of U.S. cultural relations policy and the role of private organizations see Ninkovich, *Diplomacy of Ideas*, esp. chap. 1; and Rosenberg, *Spreading the American Dream*. On U.S. efforts to thwart German influence in Latin America see Friedman, *Nazis and Good Neighbors*.

28. The original name of this agency was the Office for Coordination of Commercial and Cultural Relations between the American Republics, but the name changed to the Office of the Coordinator of Inter-American Affairs (OCIAA) in 1941 and finally to the Office of Inter-American Affairs (OIAA) in 1945. For the purposes of this chapter I will use the acronym OCIAA. Rowland, *History of the Office of the Coordinator of Inter-American Affairs*.

29. "Mexico Tours," *Art Digest*, January 15, 1940, 16; "Below the Rio Grande," *Art Digest*, March 1, 1940, 13.

30. Amigos de San Miguel de Allende, *Guía de San Miguel de Allende*. Although Dickinson is not directly credited as the author of the English-language section of this guidebook, the text bears his literary style.

31. Escuela Universitaria de Bellas Artes catalog, 1943, Box 337, Mexico City Embassy General Records, 1937–49, RG 84, NARA, College Park MD.

32. "Gay, Romantic Art Colony Develops South of the Border," *Los Angeles Times*, February 2, 1941, C8.

33. Correspondence regarding the Bracero program during World War II, Exp. 546.6/120, MAC, AGN. Also see "State of Origin of Migratory Agricultural Workers Entering the U.S., 1942–1968," Perry-Castañeda Library Map Collection, University of Texas at Austin.

34. For example, see Cohen, *Braceros*; and Orozco, "Esos altos de Jalisco!"

35. On the recruitment of Latin American students see Cossío del Pomar, *Cossío del Pomar en San Miguel de Allende*, 142–43. On inquires about the school see Gilbert Franklin to Ambassador Daniels, 1941, Box 101, Mexico City Embassy General Records, 1937–49, RG 84, NARA; and "Travel Queries Answered," *Chicago Daily Tribune*, December 31, 1941, 9; April 8, 1942, 18.

36. Correspondence regarding war censorship, 1942, 812.4035/30–41, RG 59, NARA.

37. Virtue, *Model American Abroad*, chaps. 11 and 12.

38. Cossío del Pomar, *Cossío del Pomar en San Miguel de Allende*, 156.

39. Cossío del Pomar, *Cossío del Pomar en San Miguel de Allende*, 159.

NOTES TO PAGES 53–57

40. Correspondence regarding the extension of the GI Bill abroad, 1945, Box 396, 103.9991/1-145 through 103.9992/12-3145, 1945–49, RG 59, NARA; Elías G. Garza, American Vice Consul of San Luis Potosí, to Secretary of State Byrnes, June 4, 1946, Box 397, 103.9992/6-446, 1945–49, RG 59, NARA. Also see Covert, "GI Bill Abroad."

41. Virtue, *Model American Abroad*, 137.

42. Virtue, *Leonard and Reva Brooks*, 100–105.

43. Dorothy Vidargas, interview by author, San Miguel de Allende, January 18, 2003, July 9, 2004; Leonard Brooks, interview by author, San Miguel de Allende, July 15, 2004; Virtue, *Leonard and Reva Brooks*, 121.

44. Carmen Beckmann Macías, interview by author, San Miguel de Allende, February 10, 2008.

45. Cossío del Pomar, *Cossío del Pomar en San Miguel de Allende*, 66, 152.

46. Virtue, *Model American Abroad*, 131. Several scholars have examined marriages between U.S. servicemen and foreign women abroad. For example, see Lipman, *Guantánamo*, chap. 3; Alvah, *Unofficial Ambassadors*; and Plummer, "Brown Babies."

47. Virtue, *Model American Abroad*, 177–78.

48. Dorothy Vidargas, interview by Leticia Echlin, filmed by Adeline Medalia, February 1, 1993, SMHA.

49. Correspondence regarding the GI Art Exhibition in Mexico City, 1948, Box 336, Mexico City Embassy General Records, 1937–49, RG 84, NARA.

50. "GI Paradise," *Life*, January 5, 1948, 56–58; also quoted in Virtue, *Leonard and Reva Brooks*, 120.

51. Cossío del Pomar, *Cossío del Pomar en San Miguel de Allende*, 94.

52. On Catholic appropriation of new political culture in the 1930s and 1940s see Butler, "Introduction," 11. On church-state détente in 1940 see Knight, "Mentality and Modus Operandi of Revolutionary Anticlericalism," 41; Blancarte, "Intransigence, Anticommunism, and Reconciliation"; and Reich, *Mexico's Hidden Revolution*, 55, 68. On the 1940 election of Manuel Ávila Camacho see Sherman, *Mexican Right*, chap. 8.

53. On Mexico's Catholic lay organizations see Reich, *Mexico's Hidden Revolution*, esp. chap. 7. On the role of lay organizations in Guanajuato in the 1930s see Fallaw, *Religion and State Formation*, chap. 5. For correspondence between San Miguel's municipal authorities and state authorities regarding the regulation of priests see Exp. 3.48.2–3.48.4, 1933, 1934, Serie: Cultos-Correspondencia, Sección: Gobernación, Fondo: C.P. Miguel Herrera A., AGMSMA.

54. On the Cristiada, the violent church-state conflict from 1926 to 1929, see chap. 1.

55. Luis Villa Mercadillo, interview by author, San Miguel de Allende, November 27, 2006.

56. Villa Mercadillo interview; Ruíz Valenzuela, *El reverendo Monseñor José Mercadillo Miranda*. On Mercadillo's appointment as assistant parish priest see Francisco Rocha L. to Secretario del Gobierno, October 28, 1936, Sección: Asuntos Varios, Serie: Ciudad, Julio-Diciembre, Fondo: Gobernación, AGMSMA.

57. Mojica maintained a relationship with San Miguel and returned frequently. Mojica, *I, a Sinner*; Katherine Walch, "Remembering José Mojica," *El Independiente*, BD; Max Arthur, "The Padre Who Was Mojica," *Chicago Daily Tribune*, April 18, 1948, E5.

58. Mercadillo to Jefe Subalterno Federal de Hacienda, December 30, 1940, Box 50, Correspondencia, APSMA. Cantera is a stone carving technique that was very popular in architectural design throughout the region, especially in religious architecture. The designs were often quite elaborate, and the masons skilled in the art of cantera were in high demand during the twentieth century, as it was considered a dying art. The nineteenth-century façade of the Parroquia incorporates cantera.

59. Ruíz Valenzuela, *El reverendo Monseñor José Mercadillo Miranda*; Mercadillo Miranda, *Anécdotas sin importancia*.

60. Mercadillo to Director General de Bienes Nacionales, August 13, 1942, Box 49, Correspondencia, APSMA.

61. Cossío del Pomar, *Cossío del Pomar en San Miguel de Allende*, 104–6.

62. "Monumento a Fray San Juan de San Miguel," 1942, Box 51, Correspondencia, APSMA.

63. Comité de Obreros y Empleados Sanmiguelenses en el D.F. to Mercadillo, July 22, 1942, Box 49, Correspondencia, APSMA; Comité Metropolitano Pro IV Centenario de la Fundación de San Miguel de Allende to Mercadillo, May 18, 1942, Box 49, Correspondencia, APSMA.

64. Mercadillo to de la Maza, June 29, 1942, Box 49, Correspondencia, APSMA.

65. Mojica wanted to construct an arch at the bridge that led toward Guanajuato and then erect the statue there. The Zavala family wanted the statue in front of the San Francisco church, and others thought that El Chorro, the springs that originally drew Fray Juan to San Miguel, according to legend, would be a more appropriate setting. The historian Graciela Cruz López claims that people objected to putting the statue in its present

location for several reasons, the most practical being that it disrupted a major source of water for the community. Graciela Cruz López, interview by author, San Miguel de Allende, January 23, 2008.

66. Reich, *Mexico's Hidden Revolution*, 72.

67. Hernández, *La soledad del silencio*; Mercadillo Miranda, *El venerado e histórico Santuario de Atotonilco, Guanajuato*; Cervantes Jáuregui and Crespo, *Fiesta y tradición*, 107–11. On the history of the Oratorians in San Miguel and especially Father Alfaro see Santiago Silva, *Atotonilco*, chaps. 2 and 3.

68. Mercadillo Miranda, *El venerado e histórico Santuario de Atotonilco, Guanajuato*, 80–81.

69. Hernández, *La soledad del silencio*, 120.

70. On the history of Ignatian spiritual exercises see Hernández, *La soledad del silencio*, 46, 113. For examples of the activities involved in Ignatian spiritual retreats see Ignatius of Loyola, *Spiritual Exercises of Saint Ignatius*. The 2000 translation of Saint Ignatius's guide states of "external penance" that it "would cause sensible pain to the body . . . so that it inflicts pain, but does not cause sickness" (31). For a late twentieth-century interpretation of the spiritual exercises see Skehan, *Place Me with Your Son*. In this case, prayer involving self-inflicted pain was certainly an anomalous component, but the guide does emphasize the connection between suffering and heightened emotional states. Skehan, *Place Me with Your Son*, 40.

71. Mercadillo Miranda, *El venerado e histórico Santuario de Atotonilco, Guanajuato*; Report on the Sanctuary of Atotonilco by Cap. Luis de la Barreda Moreno, December 12, 1972, H-316, L-14, Exp. 15-3-72, DFS, AGN; Agustín Martínez to Mercadillo, March 22, 1944, Box 49, Correspondencia, APSMA; R. Sánchez R. to B. Mendez, January 29, 1944, Box 49, Correspondencia, APSMA. Approximately thirty-five hundred pilgrims attended retreats each week in the early 1990s according to Hernández, *La soledad del silencio*, 144. On the early twentieth-century tradition of pilgrimages in Mexico see Butler, "Trouble Afoot?," 149–66.

72. Cárdenas and Tenorio, "Mexico 1920s–1940s," 623. Despite their differences, the following scholars all seem to concur to varying degrees with the sentiment quoted in the main text: Meyer, *El sinarquismo*, esp. 130–31; Serrano Álvarez, *La batalla del espíritu*; Newcomer, *Reconciling Modernity*; and Dormady, *Primitive Revolution*, esp. 111.

73. On U.S. government concerns about the UNS see Ambassador Daniels to Secretary Hull, March 19, 1940, 812.00/30979; Finley to Secretary Hull, February 25, 1942, 812.404/2095; Gibson to Secretary Hull, March 3,

1942, 812.404/2097; Schraud, American Consulate in San Luis Potosí,
to Secretary Hull, May 11, 1942, 812.404/2101; Gibson to Secretary Hull,
June 2, 1942, 812.404/2106, all from RG 59, NARA; and Presidente Municipal to Inspector of Gobernación in Guanajuato, May 13, 1943, 1.54.(3) 5,
Allende, Fondo: Secretaría del Gobierno, Primer Departamento, AGGEG.
The FBI also spied on the UNS, both in Mexico and in the United States,
where the organization boasted approximately fifty thousand members in
1943. See Serrano Álvarez, La batalla del espíritu, 2:79; and Vargas, Labor
Rights Are Civil Rights, 188–98. On UNS donors within the United States
see Dormady, Primitive Revolution, 116–17.

74. Serrano Álvarez, La batalla del espíritu, 1:313–16.

75. Meyer, El sinarquismo, 72, 74–96, 117, 144; Dormady, Primitive Revolution,
chap. 3.

76. Over the years Mercadillo asserted these views many times, but a 1953
letter brings together all of the facets of the argument. See Mercadillo
Miranda to Marin, July 20, 1953, Exp. 151.3/345, ARC, AGN.

77. Josemaría Escrivá founded Opus Dei in Spain in 1928. Although Opus Dei
did not officially expand to Mexico until 1949, its ideals were influential
in Mexico before then. See Meyer, El sinarquismo, 149.

78. "La Mujer y el Hogar: La Moda Corruptora de Costumbres," 1944, Box 49,
Correspondencia, APSMA.

79. For a similar argument regarding a millenarian group in Brazil see
Pessar, From Fanatics to Folk, 7. Other scholars who have emphasized the
adaptability of Catholicism in Mexico include Cervantes, "Mexico's 'Ritual
Constant,'" 57–73; Wright-Rios, Revolutions in Mexican Catholicism, esp.
the introduction; Knight, "Mentality and Modus Operandi of Revolutionary Anticlericalism," 38; and Overmyer-Velázquez, Visions of the Emerald
City, esp. 71. Dormady seems to contradict himself on this point in his
study of the UNS. While much of his evidence and analysis demonstrates
how the UNS adeptly adapted to postrevolutionary political contexts,
at times he describes the group as antimodern for idealizing village
life. However, even in cases where the UNS seems to look backward in
Dormady's account, the organization does so in the context of laying out a
different vision for Mexico's future (see, e.g., Dormady, Primitive Revolution, 110–11).

80. On the restrictions against religious pilgrimages and Mercadillo's
response, see correspondence regarding fiebre aftosa outbreak, Exp.
425.5/2-101947, MAV, AGN; Mercadillo to D. Roberto Ornelas, March
26, 1947, Box 51, Correspondencia, APSMA; "Circular 272," Gobierno

Eclesiástico de la Diócesis de León, November 14, 1947; and "Circular 271," Gobierno Eclesiástico de la Diócesis de León, November 12, 1947, both in Box 51, Correspondencia, APSMA. On the outbreak more generally see B. Torres, *Hacia la utopía industrial*, 252–69; Serrano Álvarez, *La batalla del espíritu*, 2:280–90; and Meyer, *El sinarquismo*, 213–16. On historic precedents for government discourse concerning religious practices and hygiene see Butler, "Introduction," 5; and Knight, "Mentality and Modus Operandi of Revolutionary Anticlericalism," 48n68, where he addresses such discourse by questioning the characterization of an event described in Becker, *Setting the Virgin on Fire*, 140.

81. Serrano Álvarez, *La batalla del espíritu*, 2:286–90.

82. For example, see B. Torres, *Hacia la utopía industrial*, 260–61; and González y González, *San José de Gracia*, 230.

83. Bellas Artes students and faculty to Alfredo Campanella, letter of petition, March 12, 1948, Exp. 111/1140, MAV, AGN.

84. Bellas Artes students and faculty to Alfredo Campanella, letter of petition, July 7, 1948, Exp. 111/1140, MAV, AGN.

85. Stein, *Siqueiros*.

86. Stein, *Siqueiros*, 158, 161–65. On the role of this particular site in the development of Siqueiros's ideas about integración plástica see Herner, "Siqueiros, una lección mural en San Miguel de Allende," 47–54; and de la Rosa, "David Alfaro Siqueiros en el Instituto Politécnico Nacional," 61–62.

87. There are multiple accounts of this conflict, but this view seems to be the consensus. See Cossío del Pomar, *Cossío del Pomar en San Miguel de Allende*, 159–62; Virtue, *Leonard and Reva Brooks*, 127–34; Stein, *Siqueiros*, 166–69; Smart, *At Home in Mexico*, 127–32; and Anhalt, *Gathering of Fugitives*, 108–9.

88. Veterans' grievance letter, 1949, Exp. 111/1140, MAV, AGN. The number of students voting in favor of the boycott was 130, while 5 students voted against it.

89. Veterans' grievance letter, 1949, Exp. 111/1140, MAV, AGN.

90. Memos from Veterans Administration attaché Patterson, 1949, 103.9992/1-349 through 103.9992/9-3049, 1945–49, Box 406, RG 59, NARA.

91. I was unable to locate any original copies of *El Quijote*, only English translations.

92. These quotations come from a translation of *El Quijote* enclosed with letters written by Gladys S. Bonfiglio, August 1949, 103.9992/1-349 through 103.9992/9-3049, 1945–49, Box 406, RG 59, NARA.

93. On Catholic moralization campaigns in the 1940s see Moreno, *Yankee Don't Go Home!*, chap. 7; and Rubenstein, *Bad Language, Naked Ladies, and Other Threats to the Nation*, esp. chap. 3.

94. Secretaría de Gobernación to the Governor of Guanajuato, August 15, 1949, 1.18.104.(3) 2, Allende, Fondo: Secretaría del Gobierno, Primer Departamento, AGGEG. Unfortunately, I have not located any images of this painting.

95. Gladys S. Bonfiglio letters, August 1949, 103.9992/1-349 through 103.9992/9-3049, 1945–49, Box 406, RG 59, NARA.

96. This analysis draws inspiration from Julio Capó Jr.'s call to explore "how 'the world' queered the United States," in Belmonte et al., "Colloquy"; and Cantú, *Sexuality of Migration*.

97. Dr. J. Jesus Agundis Gallegos, telegram to Lic. Amoros, August 4, 1949, Exp. 111/1140, MAV, AGN; Dr. Anastasio López, telegram to Lic. Amoros, August 4, 1949, Exp. 111/1140, MAV, AGN; Cámara Nacional de Comercio de San Miguel de Allende, telegram to Governor Luis Diaz Infante, July 30, 1949, 1.18.104.(3)1, Allende, Fondo: Secretaría del Gobierno, Primer Departamento, AGGEG; Cámara Nacional de Comercio, telegram to Lic. Amoros, August 5, 1949, Exp. 111/1140, MAV, AGN.

98. Alfredo Campanella, telegram to President Miguel Alemán, August 2, 1949, Exp. 111/1140, MAV, AGN.

99. Blancarte, "Intransigence, Anticommunism, and Reconciliation."

100. Campanella, telegrams to Lic. de la Selva and to President Miguel Alemán, both August 2, 1949, Exp. 111/1140, MAV, AGN.

101. Dorothy Vidargas, correspondence with author, March 29, 2003.

102. Goniewich to President Miguel Alemán, August 3, 1949, Exp. 111/1140, MAV, AGN.

103. Comisión del Organismo Ejecutivo de Boicot y Reorganización to Chávez and Patterson, August 2, 1949, Exp. 111/1140, MAV, AGN.

104. Chávez, memo to Gual Vidal, August 2, 1949, Exp. 111/1140, MAV, AGN. The marginal notes appear on the following document, which was forwarded with Chávez's memo: Dickinson to the Executive Committee of the Escuela Universitaria, March 19, 1948, Exp. 111/1140, MAV, AGN.

105. Secretaría de Educación Pública, translation of memo to Patterson, August 17, 1949, 103.9992/1-349 through 103.9992/9-3049, 1945–49, Box 406, RG 59, NARA.

106. On the efforts to erase or at least minimize the role foreigners played in the promotion of Mexican culture see López, *Crafting Mexico*, chap. 3. On the history of collaboration between Mexican officials and foreign residents during the Porfiriato see W. Schell, *Integral Outsiders*.

107. "Letter of Señor Alfredo Campanella to the Mexican and North American Public," translated and included as an attachment to Goniewich to Secretary Acheson, August 27, 1949, 103.9992/1–349 through 103.9992/9–3049, 1945–49, Box 406, RG 59, NARA.

108. Gladys S. Bonfiglio letters, August 1949, 103.9992/1-349 through 103.9992/9-3049, 1945–49, Box 406, RG 59, NARA.

109. Smart, *At Home in Mexico*, 129.

110. For example, see Lynch to Illinois Senator Douglas, August 20, 1949; John M. Johnson to President Harry Truman, September 17, 1949; and correspondence between Mertz and the State Department, 1949, all in 103.9992/1-349 through 103.9992/9-3049, 1945–49, Box 406, RG 59, NARA.

111. Dickinson to Madill, September 14, 1949, 103.9992/1-349 through 103.9992/9-3049, 1945–49, Box 406, RG 59, NARA.

112. Veterans Administration Attaché Patterson, memos, 1949, 103.9992/1-349 through 103.9992/9-3049, 1945–49, Box 406, RG 59, NARA. The Ministry of Public Education notified Patterson of the school's new status on August 17, 1949. See Secretaría de Educación Pública, memo to Patterson, August 17, 1949, 103.9992/1-349 through 103.9992/9-3049, 1945–49, Box 406, RG 59, NARA.

113. Department of State, memo to Veterans Administration, November 21, 1949; and Dickinson to Ramsey, November 14, 1949, both in 103.9992/10-349 through 103.9992/12-3149, 1945–49, Box 407, RG 59, NARA.

114. "Warning! Be Careful with the Deceitful Communists!," pamphlet, October 1949, 103.9992/10-349, 1945–49, Box 407, RG 59, NARA.

115. *Mexico City Herald* clipping dated October 28, 1949, 103.9992/10-349 through 103.9992/12-3149, 1945–49, Box 407, RG 59, NARA.

116. "Sept. 16 Parade, San Miguel de Allende," September 16, 1949, 103.9992/10-349 through 103.9992/12-3149, 1945–49, Box 407, RG 59, NARA.

117. Virtue, *Leonard and Reva Brooks*, 150–57. Also see Virtue, *Model American Abroad*, chap. 20; and Smart, *At Home in Mexico*, 131.

118. Virtue, *Model American Abroad*, 169.

119. On the foundation of the Instituto Allende see Cossío del Pomar, *Cossío del Pomar en San Miguel de Allende*, chap. 11; and Virtue, *Model American Abroad*, chap. 21.

120. Correspondence regarding flyers distributed by Mercadillo Miranda, April 19, 1950, 1.40.(3).4, Allende, Fondo: Secretaría del Gobierno, Primer Departamento, AGGEG.

3. Bringing the Mexican Miracle

1. Ruth Hyba, interview by author, San Miguel de Allende, July 14, 2004.
2. Hail, *To Mexico with Love*, 69.
3. Hyba interview.
4. Cossío del Pomar, *Cossío del Pomar en San Miguel de Allende*, 188.
5. On the urban industrial working class see Bachelor, "Toiling for the 'New Invaders'." On Mexico's urban middle classes see Walker, *Waking from the Dream*; and Moreno, *Yankee Don't Go Home!*
6. See Joseph, Rubenstein, and Zolov, "Assembling the Fragments," 9. Scholars have used the term "golden age" both to describe cultural production during the actual period and to refer to the nostalgic way that people look back on the period.
7. The contributors to Joseph, Rubenstein, and Zolov, *Fragments of a Golden Age*, address many of these themes. On the historiographical treatment of Mexican economic development in the twentieth century see Schmidt, "Making It Real Compared to What?" On the development of the cultural industries, including the tourism industry, see Zolov, "Discovering a Land 'Mysterious and Obvious'"; Saragoza, "Selling of Mexico"; Rubenstein, "Bodies, Cities, Cinema"; Mraz, "Today, Tomorrow, and Always"; and Fein, "Myths of Cultural Imperialism and Nationalism in Golden Age Mexican Cinema." On import substitution industrialization in Mexico see B. Torres, *Hacia la utopía industrial*; Gauss, *Made in Mexico*; Babb, *Managing Mexico*, chaps. 4 and 5; and Clancy, *Exporting Paradise*, 32–37.
8. Babb, *Managing Mexico*, chap. 5; Schmidt, "Making It Real Compared to What?" For an analysis of the contradictions of the economic miracle in relation to students see Pensado, *Rebel Mexico*, chap. 1.
9. Emigdio Ledesma Pérez, interview by author and Fredy González, San Miguel de Allende, May 5, 2015; Francisco Garay Llaguno, interview by author, San Miguel de Allende, February 9, 2008.
10. On the number of tourists see "Cuadro sinóptico de los turistas," 1968, Exp. Mayo 1969, Caja 1968–70, AGMSMA. On the unreliability of population estimates for foreigners in San Miguel see the introduction to this study. According to the Mexican census San Miguel's total population in 1950 was 11,629, and by 1970 it had reached 24,286. Marco Geoestadístico

Nacional, Descarga de información correspondiente a la localidad geoestadística: 110030001 INEGI, last accessed August 23, 2016, http://www.inegi.org.mx/geo/contenidos/geoestadistica/introduccio.aspx. One estimate placed the number of expats in the mid-1950s at 75. See Virtue, *Model American Abroad*, 178–79.

11. Richard Joseph, "Luxury-Living on $45.00 a Week," *Coronet*, October 1956, 102–6, also cited in Virtue, *Model American Abroad*, 177.

12. For examples of Spanish Civil War exiles see Dolores Danzig, "Spotlight on Dr. Francisco Olsina," *Atención*, March 10, 1981, 6; Faber, *Exile and Cultural Hegemony*, chap. 5; Carmen Masip de Hawkins, untitled essay read and recorded by Fran Rowe Robbins, n.d., SMHA; and "Empresaria Incomparable," *Atención*, March 12, 1976, 7–8. On Americans fleeing McCarthyism see James Hawkins, interview by the author, San Miguel de Allende, November 11, 2006. On other Americans who left the United States for Mexico during the Cold War years see Schreiber, *Cold War Exiles in Mexico*; and Anhalt, *Gathering of Fugitives*. On Morris see Don Pitblado, "Mister San Miguel, Everyone Knows Him," *Atención*, April 2, 1976, 2; and Jack Wall, "Spotlight on People: Jaime Morris," *Atención*, June 5,1979, 2. On Mexico as historically a land of relative opportunity for Americans of color see W. Schell, *Integral Outsiders*, 24–26.

13. Hail, *To Mexico with Love*, 60.

14. Smart, *At Home in Mexico*, 39–40.

15. Robert Maxwell and Lucha Maxwell, interview by author, San Miguel de Allende, December 6, 2006. One scholar has argued that foreign students in Europe tend to interact with local populations more than other foreign residents do. See Pells, *Not Like Us*, 146.

16. Paulina Hawkins, interview by author, San Miguel de Allende, May 5, 2015.

17. Rudolfo Fernández Harris, interview by author, San Miguel de Allende, May 2, 2015.

18. Jaime Fernández Harris, interview by author, San Miguel de Allende, July 14, 2013; Rudolfo Fernández Harris interview; Katherine Walch, "Nell Fernández, Doyen of San Miguel's Foreign Colony," *El Independiente*, BD; Sarah M. Gottlieb, "Spotlight on People," *Atención*, September 30, 1977, 6, 7.

19. See Carmen Masip de Hawkins, essay read and recorded by Fran Rowe Robbins, n.d., SMHA; "Empresaria Incomparable," *Atención*, March 12, 1976, 7–8; James Hawkins, interview by author, San Miguel de Allende,

November 11, 2006; Paulina Hawkins, interview by author, San Miguel de Allende, May 5, 2015; Sylvia Samuelson, interview by author, San Miguel de Allende, November 28, 2006; Robert Maxwell and Lucha Maxwell, interview by author, San Miguel de Allende, December 6, 2006; Dorothy Vidargas, interview by Leticia Echlin, filmed by Adeline Medalia, February 1, 1993, SMHA; Dorothy Vidargas, interview by author, San Miguel de Allende, January 18, 2003, July 9, 2004; and Hyba interview.

20. For analyses of Americans in Porfirian Mexico, many of whom explicitly saw themselves as agents of empire, see W. Schell, *Integral Outsiders*; Ruiz, *Americans in the Treasure House*; and G. González, *Culture of Empire*.

21. Virtue, *Model American Abroad*, 178–79.

22. Joseph, "Luxury-Living on $45.00 a Week," 106.

23. Smart, *At Home in Mexico*, 12–13.

24. Cossío del Pomar, *Cossío del Pomar en San Miguel de Allende*, 173–76, 187–88.

25. For example, see "Scholarship Contest," *Washington Post*, September 30, 1951, L3; and Eleanor Jewett, "1954 Art Scholarship Available in Mexico," *Chicago Daily Tribune*, November 15, 1953, G8. For a more comprehensive sample of promotional materials see the collection of news clippings in Acervo Histórico, IA.

26. Jaime Fernández Harris interview by author, San Miguel de Allende, July 14, 2013.

27. For example, see Sackett, "Two Faces of Acapulco during the Golden Age," 500–510; and Saragoza, "Selling of Mexico," 103–4.

28. Peter Olwyler, "Dateline . . . Mexico City," *Travel*, November 1957, 8–9; Olwyler, "Mexico City," *Travel*, May 1959, 12–13; Olwyler, "Dateline . . . Mexico City," *Travel*, June 1957, 8–9; Olwyler, "Dateline . . . Mexico City," *Travel*, January 1957, 9; Olwyler, "Dateline . . . Mexico City," *Travel*, August 1957, 7; and Olwyler, "Dateline . . . Mexico City," *Travel*, February 1958, 11.

29. Hail, *To Mexico with Love*, 60–61.

30. For examples of publicity see Stephanie Martin, "Mexican Town Pays Honor to Native Patriot," *Chicago Daily Tribune*, October 14, 1951, F17; La Fond, *How, When, and Where to Tour Mexico*, 53, appendix; Roland A. Goodman, "Winter in Mexico," *New York Times*, December 9, 1951, 320; Rupert Gresham, "Drive On to Mexico," *New York Times*, April 15, 1951, 265; "Mexico City Road to Open," *Los Angeles Times*, November 16, 1952, D7; Arthur Pollock, "Fast Highway into Historic Mexico," *New York Times*,

July 21, 1957, X29; and Robert H. Evans, "Circle Trip in Mexico with a Rented Car," *New York Times*, November 23, 1958, XX21.

31. Hugh Hamill Jr., "Experiment in International Living: American College Students, Mexicans for a Summer, Become Members of Households in Colonial Guanajuato," *National Geographic*, March 1953, 322–50.

32. Norman D. Ford, "Journey into Mexico's Past," *New York Times*, November 25, 1962, 423.

33. Norman, "Prologue," in *Mexican Hill Town*, 1. For other examples, see Hail, *To Mexico with Love*, 85; and Dickerson, *Sketchbook of San Miguel de Allende*, 9.

34. S. González, *Síntesis histórica de San Miguel de Allende*, 2–3.

35. On the Academia Hispano Americana see James Hawkins interview; Paulina Hawkins interview; Jeannie Schnakenberg, "Harold Black and the Escuela Ecuestre," MPWC Foundation, last accessed August 5, 2015, http://www.mpwcf.org/memories_of_sma.htm.

36. For example, see Rubirosa, "Crisol Social," *El Vocero del Norte*, January 8, 1961, 2; Rubirosa, "Crisol Social," *El Vocero del Norte*, March 12, 1961, 2; and Incrédulo, "Me cuentan que . . . ," *El Vocero del Norte*, February 26, 1961, 5.

37. On INAH see Olivé Negrete and Urteaga Castro-Pozo, *INAH, una historia*; and López, *Crafting Mexico*, chap. 4.

38. Malo Zozaya and de Vivero, *San Miguel Allende*; Cervantes Jáuregui and Crespo, *Fiesta y tradición*.

39. "Cuadro sinóptico de los turistas," 1968, Exp. Mayo 1969, Caja 1968–70, AGMSMA.

40. Malo Zozaya, *Guía turista en San Miguel de Allende*, advertisement section. For another example of how infrastructure development increased tourist flows and revenues see Sackett, "Two Faces of Acapulco," 503.

41. On the Maycotte family and the Rancho Hotel El Atascadero, see the Rancho Hotel El Atascadero website, last accessed October 5, 2015, http://www.hotelelatascadero.com/about.html. On the other hotels see the advertisement section in Malo Zozaya, *Guía turista en San Miguel de Allende*.

42. By making this distinction I do not intend to elide the important linkages between the U.S. and Mexican film industries. On these linkages see Seth Fein's work on Mexican cinema, esp. "From Collaboration to Containment"; and "Myths of Cultural Imperialism and Nationalism."

43. The Mexican film industry's most profitable foreign market was the Spanish-speaking audience in the United States. Fein, "From Collaboration to Containment," 133.

44. Jaime Fernández Harris interview.

45. Other films that were at least partially set in San Miguel during the 1950s and 1960s include *Serenade, The Wonderful Country, María Montecristo, El señor gobernador, Atrás de las nubes*, and *El padrecito*. I compiled this list using newspaper articles from the United States and San Miguel, and the Internet Movie Database, www.imdb.com. While film production in San Miguel dropped off for a while, it picked up again in the late 1990s and 2000s with films such as *Once Upon a Time in Mexico*, starring Antonio Banderas. San Miguel was also the backdrop for the season 12 (2015) finale of the Bravo reality series *Top Chef*.

46. "Se integró la Comisión de Turismo de San Miguel," *El Vocero del Norte*, February 19, 1961, 1, 6.

47. Torres Morales to Presidente Municipal Gil Vega, March 31, 1969, Exp. Mayo 1969, Caja 1968–70, AGMSMA.

48. For example, see correspondence in Exp. Marzo 1969 and Mayo 1969, Caja 1968–70, AGMSMA.

49. "Es indispensable el turismo en San Miguel de Allende, Guanajuato," *El Vocero del Norte*, February 4, 1962, 1, 6.

50. "Nuevamente sobre el tapete el asunto del turismo en San Miguel de Allende, Gto.," *El Vocero del Norte*, March 4, 1962, 1, 6.

51. "Ya es tiempo de que alguien se preocupe por darle adecuada formacióna los guías de turistas de esta ciudad, y queden garantizados sus derechos," *El Vocero del Norte*, August 9, 1964, 1, 6. For the argument against foreigners serving as tourist guides see "Una caravana de turistas de McAllen, Texas, visitó esta ciudad," *El Vocero del Norte*, May 27, 1962, 1, 6.

52. Petition to the Presidente del H. Ayuntamiento, November 27, 1950, 1.50. (3) 5, Allende, Fondo: Secretaría del Gobierno, Primer Departamento, AGGEG.

53. Presidente Municipal Malo Sautto to President Alemán, October 24, 1951, Exp. 741.5/28225, MAV, AGN.

54. "Peticiones Hechas al Sr. Presidente de la República, parte 1," *El Vocero del Norte*, February 26, 1961, 4; "Peticiones Hechas al Sr. Presidente de la República, parte 2," *El Vocero del Norte*, March 5, 1961, 4.

55. García y García, *El agua en San Miguel de Allende*, 118–19.

56. "Gobierno del Estado de Guanajuato," *Novedades*, September 19, 1961 [no page number], Archivo Económico, Biblioteca Lerdo de Tejada, Mexico City, D.F.

57. *El Fisgón Anteojudo*, June 16, 1968, 6.

58. Jaime Fernández Harris interview.

59. For more on the Plan de Guanajuato see "Ni es verdad tanta belleza; ni hay por qué descuidarse tanto," *El Vocero del Norte*, March 13, 1966, 1, 6.

60. For example, see Arthur Pollock, "Fast Highway into Historic Mexico," *New York Times*, July 21, 1957, X29; Hamill, "Experiments in International Living," 322–50; and Martin, "Mexican Town Pays Honor to Native Patriot," F17.

61. Ford, "Journey into Mexico's Past," 423. American writers still use this rhetoric into the twenty-first century. See Virtue, *Model American Abroad*, 54.

62. For an overview of these efforts see Covert, "Political Economy of Mexico's Independence Heroes." For a similar case in which a Mexican town attempted, and mostly failed, to use a claim to historic significance in order to obtain federal resources see Gillingham, *Cuauhtémoc's Bones*, esp. chap. 2.

63. For correspondence related to both of these conflicts see Exp. Sept. 1969, Caja Correspondencia Presidencia Julio a Diciembre 1969, AGMSMA; and Folder 8, Exp. 1970, Caja 1968–70, AGMSMA.

64. Newcomer, *Reconciling Modernity*, 22.

65. Valencia García, *Guanajuato*, 72–73. On the industrialization of Mexico's agricultural sector more broadly see B. Torres, *Hacia la utopía industrial*, 69–77.

66. "State of Origin of Migratory Agricultural Workers Entering the U.S., 1942–1968," Perry-Castañeda Library Map Collection, University of Texas at Austin. Also see B. Torres, *Hacia la utopía industrial*, 236–51.

67. On the Mexican textile industry and import substitution industrialization (ISI) see Gauss, *Made in Mexico*, chap. 4.

68. Ledesma Pérez interview; Garay Llaguno interview; Ernesto López Arteaga, interview by author, San Miguel de Allende, February 12, 2008.

69. Malo Sautto, telegram to the Secretaría General del Gobierno, July 24,1951; Malo Sautto to the Secretaría General del Gobierno, August 22, 1951, both in CI-260-E6, Sección: Municipios, Fondo: Secretaría del Gobierno, AGGEG.

70. Snodgrass, "Patronage and Progress"; Snodgrass, "Golden Age of Charrismo." For a discussion of these larger national trends see Cohen, *Braceros*, 22.

71. As one scholar points out, industrialism was often perceived as a solution to problems such as poverty and emigration. Gauss, *Made in Mexico*, 94.

72. Incrédulo, "Me cuentan que . . . ," *El Vocero del Norte*, August 27, 1967, 5.

73. Donato Almanza M., "Quienes son los beneficiados conque nuestra ciudad sea Colonial, Turística e Histórica," *El Vocero del Norte*, October 6, 1968, 3.

74. On the demise of San Miguel's industries see Tutino, *Making a New World*, chap. 6; and Chowning, *Rebellious Nuns*, 226.

75. Data compiled from reports by the Servicio Militar Nacional, Exp. Servicio Militar Nacional Clase 50 Año 1968 and Clase 51 Año 1969, Caja 1968–70, AGMSMA.

76. On these and other considerations that went into the establishment of nineteenth-century textile mills see Potash, *Mexican Government and Industrial Development in the Early Republic*, 149–50.

77. Garay Llaguno interview.

78. Ledesma Pérez interview; Carmen Morales and Nicolás Tovar Sánchez, interview by author and Fredy González, San Miguel de Allende, May 5, 2015. On female textile workers during the early twentieth century in Colombia and Chile, respectively, see Farnsworth-Alvear, *Dulcinea in the Factory*; and Winn, *Weavers of Revolution*. On the relatively low numbers of female textile workers in Mexico see Gómez-Galvarriato, *Industry and Revolution*, 74–78. It is important to note, however, that this practice has shifted, and most twenty-first-century Mexican textile workers (who now mostly sew in *maquilas*) are female; see Byrnes, *Driving the State*, esp. chap. 7.

79. On the Garay family's linkages to nineteenth-century textile mills see Potash, *Mexican Government and Industrial Development in the Early Republic*, 152. On protectionist policies in the 1930s see Gauss, *Made in Mexico*, 139, and on textiles as the largest manufacturing sector, 148.

80. Ledesma Pérez interview.

81. Ledesma Pérez interview; Morales and Tovar Sánchez interview. For an example of exploitative company-owned services see Santiago, *Ecology of Oil*, 177–78. One scholar argues that the power of company stores in the Orizaba valley was never as great as historians have assumed, in part because of the shift to the cooperative model; see Gómez-Galvarriato, "From Company Towns to Union Towns," 54–58. Another argues that

during certain periods of the colonial era employee debt served as an indicator of positive working conditions in the Bajío; see Tutino, *From Insurrection to Revolution*, 59. For a broader historical analysis of company towns and company stores see Dinius and Vergara, "Company Towns in the Americas."

82. Ledesma Pérez interview.

83. López Arteaga interview.

84. On the presence of artisan guilds and confraternities in eighteenth-century San Miguel see Chowning, *Rebellious Nuns*, 37–38.

85. Garay Llaguno interview; Samuel Rangel Gómez, "Historia de la negociación fabril 'La Aurora' clausurada el sábado 11 de marzo de 1991," *Ciudadano Informa*, September 2014, 18–20; Cervantes Jáuregui and Crespo, *Fiesta y tradición*, 137–38.

86. Cervantes Jáuregui and Crespo, *Fiesta y tradición*, 135–36.

87. Potash, *Mexican Government and Industrial Development in the Early Republic*, 157.

88. Incrédulo, "Me cuentan que . . . ," *El Vocero del Norte*, October 2, 1960, 5.

89. Incrédulo, "Me cuentan que . . . ," *El Vocero del Norte*, August 27, 1961, 7.

90. "Se sabe que van a establecerse otras industrias en diversas lugares del Estado," *El Vocero del Norte*, March 1, 1970, 1.

91. Incrédulo, "Me cuentan que . . . ," *El Vocero del Norte*, September 27, 1964, 5.

92. Antonio Ruíz Valenzuela, "San Miguel de Allende necesita industrias," *El Vocero del Norte*, March 20, 1966, 2.

93. Incrédulo, "Me cuentan que . . . ," *El Vocero del Norte*, October 2, 1960, 5.

94. On the history of the workers and worker-owner relations in San Miguel's textile workshops see Salvucci, "Aspectos de un conflicto empresarial"; Tutino, *Making a New World*, 190–91; and Chowning, *Rebellious Nuns*, 37. On the history of the textile industry in the Bajío more broadly up to 1810 see Tutino, *From Insurrection to Revolution*, 90–94. On the use of slave labor in San Miguel and the surrounding area see Tutino, *From Insurrection to Revolution*, 69–70. On the presence of Africans in colonial Guanajuato more broadly see Guevara Sanginés, "Participación de los africanos en el desarollo del Guanajuato colonial," 133–98.

95. Ruíz Galindo, "Nuestras problemas," *El Vocero del Norte*, June 14, 1964, 6.

96. Incrédulo, "Me cuentan que . . . ," *El Vocero del Norte*, January 16, 1966, 5.

97. "Una caravana de turistas de McAllen, Texas, visitó esta ciudad," *El Vocero del Norte*, May 27, 1962, 1, 6. Mexicans typically do not consider themselves "North Americans" even though people in the United States

frequently include Mexico in their understanding of North America, and therefore, the author's use of *norteamericanos* here is another iteration of terms such as *americanos* or *gringos*, with *gringos* usually having the most negative connotation.

98. On the cultural center in Celaya and the types of activities and services provided by these centers in general see the report on the various facilities coordinated by INBA, 1964, Caja 1, Serie: Coordinación General, 1962–72, Sección: INBA, Archivo Histórico, SEP.

99. "Quizá el fomento de las artesanías podría mejorar la economía de la población," *El Vocero del Norte*, December 24, 1961, 1. See López, *Crafting Mexico*, on how artesanía production could bring economic benefits to Mexican communities.

100. Rubirosa, "Crisol social," *El Vocero del Norte*, March 12, 1961, 2.

101. "Ya está próxima la fecha de la apertura de la escuela de artesanías," *El Vocero del Norte*, June 3, 1962, 1.

102. Schedule of Inaugural Events, Centro Cultural Ignacio Ramírez, 1962, uncatalogued files, AJMFMZ; Zavala Zavala, "Sucesos, sucedidos, o qué van a suceder," Radio XESQ transcripts, August 16, August 18, 1962.

103. During 1963 the center in Acapulco had the largest enrollment, 700 students, followed by Aguascalientes with 684 and Tampico with 645. Overall San Miguel fell in the middle in terms of enrollment numbers, but when compared to cities of comparable size, it had substantially larger numbers. For the sake of comparison the larger cities of Celaya and Guanajuato had 177 and 63 students per capita, respectively. Report on the various facilities coordinated by INBA, 1964, Caja 1, Serie: Coordinación General, 1962–1972, Sección: INBA, Archivo Histórico, SEP.

104. The following archives contain numerous event flyers and invitations that demonstrate the international nature of the center's programming: Exp. 1940-72, CCIR; and Centro Cultural Ephemera, Fondo Centro Cultural Ignacio Ramírez, AJMFMZ.

105. Erasto Cortés Juárez, "Crónica cultural," *El Vocero del Norte*, April 14, 1963, 1, 3.

106. For examples, see sponsorship listed on various event announcements in Exp. 1940–72, CCIR. On San Miguel's Centro Cultural as a model, see the report on the various facilities coordinated by INBA, 1964, Caja 1, Serie: Coordinación General, 1962–72, Sección: INBA, SEP.

107. On the Institute for Continuing Adult Education see the announcements in Exp. 1940–72, CCIR; Zavala Zavala, *El Fisgón Anteojudo*, February 25, 1968, 6.

108. Virtue, *Leonard and Reva Brooks*, 227–34.

109. On the weaknesses of ISI see Gauss, *Made in Mexico*; and Babb, *Managing Mexico*.

110. Ledesma Pérez interview; Garay Llaguno interview.

111. Clancy, *Exporting Paradise*, chaps. 3 and 4; Castellanos, "Cancún and the Campo."

112. "Bus Terminal/Bypass Plans Announced," *Atención*, July 29, 1980.

113. On the controversy over Malo's collection see Folleto 6, Caja 6, and other uncatalogued items, AJMFMZ. For more context on the creation of the Allende museum see Covert, "Political Economy of Mexico's Independence Heroes," 37–38.

114. The founding of the Sanmiguelada was discussed in the Ledesma Pérez interview. On eighteenth-century bullfights in the plaza see Tutino, *Making a New World*, 321.

115. José Guadalupe Ramírez, interview by author, San Miguel de Allende, November 6, 2007. I also draw from my own observations of the Sanmiguelada in 2006.

4. Containing Threats

1. Report compiled by Schimel and submitted to Hugo Margáin, Mexican ambassador to the United States, August 7, 1969, III-5933-24, SRE.

2. For example, see Boyle Dooley to Carrillo Flores, September 26, 1969; Witenberg to Margáin, August 5, 1969; and Alan S. (last name illegible) to Mexican Embassy, August 8, 1969, all in III-5933-24, SRE.

3. On the general anxieties of Mexico's ruling elites over national identity see Lomnitz, *Deep Mexico, Silent Mexico*, 143; and Zolov, *Refried Elvis*, 5, 14. On the relationship between elites' perceived loss of control and the democratization of consumer culture see P. Schell, "Social Catholicism, Modern Consumption, and the Culture Wars in Postrevolutionary Mexico City," 1587.

4. For example, see Gutmann, *Meanings of Macho*, 68; Vaughan, "Modernizing Patriarchy"; Johnson, *Lavender Scare*, 43–44; Rosemblatt, *Gendered Compromises*.

5. For example, see Johnson, *Lavender Scare*; Cowan, "Sex and the Security State"; Cowan, "'Why Hasn't This Teacher Been Shot?'"; Manzano, "Sexualizing Youth"; and Langland, "Birth Control Pills and Molotov Cocktails," 308–49.

6. Mercadillo to the Reverend Mothers, February 21, 1948, Box 51, Correspondencia, APSMA.

7. Zolov, *Refried Elvis*. Also see Adams, "Hipsters and jipitecas"; Pensado, *Rebel Mexico*, chap. 2; González y González, *San José de Gracia*, 101; and Gutmann, *Meanings of Macho*, 134. Similarly, on Brazil see J. Green, *Beyond Carnival*, 68; and on the Dominican Republic see Hoffnung-Garskof, *Tale of Two Cities*, 81–82.

8. Zolov, *Refried Elvis*, 55, 62, 96.

9. Don Patterson, interview by author, San Miguel de Allende, November 12, 2006.

10. Langland, *Speaking of Flowers*, 8–10. Also see Gould, "Solidarity under Siege," 348–75. For a variety of perspectives on the 1960s as a global phenomenon see the AHR Forum, "International 1968." On international youth culture as a broader conspiracy see Cowan, "'Why Hasn't This Teacher Been Shot?'"

11. On anti-Chinese sentiment see Chao Romero, *Chinese in Mexico, 1882–1940*, chap. 6; and Carey, "'Selling Is More of a Habit Than Using,'" 66–67. On religious precedents see Fallaw, *Religion and State Formation in Postrevolutionary Mexico*.

12. "Pasan películas muy viejas y sumamente inmorales," *El Vocero del Norte*, May 21, 1961, 1; Armando Ruíz Galindo, "El mal empieza en la familia," *El Vocero del Norte*, June 18, 1961, 3; Ruíz Galindo, "Nuestros problemas," *El Vocero del Norte*, July 9, 1961, 3. On the role of the Catholic press in debates over consumption and morality see P. Schell, "Social Catholicism, Modern Consumption, and the Culture Wars." On concerns over the relationship between popular culture, specifically films and movie theaters, and morality in Mexico City see Zolov, *Refried Elvis*, 55–59; Rubenstein, "Bodies, Cities, Cinema," 217–18; and Pilcher, *Cantinflas and the Chaos of Mexican Modernity*, 41. On similar concerns over films, theaters, and vice in Brazil see J. Green, *Beyond Carnival*, 97.

13. Police reports, Folder 12, Box 1973–76, AGMSMA.

14. Armando Ruíz Galindo, "Un problema más," *El Vocero del Norte*, April 2, 1961, 3; Ruíz Galindo, "En el hogar empieza el mal," *El Vocero del Norte*, March 26, 1961, 3.

15. Armando Ruíz Galindo, "La sagrada misión de la madre," *El Vocero del Norte*, May 7, 1961, 4.

16. On motherhood in Mexico see Sanders, "Mothering Mexico." On *desmadre* see Zolov, *Refried Elvis*, 27–28; and Pensado, *Rebel Mexico*, 75–77. On concerns over women as consumers see P. Schell, "Social Catholicism, Modern Consumption, and the Culture Wars," 1588, 1591. On Mexican women in the postrevolutionary popular imagination see Olcott,

Revolutionary Women in Postrevolutionary Mexico, 15–16; Rubenstein, *Bad Language, Naked Ladies, and Other Threats to the Nation*; Hershfield, *Imagining la Chica Moderna*; Gutmann, *Meanings of Macho*, 92; Sherman, *Mexican Right*, 91; and Olcott, Vaughan, and Cano, *Sex in Revolution*. On concerns over the threats women posed to the nation in other contexts see Manzano, "Sexualizing Youth"; Oever, *Mama's Boy*, introduction; and Johnson, *Lavender Scare*, 95. On the use of La Malinche in Mexican American culture see Ramírez, *Woman in the Zoot Suit*, 6–7, 38–39.

17. McNally and McNally, *This Is Mexico*, 38; Hail, *To Mexico with Love*, 87. Scholars have also observed that these practices persisted in other towns in the region. González y González, *San José de Gracia*, 118, 309–10; Gordillo, *Mexican Women and the Other Side of Immigration*, 68–70.

18. For example, see Martin and Martin, *Standard Guide to Mexico and the Caribbean*, 64.

19. For example, see Petition to the H. Ayuntamiento, May 10, 1933, Exp: 3.18.55, Serie: Acuerdos de Ayuntamiento, Sección: Gobernación, Fondo: C.P. Miguel Herrera A., AGMSMA.

20. Mexican women officially received full suffrage rights in 1953, but the first presidential election in which they were eligible to participate was not until 1958. For a general overview of women's suffrage in Mexico see Morton, *Woman Suffrage in Mexico*, 9–10, 45–46, 86; and Olcott, *Revolutionary Women*, chap. 5 and the conclusion (on women's suffrage in Guanajuato see 166).

21. For example, see Pilcher, "Mexico's Pepsi Challenge"; Rubenstein, "War on 'Las Pelonas,'" 57–80; Zolov, *Refried Elvis*; and Gordillo, *Mexican Women and the Other Side of Immigration*, 46, 105.

22. "No debemos ayancarnos ni gringolizarnos," *El Vocero del Norte*, March 14, 1965.

23. Incrédulo, "Me cuentan que . . . ," *El Vocero del Norte*, July 23, 1967.

24. One of the most scathing critiques of the pachuco was the essay "The Pachuco and Other Extremes," by the Mexican intellectual Octavio Paz in *The Labyrinth of Solitude and Other Writings*, 9–28. On the pachuco in Mexican popular culture see Mraz, "Today, Tomorrow, and Always," 132; and Pilcher, *Cantinflas and the Chaos of Mexican Modernity*, 148–50. On pachucos as antecedents of Mexican counterculture see Agustín, *La contracultura en México*, 17–19. On Mexicans being called malinchistas see Paz, "Sons of La Malinche," in *Labyrinth of Solitude*, 65–88; Bachelor, "Toiling for the 'New Invaders,'" 313–14; and Hershfield, *Imagining la Chica Moderna*, 59.

25. Mercadillo Miranda to President Ruiz Cortines, July 28, 1953, Exp. 151.3/345, ARC, AGN. Catholic leaders in Latin America frequently pressured local and national governments to police morality. For example, see Rubenstein, *Bad Language, Naked Ladies, and Other Threats to the Nation*; Manzano, "Sexualizing Youth"; and Moreno, *Yankee Don't Go Home!*, 220–21.

26. On deportations from San Miguel see Virtue, *Model American Abroad*, 224. On the drug-trafficking network see "Batida de hipies drogadictos," *El Heraldo de León*, July 27, 1969, 1, Estado de Guanajuato, Information periodística, Folio: 13 febrero 1969–13 agosto 1969, 27 de julio 1969, 12.05 horas, Exp. 4333, Caja. 549, Serie: Información General de los Estados, Guanajuato-Guerrero, 1969, DGIPS, AGN.

27. "Se hace una propaganda injusta y exagerada en contra de S. Miguel," *El Vocero del Norte*, April 10, 1960, 1; Incrédulo, "Me cuentan que . . . ," *El Vocero del Norte*, April 10, 1960, 5; Rubirosa, "Crisol social," *El Vocero del Norte*, April 17, 1960, 2. On a similar incident several years later see "En esta ciudad de San Miguel de Allende, Gto., hay mucho quehacer para la ciudadanía y para las autoridades," *El Vocero del Norte*, June 11, 1967, 1.

28. Cornelio Plas, "Conceptos," *El Vocero del Norte*, July 31, 1966, 5; January 29, 1967, 6; November 23, 1969, 4. On the demonization of nightclubs and rock and roll music in Mexico City see Agustín, *La contracultura en México*, 35.

29. "Encomiable labor contra la vagancia y el vicio hace la actual administración," *El Vocero del Norte*, March 12, 1961, 1. Scholars have observed that in the United States, men of color represented youthful rebellion before James Dean and Elvis came on the scene. For example, see Ramírez, *Woman in the Zoot Suit*, 88.

30. Cuba's revolutionary government was also concerned about the potentially negative influence of "rebels without a cause." See Guerra, *Visions of Power in Cuba*, 253.

31. "Suceden cosas extrañas que antes no sucedían, debido a varios factores," *El Vocero del Norte*, July 3, 1966, 1; "Es necesario prestar atención a las voces de sensatez, para q' se ponga un hasta aquí a tanta inmoralidad," *El Vocero del Norte*, August 13, 1967, 1. Anne Rubenstein claims that out-of-wedlock pregnancies were such a common preoccupation in Mexico that it appeared as a plot device in nearly half of the romance and true-life genres of Mexican comics after 1950. Rubenstein, *Bad Language, Naked Ladies, and Other Threats to the Nation*, 50.

32. For example, see "Sigue adelante la labor de limpia emprendida por la policía local; lástima que sea tanto lo que hay que corregir," *El Vocero del Norte*, August 22, 1965, 1, 6; and James Egan, "San Miguel Is Where the Action Is for Art Students and Other Swingers," *New York Times*, May 2, 1971, XX1, 15. Paulina Hawkins corroborated this phenomenon. Paulina Hawkins, interview by author, San Miguel de Allende, May 5, 2015.

33. Galindo, *Nudo*, 58–59.

34. Galindo, *Nudo*, 141.

35. Correspondence regarding flyers distributed by Mercadillo Miranda, April 19, 1950, 1.40.(3).4, Allende, Fondo: Secretaría del Gobierno, Primer Departamento, AGGEG; Mercadillo Miranda to President Ruiz Cortines, July 28, 1953, Exp. 151.3/345, ARC, AGN.

36. For example, see Plas, "Conceptos," *El Vocero del Norte*, September 11, 1966, 6; July 31, 1966, 5; July 17, 1966, 3. While conservative Catholics across the globe warned of the supposed relationship between homosexuality and communism, many on the Left also stigmatized homosexuality as a threat to ideological orthodoxy, patriarchal order, and national security. See Guerra, *Visions of Power in Cuba*, chap. 7; and J. Green, "'Who Is the Macho Who Wants to Kill Me?'"

37. It is unclear whether these articles were transcripts of his radio programs. Lombardi, "Importantísimo edicto cuaresmal del Excelentísimo Señor Obispo Dr. D. Manuel Martín del Campo," *El Vocero del Norte*, February 19, 1961, 1; Lombardi, "Es necesario conocer el sistema comunista para convencerse de sus errores," *El Vocero del Norte*, June 11, 1961, 4; Lombardi, "Africa y América bajo el comunismo," *El Vocero del Norte*, June 18, 1961, 4; and "Las últimas agitaciones comunistas nos obliga a examinarlo y analizarlo," *El Vocero del Norte*, June 4, 1961, 1.

38. This translates to "Yes to Christianity, down with communism!" Juan A. Serrano, "Cristianismo sí, Comunismo, no," *El Vocero del Norte*, 28 May 1961, 4, 6. On the rise of Catholic anticommunism in Mexico in the 1950s and 1960s see Blancarte, "Intransigence, Anticommunism, and Reconciliation," 81–83.

39. Lombardi, "Africa y América bajo el comunismo," *El Vocero del Norte*, June 18, 1961, 4.

40. "Tratáronse temas de vital importancia y de palpitante actualidad sobre el agro y la industria, en el II Congreso Mariano que terminó el día 12 en la Ciudad de México," *El Vocero del Norte*, October 15, 1961, 1.

41. Lombardi, "La familia base de la nueva sociedad," *El Vocero del Norte*, August 13, 1961, 4. On the relationship between the Catholic Church and

the Left see Gould, "Solidarity under Siege." On the influence of Vatican II and liberation theology in Mexico see Palacios, *Catholic Social Imagination*, 158–60.

42. On the perceived communist threats on a national level see Fallaw, *Religion and State Formation in Revolutionary Mexico*; Blancarte, "Intransigence, Anticommunism, and Reconciliation"; and Sherman, *Mexican Right*. On Catholics and the perceived Catholic threat on an international level see Pensado, *Rebel Mexico*, 220–22; Manzano, "Sexualizing Youth"; and Cowan, "'Why Hasn't This Teacher Been Shot?'"

43. Pilcher, *Cantinflas and the Chaos of Mexican Modernity*.

44. On the history of Catholic anticommunism in Mexico more broadly see Sherman, *Mexican Right*. On Catholics who sounded similar warnings in other national contexts see Johnson, *Lavender Scare*, 103; and J. Green, *Beyond Carnival*, 114.

45. Smart, *At Home in Mexico*, 32.

46. Kerouac, *On the Road*, 276.

47. For an example of the myths about the Beats in San Miguel see Virtue, *Model American Abroad*, 225; and Greenhaw, *My Heart Is in the Earth*, 153–61. For an example of how contentious some of the debates are about the Beats in San Miguel, see the following article and its comments section: Peter Ferry, "Searching for Neal Cassady," WorldHum, May 6, 2010, http://www.worldhum.com/features/travel-stories/searching-for-neal-cassady-in-san-miguel-de-allende-20100503/#comments.

48. Kesey, *Demon Box*, 64–90. Harry Burrus, one of the individuals who painstakingly dismantles claims that Kerouac, Ginsberg, and Cassady ever spent time together in San Miguel, shared his research notes with me through personal correspondence in July 2013.

49. Dean, *Douglas Dean's Gay Mexico*, 7–9. For a scholarly analysis that challenges these stereotypes see Gutmann, *Meanings of Macho*; and Cantú, *Sexuality of Migration*, chap. 5.

50. Cantú, *Sexuality of Migration*, chap. 5. Flannery Burke explores this theme in a gay man's portrayal of nonwhite New Mexicans in "Spud Johnson and a Gay Man's Place in the Taos Creative Arts Community," 106–10. Also see the analysis of masculinity and conquest in Beat travel narratives in Carden, "'Adventures in Auto-Eroticism.'"

51. Macías-González, "Transnational Homophile Movement," 523.

52. Dean, *Douglas Dean's Gay Mexico*, 8. Cantú, *Sexuality of Migration*, 110–13, also supports this claim.

53. Dean, *Douglas Dean's Gay Mexico*, 43.

54. Macías-González, "Transnational Homophile Movement."
55. *Últimas Noticias*, July 7, 1950, cited in Virtue, *Model American Abroad*, 161.
56. Dean, *Douglas Dean's Gay Mexico*, 43–45.
57. Dean, *Douglas Dean's Gay Mexico*, 43.
58. Macías-González, "Transnational Homophile Movement," 521.
59. Virtue, *Model American Abroad*, chap. 15. With the exception of their dissimilar economic status, Dickinson lived a life that shares many parallels with that of William "Spud" Johnson in 1930s Taos, New Mexico. See Burke, "Spud Johnson and a Gay Man's Place in the Taos Creative Arts Community."
60. Virtue, *Model American Abroad*, 160.
61. Virtue, *Model American Abroad*, 132. Dickinson was not openly gay.
62. On Dorsey Fisher and the links between red-baiting and accusations about homosexuality in the Foreign Service, see Virtue, *Model American Abroad*, chap. 22; and Johnson, *Lavender Scare*, chap. 3. For one of the newspaper articles see a story from the Herald Tribune News Service: Bert Quint, "More Than 100 Expatriate Reds in Mexico Viewed as Peril to U.S.," *Washington Post and Times Herald*, August 30, 1957, A4. Although embassy officials denied playing a role in red-baiting, one scholar notes that newspapers often obtained their information on Americans in Mexico from the U.S. embassy. Schreiber, *Cold War Exiles in Mexico*, 182.
63. Joe Hyams, "The 'Sorbonne' of Latin America," *Washington Post and Times Herald*, February 23, 1958, C12. Also see Virtue, *Model American Abroad*, chaps. 22 and 23.
64. See Overmyer-Velázquez, *Visions of the Emerald City*, 109; and Guy, *Sex and Danger in Buenos Aires*, 46.
65. Olcott, *Revolutionary Women*, 19. In the United States a woman's nationality legally "followed" her husband's nationality in the early twentieth century (until 1931 in some cases). N. Green, "Expatriation, Expatriates, and Expats," 318.
66. Cossío del Pomar, *Cossío del Pomar en San Miguel de Allende*, 153.
67. Robert Maxwell and Lucha Maxwell, interview by author, San Miguel de Allende, December 6, 2006.
68. These requests are scattered throughout the municipal records I consulted for the 1960s and 1970s, which were clearly incomplete. Therefore it is impossible to offer an accurate estimate of how many of these couples existed during this period. For a sample of these letters see Box 1969, AGMSMA.

69. Dorothy Vidargas, interview by Leticia Echlin, filmed by Adeline Medalia, February 1, 1993, SMHA.

70. Hartwell, *Señorita Okay*, 141.

71. Hartwell, *Señorita Okay*, 36–37.

72. On gendered representations of foreign relations in the national mythology and for the Mexican tourist industry, respectively, see Lomnitz, *Deep Mexico, Silent Mexico*, 53; and Berger, *Development of Mexico's Tourism Industry*, chap. 5. For an example of how the Mexican film industry inverted these representations see analysis of the films *¡Espionaje en el golfo!* and *Los tres García* in Fein, "Myths of Cultural Imperialism and Nationalism," 159–98. For other analyses of gendered representations of U.S.–Latin American relations see Ruiz, *Americans in the Treasure House*, esp. chap. 4; Pérez, *On Becoming Cuban*, 189–95; Schwartz, *Pleasure Island*; Schwartz, *Flying Down to Rio*, chap. 7; and de la Cadena, *Indigenous Mestizos*, chap. 6. On the gendering of foreign relations from a U.S. perspective see Klein, *Cold War Orientalism*; Streeby, *American Sensations*; Renda, *Taking Haiti*; Murphy, *Hemispheric Imaginings*, esp. chap. 1; and Hunt, *Ideology and U.S. Foreign Policy*. Despite the scholarly attention given to this subject, the attempts to extend these analyses to the actual lived experiences of men and women have fallen short. Exceptions include Alvah, *Unofficial Ambassadors*; and Lipman, *Guantánamo*.

73. I draw my conclusions in this section from oral histories and several informal conversations in San Miguel. I have chosen not to identify specific families or individuals by name because in several cases I spoke only with the parents and do not have the consent of the (now adult) children to share their stories, and in other cases the individuals wished to remain anonymous.

74. However, in a 1981 study of cross-cultural families in San Miguel one respondent said that his children had a difficult time fitting in with both cultures. Debbie Baldwin, "Cross-Cultural Marriages in San Miguel," *Atención*, February 3, 1981, 3–4. Chapter 5 explores bilingualism in the workplace in greater detail.

75. On the limited access to public education beyond primary school in Mexico see Levinson, *We Are All Equal*, 16–17. On the relationship between educational opportunities and class in midcentury Mexico see Walker, *Waking from the Dream*, 6–7.

76. Paulina Hawkins interview.

77. Bob Mosher, "The International Set," *Atención*, November 18, 1980, 5.

78. On class-based linkages between Mexicans and foreigners formed through educational settings in Mexico City see Buchenau, "Small Numbers, Great Impact," 43; and Scanlon, *Un enclave cultural*.

79. Eva Fernández, interview by author, San Miguel de Allende, May 2, 2015.

80. This situation resonates with observations about "Third Culture Kids" in Bell-Villada, *Overseas American*, foreword. It also shares similarities with findings on the self-identification of the "second generation" in the American colony in Porfirian Mexico City. See W. Schell, *Integral Outsiders*, xvii–xviii. On laws regarding dual citizenship see N. Green, "Expatriation, Expatriates, Expats," 324–25. On the difficulty of categorizing children of a mixed racial background in a colonial context see Hall, *Civilising Subjects*, 10; and Stoler, *Carnal Knowledge and Imperial Power*, chap. 4.

81. On the supposed harmony between Mexicans and foreigners in San Miguel see Aguilar et al., *San Miguel de Allende*, 61–65. While only one individual explicitly commented that her generation felt a responsibility to act as stewards of San Miguel, my own observations led to the conclusion that this was a more widely shared sentiment. Eva Fernández interview.

82. For example, see the registry of public women, 1936, Serie: Registros; and correspondence regarding local prostitutes, 1936, Serie: Disposiciones, both in Sección: Casas de Asignación, Fondo: Gobernación, AGMSMA.

83. In her study of prostitution in late nineteenth- and early twentieth-century Argentina Donna Guy demonstrates that foreigners there also received blame for social problems, although in that case many of the individuals involved in the sex trade were foreign, whereas in San Miguel the workers (at least those who registered with the municipal authorities) were all Mexican. Therefore the workers could be portrayed uniformly as victims of foreign desires and exploitation, rather than as the source of vice. See Guy, *Sex and Danger in Buenos Aires*, esp. chaps. 1, 2, and 4. On the nationality of San Miguel's sex workers see the registry of public women, 1936, Serie: Registros, Sección: Casas de Asignación, Fondo: Gobernación, AGMSMA.

84. Información de San Miguel Allende, Estado de Guanajuato, 15 de agosto 1969, 20:30 horas, Folio: 13 febrero 1969–13 agosto 1969, Exp. 4333, Caja 549, Guanajuato-Guerrero, 1969, Serie: Información General de los Estados, DGIPS, AGN.

85. Petition to the H. Ayuntamiento, May 10, 1933, Exp. 3.18.55, Serie: Acuerdos de Ayuntamiento, Sección: Gobernación, Fondo: C.P. Miguel Herrera A., AGMSMA.

86. The government of Mexico's Federal District took steps to legislate "tolerance zones" in Mexico City as early as the 1910s. Bliss, *Compromised Positions*, 66.

87. Correspondence regarding local prostitutes, 1936, Serie: Disposiciones, Sección: Casas de Asignación, Fondo: Gobernación, AGMSMA. On the attempts to regulate prostitution in Porfirian Oaxaca and revolutionary Yucatán, respectively, see Overmyer-Velázquez, *Visions of the Emerald City*, chap. 4; and Smith, *Gender and the Mexican Revolution*, chap. 5. On the masculinization of Mexico's sex industry see Bliss, *Compromised Positions*, esp. chaps. 1 and 5. For the way early nineteenth-century European policies regarding the regulation of sex workers influenced Latin American policies see Guy, *Sex and Danger in Buenos Aires*, 47.

88. Registry of public women, 1936, Serie: Registros, Sección: Casas de Asignación, Fondo: Gobernación, AGMSMA.

89. The municipal archives did not contain documents on prostitution past the 1940s, so I rely on anecdotal evidence compiled from the sources cited below to make this claim. The absence of archival material related to prostitution can probably be attributed in part to the fact that in 1940 the government suspended the law that mandated the registration of prostitutes. See Bliss, *Compromised Positions*, chap. 6 and the postscript. For another example of the role of prostitution in the context of a foreign presence see Lipman, *Guantánamo*, 109–15.

90. On the difficulties of getting Mexicans to admit that they paid women for sex see Gutmann, *Meanings of Macho*, 133. For a fictionalized account, which the author claims is based in part on the experiences of anonymous informants, see Hayward, "La Casa de la Turca," 153–63.

91. Greenhaw, *My Heart Is in the Earth*, 145–46.

92. One source that explicitly addresses the clandestine sex trade is "Es punto más que delicado el de moralizar las costumbres; pero de vez en cuando, se debe abordar," *El Vocero del Norte*, July 25, 1965, 1, 6.

93. Barbara Edell Poole, interview by author, San Miguel de Allende, January 31, 2008. Poole shared her own informal research on the history of the Casa de la Turca during the interview. On the establishments in San Miguel that had extralegal prostitution arrangements see "Encomiable labor contra la vagancia y el vicio hace la ctual administración," *El Vocero del Norte*, March 12, 1961, 1.

94. During discussions about my project in Mexico City several individuals brought this unsolicited information to my attention, all using the phrase *turismo de infidelidad*.

95. On business complaints see Información de San Miguel Allende, Estado de Guanajuato, Report: 15 de agosto 1969, 20:30 horas, Folio: 13 febrero 1969–15 agosto 1969, Exp. 4333, Caja 549, Serie: Información General de los Estados, Guanajuato-Guerrero, 1969, DGIPS, AGN.

96. For example, see Erika Schedel, "By the Way," *El Vocero del Norte*, December 19, 1965, 4; and Schedel, "Open the Window," *El Vocero del Norte*, July 17, 1966, 4.

97. Información de San Miguel Allende, Estado de Guanajuato, Report: 15 de agosto 1969, 20:30 horas, Folio: 13 febrero 1969–15 agosto 1969, Exp. 4333, Caja 549, Serie: Información General de los Estados, Guanajuato-Guerrero, 1969, DGIPS, AGN.

98. Información de San Miguel Allende, Estado de Guanajuato, 15 de agosto 1969, 20:30 horas, Folio: 13 febrero 1969–13 agosto 1969, Exp. 4333, Caja 549, Serie: Información General de los Estados, Guanajuato-Guerrero, 1969, DGIPS, AGN. Also see police reports in Box 1968–70 and Box 1969, Tesorería/Correspondencia, AGMSMA.

99. Report submitted to Margáin, August 7, 1969, III-5933-24, SRE.

100. Información de San Miguel Allende, Estado de Guanajuato, 16 de agosto 1969, 12:45 horas, Folio: 13 febrero 1969–13 agosto 1969, Exp. 4333, Caja 549, Serie: Información General de los Estados, Guanajuato-Guerrero, 1969, DGIPS, AGN.

101. Luis Caballero V., "He oído platicar que . . ." *El Vocero del Norte*, August 10, 1969, 1, 6.

102. Virtue, *Model American Abroad*, 225–26.

103. Zolov claims that these haircutting incidents "became legion" in Mexico. Zolov, *Refried Elvis*, 165. Also see Agustín, *La contracultura en México*, 78.

104. Leach, "Magical Hair," 177–201.

105. For examples of head-shaving incidents at the U.S.-Mexican border see Stern, "Buildings, Boundaries, and Blood," 46; and Rak, *Border Patrol*, 35. California ordinances in the 1870s that forced Chinese men to cut their hair are an important precedent; see Dennis, "Anti-Chinese Campaigns in Sonora, Mexico," 72. On the role of head shaving in the Zoot Suit Riots and in Mexican American popular culture see Ramírez, *Woman in the Zoot Suit*, x–xii, 74–75, 90.

106. For example, see Manzano, "Sexualizing Youth," 457; Hoffnung-Garskof, *Tale of Two Cities*, 89; J. Green, *Beyond Carnival*, 227–28; Cowan, "Sex and the Security State," 474; Bruey, "Neoliberalism and Repression in 'Poblaciones' of Santiago de Chile," 22–24; and Guerra, *Visions of Power in Cuba*, chap. 7.

107. "Hablan de hippies los astronautas," *El Sol de Bajío,* July 18, 1969, 1, 6.

108. Pearl to Governor Moreno, September 17, 1969, III-5933-24, SRE.

109. Jack McDonald, "Hippies Get in the Artists' Hair in Mexico's San Miguel Allende," *New York Times,* January 25, 1970, 370. The 1969 head-shaving incident was also portrayed in a comical light in a fictionalized account published in 2013. See Denham, *Secrets of San Miguel,* 19–30. William Schell has demonstrated that rifts also emerged between Mexico's American colony and what they perceived as uncouth American tourists and transients during the Porfiriato. See W. Schell, *Integral Outsiders,* 28, 120.

110. Caballero V., "He oído placticar que . . . ," *El Vocero del Norte,* August 10, 1969, 1, 6.

111. "A la opinión pública," *El Fisgón Anteojudo,* August 10, 1969, 4; "Telegrama abierto," *El Fisgón Anteojudo,* August 10, 1969, 4.

112. Margáin to Schimel, August 19, 1969, III-5933-24, SRE.

113. May, *Homeward Bound,* 220. On Mexican responses to youth culture in the 1950s and 1960s see Pensado, *Rebel Mexico.*

114. Correspondence regarding preparations for the 1968 Olympics, 1967, XV-88-4, SRE. For more on the preparations for the 1968 Olympic Games see Zolov, "Showcasing the 'Land of Tomorrow.'"

115. Incrédulo, "Me cuentan que . . . ," *El Vocero del Norte,* June 23, 1968, 5.

116. Pancho Cuéllar González, "Proyecciones Olímpicas," reprinted in *El Fisgón Anteojudo,* February 18, 1968, 7–8.

117. Zolov, *Refried Elvis,* 107–10.

118. Quoted in Zolov, *Refried Elvis,* 116.

119. The number of individuals killed remains disputed, but most independent estimates challenge the government claim that fewer than fifty were killed and place the estimate at hundreds. See Carey, *Plaza of Sacrifices,* 1.

120. On the student movement and the subsequent government repression of leftist groups see Pensado, *Rebel Mexico;* Carey, *Plaza of Sacrifices;* and Walker, *Waking from the Dream,* introduction and chap. 1. On foreign praise for the Mexican government see Zolov, "Discovering a Land 'Mysterious and Obvious,'" 260; and Buchenau, *Mexico OtherWise,* 237–39.

121. Zolov, *Refried Elvis,* 133. For an analysis that links countercultural movements with armed political struggles see Zolov, "Expanding Our Conceptual Horizons," 47–73.

122. Correspondence regarding restrictions on foreign visitors, 1971, IV-1280-6, SRE. For examples of Americans seeking vice and pleasure in Mexico during the 1960s and Mexican responses to these travelers see Cadava, *Standing on Common Ground,* 146–49.

123. For example, see "Entrada de hippies a territorio nacional," 1970, A/048/1, no. 80, Caja 31; and "Hippies," 1971–73, A/048/1, no. 498, Caja 151, both in SEDENA, AGN.

124. Cervantes Jáuregui and Crespo, *Fiesta y tradición*, 113.

125. On his economic dealings in Atotonilco see Cervantes Jáuregui and Crespo, *Fiesta y tradición*, 112. Hernández, *La soledad del silencio*, raises many questions about Mercadillo's practices; see esp. 96–97. On transitions within the Catholic Church in the late 1960s see Blancarte, "Intransigence, Anticommunism, and Reconciliation," 83–84.

5. San Miguel's Two Service Economies

1. Galloway, *Margaret Cecilia Galloway*, 78–83.

2. "Population of SMA Exceeds 75,000," *Atención*, July 22, 1980, 1. The 1980 Mexican census counted San Miguel's urban population at 30,003. Marco Geoestadístico Nacional, Descarga de información correspondiente a la localidad geoestadística: 110030001 INEGI, last accessed August 23, 2016, http://www.inegi.org.mx/geo/contenidos/geoestadistica/introduccio.aspx.

3. This number is based on the population growth trends and estimates in a number of other sources, but even in the late twentieth century reliable statistics on the foreign population are difficult to locate.

4. The first issues of *Atención* were titled *This Week in San Miguel/Esta Semana en San Miguel*.

5. For more detailed analyses of Mexico's transition to neoliberalism see Harvey, *Brief History of Neoliberalism*, 98–104; Babb, *Managing Mexico*, chap. 7; and Vázquez Castillo, *Land Privatization in Mexico*, chap. 4. For an analysis of the effect of Mexico's economic policies on the middle classes in the 1970s and 1980s see Walker, *Waking from the Dream*.

6. On the reforms to Article 27 and the subsequent effects on various Mexican communities see Vázquez Castillo, *Land Privatization in Mexico*.

7. "Some Classes at Instituto Continue," *Atención*, March 26, 1982, 1; Virtue, *Model American Abroad*, 223.

8. On government investment in Cancún see Clancy, *Exporting Paradise*; R. Torres and Momsen, "Gringolandia"; and Sackett, "Making of Acapulco," 289–90.

9. On the Mexican economy in the late 1970s see Walker, *Waking from the Dream*, chap. 3. On Sanmiguelenses in the state tourism apparatus and some of the benefits that their presence entailed see Nina Martino, "News

Notes," *Atención*, August 3, 1977, 1; Quetzalcoatl, "Reunión de turismo," *Atención*, February 25, 1977, 1, 9; and Nina Martino, "News Notes," *Atención*, October 21, 1977, 2, 7.

10. "La actividad turística en San Miguel de Allende, Gto.," Exp. 12, Caja 01/ 123507/12, Dirección general de política y programas sectorales, 21.02.01.00, SECTUR, MMH, AGN.

11. "Cambio de domicilio de turismo," *Atención*, July 22, 1980, 1; "Plans for SMA Tourist Department," *Atención*, August 5, 1980, 1.

12. Nina Martino, "News Notes," *Atención*, October 21, 1977, 2, 7. For a schedule of events for the Fiestas Patrias in 1977, see "Fiestas Patrias," *Atención*, September 2, 1977, 3.

13. "Aero Taxi Coming Soon," *Atención*, November 11, 1980, 1. This service was also short-lived.

14. Nina Martino, "News Notes," *Atención*, October 21, 1977, 2, 7.

15. "A Word from the Mayor, Lic. Silvestre Bautista López," *This Week in San Miguel*, May 30, 1975, 1.

16. Javier Zavala Ortíz, interview by author, San Miguel de Allende, December 6, 2006; "More Blackouts," *Atención*, July 29, 1980, 1.

17. On the history of San Miguel's urban water distribution system see García y García, *El agua en San Miguel de Allende*, 40–44; López Espinoza, *Estampas sanmiguelenses*, 191–93, 211–18; Cervantes Jáuregui and Crespo, *Fiesta y tradición*, 95–96; and José Guadalupe Ramírez, interview by author, San Miguel de Allende, November 6, 2007.

18. For another example of the chaotic development of urban spaces in Mexico see Sackett, "Making of Acapulco," chap. 2. For an analysis of what Alan Gilbert refers to as "spontaneous housing" in the third world see Gilbert, "Housing of the Urban Poor," 81–115.

19. García y García, *El agua en San Miguel de Allende*, 124–38. Information on the migration of rural populations is from César Arias de la Canal, interview by author, San Miguel de Allende, January 17, 2008.

20. "Primer informe del Presidente Municipal," *Atención*, January 13, 1978, 4, 5.

21. "Editorial," *Atención*, March 20, 1979, 6; George K. Ford, "Letters to the Editor," *Atención*, March 20, 1979, 8.

22. "Editorial," *Atención*, August 21, 1979, 5.

23. For examples of letters sent to the newspaper and the radio station see "Citizens of San Miguel Speak Out," *Atención*, July 3, 1979, 1, 5, 10; "La Voz del Pueblo," *Atención*, July 10, 1979, 1, 9; "Nor Any Drop to Drink,"

Atención, July 17, 1979, 1, 8; and "Letters to the Editor," *Atención*, July 24, 1979, 8, 12.

24. Ben Stahl, "Letters to the Editor," *Atención*, July 24, 1979, 8, 12.

25. Nina Martino, "News Notes," *Atención*, October 21, 1977, 2, 7.

26. Gary Jennings, "My Turn," *Atención*, November 4, 1977, 5–6.

27. For example, see John Beadle, *Atención*, November 18, 1977, 4, 6; and Brewer Grant, "My Turn," *Atención*, December 2, 1977, 6–7.

28. "Bus Terminal/Bypass Plans Announced," *Atención*, July 29, 1980, 1; "City Plans for Future," *Atención*, October 14, 1980, 1, 10; "Mayor's Year-End Report," *Atención*, January 13, 1981, 5–6.

29. "Senator Asks for Citizens' Help, Sees Need to Reinforce SMA Cultural Image," *Atención*, July 14, 1981, 1, 9. Rivera de Iturbe is Diego Rivera's daughter.

30. Patterson, *Journey to Xibalba*, 252–53.

31. David Watt, "Restoration at Atotonilco," *Atención*, October 28 1980, 1, 8. On the federal government's creation of the Ministry of Human Settlements and Public Works and the attempts to formalize urban planning see Vázquez Castillo, *Land Privatization in Mexico*, 67.

32. Patterson, *Journey to Xibalba*, 12–13.

33. "San Miguel to Be National Monument?" *Atención*, October 23, 1981, 1, 10.

34. Quoted in López Espinoza, "Sucesos importantes en San Miguel de Allende en el Siglo XX," 242–43.

35. Bloom, "To Be Served and Loved," 192; "San Miguel de Allende, Colonial Retirement Spot," AIM: *A Newsletter on Retirement and Travel in Mexico* 22, no. 3 (1995), BD.

36. Buchenau, "Small Numbers, Great Impact," 43.

37. These demographic trends continued into the 1990s and 2000s. Croucher, *Other Side of the Fence*, chap. 1. The 1990 Mexican census counted in San Miguel 854 foreigners born in the Americas (783 of those from the United States), 17 born in Asia, and 106 born in Europe. For reasons discussed in the introduction these numbers do not accurately represent the number of San Miguel's foreigners, whose numbers were actually nearing 10 percent of the total population at this time. Censo General de Población y Vivienda 1990, Población total, Por: entidad, municipio, y localidad, Según: lugar de nacimiento, INEGI, last accessed August 23, 2016, http://www.inegi.org.mx/est/lista_cubos/consulta.aspx?p =pob&c=5.

38. "Obituary: John W. Kenney," *Atención*, October 14, 1977, 10; Gael Gibney, "Spotlight on People: Von Charlton," *Atención*, August 5, 1977, 2.

39. "William J. Fox, 95, a War Hero, Engineer, Stunt Man and Cowboy," *New York Times*, April 17, 1993, 10; Ed Ainsworth, "Gen. Fox Joins the Charros," *Los Angeles Times*, August 1, 1963, 22; Phil Roettinger, "Un poquito de todo," *Atención*, March 27, 1979, 2.
40. For example, on the role of charitable activities in the context of the U.S. military presence abroad see Lipman, *Guantánamo*, 105–6.
41. Mathias J. Ortwein, "Letter to the Editor," *Atención*, September 2, 1977, 4; "Forty-Two Residents Meet with Consul General," *Atención*, June 9, 1978, 1; Francis F. Brodigan, "Letter to U.S. Ambassador in Mexico Patrick J. Lucey," *Atención*, May 12, 1978, 8. For examples of the bureaucratic challenges of living abroad see Roettinger, "Un poquito de todo," *Atención*, May 1, 1979, 2; and Charles T. Pratt, "Letter to President López Portillo," *Atención*, March 10, 1978, 12.
42. Personal correspondence with Edward Clancy, U.S. consular agent in San Miguel, January 21, 2010.
43. Palma Mora, *Veteranos de guerra norteamericanos en Guadalajara.*
44. Cheri Steffeck, "Making the Move to Mexico," *Washington Post*, May 27, 1973, H12. Also see Roettinger, "Un poquito de todo," *Atención*, March 27, 1979, 2; and Carl D. Ross, "Retirement Is Sweet in the Land of the Aztecs," *Washington Post*, June 15, 1972, AS12.
45. See especially *Atención* issues from 1982 through 1984, during the height of the economic crisis.
46. Margaret Nevin, "Retirement—Most Like It—Some Like it Not," *Atención*, October 14, 1980, 8–9.
47. For example, on San Miguel's expat theater scene see Susan Beere, interview by Fran Robbins, April 25, 2002, SMHA; and Galloway, *Margaret Cecilia Galloway*, 76. On the history of San Miguel's Chamber Music Festival, see Katherine Walch, "How It All Began," *Atención*, 1999, BD. On writing groups in San Miguel, see Bixler and Bradley, *San Miguel Writer*; "Centro Internacional San Miguel Writing Center," *Atención*, January 13, 1978, advertisement; and "Centro Internacional," *Atención*, January 29, 1980, 6. For more general musings about why foreigners liked San Miguel see Galloway, *Margaret Cecilia Galloway*, 71–75.
48. See Virtue, *Model American Abroad.*
49. Sylvia Samuelson, interview by author, San Miguel de Allende, November 28, 2006. On Leonard Brooks and the Centro Cultural see chap. 3.
50. Peter Olwyler, "Dateline . . . Mexico City," *Travel*, December 1958, 10–11.
51. This is true of expatriates in other parts of Mexico as well, although as the quotations cited in the beginning of this section indicate, the expats

in San Miguel have a reputation among scholars and other expat communities for participation in charitable projects. See Bloom, "To Be Served and Loved"; "San Miguel de Allende, Colonial Retirement Spot," *AIM: A Newsletter on Retirement and Travel in Mexico* 22, no. 3 (1995), BD; and "Social Consciousness Meets Conspicuous Consumption in Competitive San Miguel de Allende," *AIM: A Newsletter on Retirement and Travel in Mexico* 33, no. 1 (2006), BD. For a discussion of philanthropy in another Mexican expatriate community see Croucher, *Other Side of the Fence*; and Truly, "Lake Chapala Riviera."

52. "25th Anniversary of the Biblioteca Pública," *Atención*, November 6, 1979, 1. This entire issue of *Atención* was dedicated to articles about the library and the reminiscences of some of the early expats.

53. I attended many events at the Biblioteca Pública during my time in San Miguel, and some weeks I spent nearly every afternoon working in the courtyard.

54. The expat was quoted in Gille, *View from Casa Chepitos*, 113–14. Blum, "Conspicuous Benevolence," 32. On the "performance of charity" as a way to accrue social status in Argentina see Guy, *Women Build the Welfare State*, chap. 3.

55. My thinking about the relationships between expatriates and their employees, particularly household employees, has been influenced by Ann Laura Stoler's work, especially "Tense and Tender Ties."

56. Ruiz, *Americans in the Treasure House*, 31–32.

57. On benevolent colonialism see Stoler, "Tense and Tender Ties," 845–46. For an analysis of how Americans understood their presence in late nineteenth- and early twentieth-century Mexico as an extension of an imperial project see Ruiz, *Americans in the Treasure House*. On imperial progressivism see Huyssen, *Progressive Inequality*, 14; and Irwin, *Making the World Safe*, chap. 5. On the relationship between philanthropic efforts and social capital in an international context see Tomazos and Cooper, "Volunteer Tourism," 408.

58. Tony Adlerbert, interview by Katherine Walch, September 3, 2001, SMHA.

59. For example, see Jack McDonald, "Hippies Get in the Artists' Hair in Mexico's San Miguel Allende," *New York Times*, January 25, 1970, 370.

60. "International Good Neighbor Council," *Atención*, August 19, 1977, 2.

61. *El Fisgón Anteojudo*, n.d., 1968, 5; Nina Martino, "News Notes," *Atención*, April 3, 1979, 2; Stirling Dickinson, "Ayudando a los que se ayudan," *Atención*, April 24, 1979, 11; Katherine Walch, "Two San Miguel

Foreigners Honored by Mexican Government," *Atención*, 1999, BD. Also see Virtue, *Model American Abroad*.

62. "Jaime Morris Honored," *Atención*, November 4, 1980, 1; Katherine Walch, "Two San Miguel Foreigners Honored by Mexican Government," *Atención*, 1999, BD.

63. On the tensions at the national level, especially during the Salinas administration, see Piester, "Targeting the Poor," 486.

64. On the social spending data see Piester, "Targeting the Poor," 474. On the impact of these austerity measures on Mexico's middle classes see Walker, *Waking from the Dream*; on women specifically see Sanders, *Gender and Welfare in Mexico*, 138–39. On the impact of debt politics internationally see Enloe, *Bananas, Beaches and Bases*, 184–85.

65. Although international NGOs also played an important role in supplying resources previously provided by the Mexican government (including, at times, in San Miguel), they are outside the purview of this chapter. For a brief discussion of the relationship between NGOs and the rise of neoliberal economic policies in Mexico see Stephen, "Epilogue." For a critique of the relationship between NGOs and privatization see Harvey, *Brief History of Neoliberalism*, 177.

66. Rubirosa, "Crisol social," *El Vocero del Norte*, August 14, 1960, 2. For a foreigner's critical reflections on the role of charitable giving in San Miguel see Gille, *View from Casa Chepitos*, 267–70.

67. Erika Schedel, "Open the Window," *El Vocero del Norte*, August 21, 1966, 4.

68. For example, see *El Fisgón Anteojudo*, October 27, 1968, 2; and "La Casa Hogar 'Don Bosco' es una institución Benéfica, que, desde hace cerca de diez años viene cubriendo de cariño, educación e instrucción a la niñez," *El Vocero del Norte*, May 5, 1968, 1.

69. For a more common example of the role that immigrants played in the economies of their communities of origin see Gordillo, *Mexican Women and the Other Side of Immigration*, 127–31.

70. Melissa Cannon, "Fashion Flourishes in San Miguel Jail," *Atención*, April 2, 1976, 6; "Letters from 'El Fisgon,'" *Atención*, April 30, 1976, 6.

71. On government efforts to centralize control over charitable organizations see Blum, "Conspicuous Benevolence"; and Sanders, *Gender and Welfare in Mexico*. On public-private collaboration in the realm of charity more broadly in Mexico see Sanders, *Gender and Welfare in Mexico*, 53–55.

72. Ezequiel López, interview by Leonardo Rosen, September 17, 2002, SMHA; Mercedes Ramírez, "Gracias al Club Rotario," *Atención*, June 30, 1981, 11. On the introduction of service organizations such as the Rotary

Club and the "service ethic" into Europe see de Grazia, *Irresistible Empire*, chap. 1.

73. *El Fisgón Anteojudo*, October 27, 1968, 2; Angelina Correa, "Club de Leones," *Atención*, January 20, 1981, 6.

74. "Hernandez, Primer Presidente Mexicano," *Atención*, March 3, 1978, 1; Susan Beere, "Spotlight on People: Celia Hoyos de Téllez," *Atención*, October 31, 1978, 5.

75. Galloway, *Margaret Cecilia Galloway*, 79–83.

76. Correa, "Sharecropping and Agrarian Reform," 167. For a more general discussion of the changes to Article 27 see Stephen, "Epilogue," 254; and on changes to foreign property ownership restrictions see Bantman-Masum, "'You Need to Come Here,'" 19–20. For an analysis of how changes to Article 27 affected labor in the region surrounding Acapulco see Vázquez Castillo, *Land Privatization in Mexico*, chap. 6.

77. Francisco Garay Llaguno, interview by author, San Miguel de Allende, February 9, 2008.

78. For a discussion of a similar process in the town of Tepoztlán, south of Mexico City, see Lomnitz, *Deep Mexico, Silent Mexico*, chap. 8. On the potential profitability of place-bound identities see Harvey, *Condition of Postmodernity*, 303.

79. Address before the Cámara de Diputados, Chapultepec, February 9, 1983, Fojas 84–88, Exp. 03/123497/3/14, Caja 01, 21.01.00.00, SECTUR, MMH, AGN.

80. Address before elected officials in Oaxaca, February 12, 1983, Fojas 84–88, Exp. 03/123497/3/14, Caja 01, 21.01.00.00, SECTUR, MMH, AGN.

81. John Windsor, "Commuting to and from Mexico," *Atención*, January 28, 1977, 12, reprinted from the *St. Louis Post-Dispatch*.

82. Sassen, *Global City*, chap. 9.

83. On the relative instability and temporality of tourist-industry related jobs see Vázquez Castillo, *Land Privatization in Mexico*, 124.

84. On tourism and the gendered division of labor and on the depression of women's wages see Enloe, *Bananas, Beaches and Bases*, 33–35, 162–66. For another example of how tourism feminized a local economy see Brennan, *What's Love Got to Do with It?*, esp. chap. 4. For an example of how men historically were gendered as breadwinners and women as homemakers in the Chilean context see Rosemblatt, *Gendered Compromises*.

85. For example, see Phil Roettinger, "Un poquito de todo," *Atención*, February 19, 1980, 2. For a similar analysis of relationships between domestic

labor and foreign employers in the context of U.S. military bases see Alvah, *Unofficial Ambassadors*, 109.

86. I was able to locate labor grievances for the 1970s only in the municipal archive, but others will likely emerge once the materials are organized.

87. For these and other examples see "Demandas de los Ciudadanos a sus Patrones," Folder 6, Box 1976; and Folder "Laborales 1973," Box 1973–76, both in AGMSMA.

88. Report and documents presented by Imelda Juárez Ramírez to the presidente municipal, Lic. Silvestre Bautista López, February 2, 1976, "Demandas de los Ciudadanos a sus Patrones," Folder 6, Box 1976, AGMSMA.

89. Report and documents compiled for the presidente municipal, Lic. Silvestre Bautista López, on February 13, 1976, "Demandas de los Ciudadanos a sus Patrones," Folder 6, Box 1976, AGMSMA. For another example of a foreigner making assumptions about a friendship with a Mexican maid because she left generous tips, see Denham, *Secrets of San Miguel*, 102.

90. "Letters to the Editor," *This Week in San Miguel*, August 1, 1975, 2.

91. Dolores Danzig, "Spotlight on the Garcia Sisters," *Atención*, June 10, 1980, 3.

92. Dolores Danzig, "Spotlight on the Garcia Sisters," *Atención*, June 10, 1980, 3.

93. Paulina Hawkins, interview by author, San Miguel de Allende, May 5, 2015.

94. Don Patterson, interview by author, San Miguel de Allende, November 12, 2006. Also see his account in Patterson, *Journey to Xibalba*, 253–54.

95. Byrnes, *Driving the State*, 77.

96. For example, see Roettinger, "Un poquito de todo," *Atención*, February 19, 1980, 2; and Gille, *View from Casa Chepitos*.

97. As Alicia Schmidt Camacho has argued, migrants found that neoliberalism also restructured the U.S. economy in similar ways. See Schmidt Camacho, *Migrant Imaginaries*, 198–203, 288–98, on the relationship between NAFTA, undocumented migration, and the militarization of the border. Also see Dunn, *Militarization of the U.S.-Mexico Border, 1978–1992*.

98. In informal conversations several informants in San Miguel reported that family members or friends who had moved to the United States stopped sending promised money, and some even cut off contact altogether. On the broader effects on those left behind in Guanajuato see Byrnes, *Driving the State*, esp. chap. 5; and for an analysis of "those left behind" in Jalisco see Gordillo, *Mexican Women and the Other Side of Immigration*.

99. Mujeres en Cambio, interview by Katherine Walch and Pakina Langensheidt, October 2003, SMHA; "The Rug Hook Project," last accessed October 9, 2015, http://rughookproject.com.

100. For example, see "Local Cooperatives and Organic Food Stores and Restaurants," Center for Global Justice, last accessed October 9, 2015, http://www.globaljusticecenter.org/local.

101. See Sanders, *Gender and Welfare in Mexico*, 55. For a similar analysis of how white communities in the United States deemed certain groups more deserving of charity see Weise, *Corazón de Dixie*, chap. 4.

102. On how philanthropic pursuits can reinforce class divisions see Guy, *Women Build the Welfare State*, chap. 4. On government welfare programs reinforcing patriarchal structures see Sanders, *Gender and Welfare in Mexico*.

103. CASA, last accessed September 14, 2015, http://www.empowercasa.org. On the importance of including the beneficiaries in the decision-making process see Piester, "Targeting the Poor," 486–87; Byrnes, *Driving the State*, 49–50; and Burkey, *People First*, 53.

104. Jesús Gutiérrez, interview by author, San Miguel de Allende, July 8, 2013. Byrnes, *Driving the State*, has also elaborated on the roles that gender played in economic development efforts across Guanajuato in the early 2000s (see esp. chaps. 3 and 7). On the perception that immigrants' patriarchal authority declines while they are abroad see Gordillo, *Mexican Women and the Other Side of Immigration*, 104.

105. Virtue, *Model American Abroad*, 230.

106. Blum, "Conspicuous Benevolence," 16. On the question of providing a temporary solution versus enabling structural change to take place see the comparison of the efforts of elite philanthropists and middle-class feminists in Guy, *Women Build the Welfare State*, chap. 3. For an example of the complicated issues that arise when a charitable organization's founder passes away, when foundations lack transparency, when sources of funding dry up, or when gossip and rivalries influence charitable giving see the discussions and commentary on the website for the Michael Paul Wein Charitable Foundation, based in San Miguel, last accessed September 14, 2015, http://www.mpwcf.org/index.html.

107. The government's objectives and expenditures were last accessed by the author at "Pueblos Mágicos," SECTUR, December 23, 2009, http://www.sectur.gob.mx/wb2/sectur/sect_Pueblos_Magicos. These reports are no longer available at this web address, but the author has copies in her possession.

108. On the Nautical Ladder initiative see Saragoza, "Golfing in the Desert." Saragoza argues that the sense of placelessness in this development

scheme signals an important shift in Mexican tourist development, but when viewed in the context of the Pueblos Mágicos program it seems more like a continuation of a decades-old attempt to provide the traveler with both cosmopolitan amenities and folkloric day trips.

109. Saragoza, "Golfing in the Desert," 295.

110. Castellanos, "Adolescent Migration to Cancún," 5.

111. "Pueblos Mágicos," SECTUR.

112. Sackett, "Making of Acapulco," chap. 6.

113. The Mexican government invested a total of 12.3 million pesos from 2002 to 2006, compared to 39.6 million pesos from other sources, which the report did not disclose. See "Pueblos Mágicos," SECTUR.

114. For example, see the discussion of the private-public collaboration in San Miguel's Centro Cultural in chapter 3.

115. Bantam-Masum, "'You Need to Come Here,'" 44. See the entire article for discussion of the "San Miguel model."

Epilogue

1. United Nations Educational, Scientific, and Cultural Organization, "Decisions Adopted at the 32nd Session of the World Heritage Committee," 2009, last accessed October 10, 2015, http://whc.unesco.org/en/sessions /32com/documents/.

2. José Guadalupe Ramírez, interview by author, San Miguel de Allende, November 6, 2007. On the local opposition to the Sanmiguelada see David Agren, "Annual Event Re-Examined," *El Universal*, September 24, 2006, posted at http://agren.blogspot.com/2006/09/sanmiguelada-lots-of -hype-drinking-and.html.

3. Ramírez interview.

4. "Protective Town of San Miguel and the Sanctuary of Jesús Nazareno de Atotonilco," UNESCO Nomination Dossier, 2008, 228, last accessed October 10, 2015, http://whc.unesco.org/en/list/1274 /documents/.

5. Virtue, *Model American Abroad*, 235–36.

6. For example, see a report on the conflict over the Rio Blanco textile mill in Veracruz in Kreitlow, "Political Economy of Preserving the Past."

7. Emigdio Ledesma Pérez, interview by author and Fredy González, San Miguel de Allende, May 5, 2015.

8. Cervantes Jáuregui and Crespo, *Fiesta y tradición*, 67. The original Spanish captures the sentiment better, but it roughly translates to: "Traditions should be preserved because of what one feels, not because it is in one's interest."

BIBLIOGRAPHY

Archival Sources

AGGEG: Archivo General del Gobierno del Estado de Guanajuato, Guanajuato, Gto.

AGMSMA: Archivo General del Municipio de San Miguel de Allende, San Miguel de Allende, Gto.

AGN: Archivo General de la Nación, Mexico City, D.F.
- ALR: Abelardo L. Rodríguez
- ARC: Adolfo Ruiz Cortines
- DFS: Dirección Federal de Seguridad
- DGIPS: Dirección General de Investigaciones Políticas y Sociales
- LCR: Lázaro Cárdenas
- MAC: Manuel Ávila Camacho
- MAV: Miguel Alemán Valdés
- MMH: Miguel de la Madrid Hurtado
- PGR: Procuraduría General de la República
- SECTUR: Secretaría del Turismo
- SEDENA: Secretaría de la Defensa Nacional

AJMFMZ: Archivo José Miguel Francisco Malo Zozaya, in the possession of César Arias de la Canal, San Miguel de Allende, Gto.

APSMA: Archivo de la Parroquia de San Miguel Arcángel, San Miguel de Allende, Gto.

BD: Betse Davies Collection (newspaper clippings), in the possession of Betse Davies, San Miguel de Allende, Gto.

Biblioteca Lerdo de Tejada, Archivo Económico, Mexico City, D.F.

CCIR: Centro Cultural Ignacio Ramírez, Acervo Histórico, San Miguel de Allende, Gto.

Hemeroteca Nacional, Mexico City, D.F.

IA: Instituto Allende, Acervo Histórico, San Miguel de Allende, Gto.

INEGI: Instituto Nacional de Estadística y Geografía, Digital Archive
- Censos y Conteos de Población y Vivienda
- Marco Geoestadístico Nacional, Localidades Geoestadísticas, Archivo Histórico, Consulta de Localidades
- México en Cifras

NARA: National Archives and Records Administration, College Park, Maryland
- RG 59, General Records of the Department of State
- RG 84, Mexico City Embassy General Records

Radio XESQ Transcripts, in the possession of Javier Zavala Ortíz, San Miguel de Allende, Gto.

SEP: Secretaría de Educación Pública, Archivo Histórico, Mexico City, D.F.

SMHA: San Miguel History Archive, in the possession of Susan Beere, San Miguel de Allende, Gto.

SRE: Secretaría de Relaciones Exteriores, Archivos Concentraciones, Mexico City, D.F.

Sterling Memorial Library Map Collection, Yale University, New Haven, Connecticut

University of Texas at Austin, Perry-Castañeda Library Map Collection, Digital Archive

Yale Collection of American Literature, Beinecke Rare Book and Manuscript Library, New Haven, Connecticut
- Katharine Kuh Papers
- Mabel Dodge Luhan Papers

Published Works

Adams, Kathleen M. *Art as Politics: Re-Crafting Identities, Tourism, and Power in Tana Toraja, Indonesia.* Honolulu: University of Hawai'i Press, 2006.

Adams, Rachel. "Hipsters and *jipitecas*: Literary Countercultures on Both Sides of the Border." *American Literary History* 16, no. 1 (Spring 2004): 58–84.

Aguilar, Rosalia, et al. *San Miguel de Allende: Guía del visitante.* Mexico City: P.C. Editorial, 1993.

Agustín, José. *La contracultura en México: La historia y el significado de los rebeldes sin causa, los jipitecas, los punks y las bandas.* Mexico City: Editorial Grijalbo, 1996.

AHR Forum. "The International 1968." *American Historical Review* 114, nos. 1 and 2 (2009).

Alvah, Donna. *Unofficial Ambassadors: American Military Families Overseas and the Cold War, 1946–1965*. New York: New York University Press, 2007.

Amigos de San Miguel de Allende. *Guía de San Miguel de Allende*. Mexico City: Editorial Stylo, 1942.

Anhalt, Diana. *A Gathering of Fugitives: American Political Expatriates in Mexico, 1948–1965*. Santa Maria CA: Archer Books, 2001.

Archer, Christon I. "Death's Patriots—Celebration, Denunciation, and Memories of Mexico's Independence Heroes: Miguel Hidalgo, José María Morelos, and Agustín de Iturbide." In *Death, Dismemberment, and Memory: Body Politics in Latin America*, edited by Lyman L. Johnson, 63–104. Albuquerque: University of New Mexico Press, 2004.

Aveleyra Santos, Luis R., et al., eds. *Guanajuato en la voz de sus gobernadores: Compilación de Informes de Gobierno, 1917–1991*. Guanajuato: Gobierno del Estado de Guanajuato, 1991.

Avery, Kevin J. "Movies for Manifest Destiny: The Moving Panorama Phenomenon in America." In *The Grand Moving Panorama of Pilgrim's Progress*. Montclair NJ: Montclair Art Museum, 1999.

Babb, Sarah. *Managing Mexico: Economists from Nationalism to Neoliberalism*. Princeton: Princeton University Press, 2001.

Bachelor, Steven J. "Miracle on Ice: Industrial Workers and the Promise of Americanization in Cold War Mexico." In *In from the Cold: Latin America's New Encounter with the Cold War*, edited by Gilbert Joseph and Daniela Spenser, 253–72. Durham: Duke University Press, 2008.

———. "Toiling for the 'New Invaders': Autoworkers, Transnational Corporations, and Working-Class Culture in Mexico City, 1955–1968." In *Fragments of a Golden Age: The Politics of Culture in Mexico since 1940*, edited by Gilbert Joseph, Anne Rubenstein, and Eric Zolov, 273–326. Durham: Duke University Press, 2001.

Balderrama, Francisco E., and Raymond Rodríguez. *Decade of Betrayal: Mexican Repatriation in the 1930s*. Albuquerque: University of New Mexico Press, 1995.

Bandeira, Manuel. *Guia de Ouro Preto*. Rio de Janeiro: Ministerio da Educação e Saude, 1938.

Banks, Stephen P. "Identity Narratives by American and Canadian Retirees in Mexico." *Journal of Cross-Cultural Gerontology* 19, no. 4 (December 2004): 361–81.

Bantjes, Adrian A. "The Regional Dynamics of Anticlericalism and Defanaticization in Revolutionary Mexico." In *Faith and Impiety in Revolutionary Mexico*, edited by Matthew Butler, 111–30. New York: Palgrave Macmillan, 2007.

Bantman-Masum, Eve. "'You Need to Come Here . . . to See What Living Is Really About': Staging North American Expatriation in Merida (Mexico)." *Miranda* 5 (November 2011): 1–44. http://miranda.revues.org/2494.

Bastian, Jean-Pierre. "Protestants, Freemasons, and Spiritists: Non-Catholic Religious Sociabilities and Mexico's Revolutionary Movement, 1910–1920." In *Faith and Impiety in Revolutionary Mexico*, edited by Matthew Butler, 75–92. New York: Palgrave Macmillan, 2007.

Becker, Marjorie. *Setting the Virgin on Fire: Lázaro Cárdenas, Michoacán Peasants, and the Redemption of the Mexican Revolution*. Berkeley: University of California Press, 1995.

Bell-Villada, Gene H. *Overseas American: Growing Up Gringo in the Tropics*. Jackson: University Press of Mississippi, 2005.

Belmonte, Laura A., Mark Philip Bradley, Julio Capó Jr., Paul Farber, Shanon Fitzpatrick, Melani McAlister, David Minto, Michael Sherry, Naoko Shibusawa, and Penny Von Eschen. "Colloquy: Queering America and the World." *Diplomatic History* 40, no. 1 (January 2016): 19–80.

Berger, Dina. *The Development of Mexico's Tourism Industry: Pyramids by Day, Martinis by Night*. New York: Palgrave Macmillan, 2006.

Berger, Dina, and Andrew G. Wood, eds. *Holiday in Mexico: Critical Reflections on Tourism and Tourist Encounters*. Durham: Duke University Press, 2010.

Bixler, James P., and Virginia Bradley, eds. *The San Miguel Writer*. San Miguel de Allende: Instituto Allende, 1972.

Blancarte, Roberto. "Intransigence, Anticommunism, and Reconciliation: Church/State Relations in Transition." In *Dictablanda: Politics, Work, and Culture in Mexico, 1938–1968*, edited by Paul Gillingham and Benjamin T. Smith, 70–88. Durham: Duke University Press, 2014.

Blanco, Mónica. *Revolución y contienda política en Guanajuato (1908–1913)*. Mexico City: El Colegio de México and la Universidad Nacional Autónoma de México, 1995.

Blanco, Mónica, Alma Para, and Ethelia Ruiz Medrano. *Breve historia de Guanajuato*. Mexico City: Fideicomiso Historia de las Américas, 2000.

Bliss, Katherine Elaine. *Compromised Positions: Prostitution, Public Health, and Gender Politics in Revolutionary Mexico City*. University Park: Pennsylvania State University Press, 2001.

Bloom, Nicholas Dagen, ed. *Adventures into Mexico: American Tourism beyond the Border*. Lanham MD: Rowman & Littlefield, 2006.

Bloom, Nicholas Dagen. "To Be Served and Loved: The American Sense of Place in San Miguel de Allende." In *Adventures into Mexico: American Tourism beyond the Border*, edited by Nicholas Dagen Bloom, 191–218. Lanham MD: Rowman & Littlefield, 2006.

Blum, Ann S. "Conspicuous Benevolence: Liberalism, Public Welfare, and Private Charity in Porfirian Mexico City, 1877–1910." *The Americas* 58, no. 1 (July 2001): 7–38.

Bowman, Heath. *Death Is Incidental: A Story of Revolution*. Chicago: Willett, Clark & Company, 1937.

Brading, D. A. *Church and State in Bourbon Mexico: The Diocese of Michoacán, 1749–1810*. Cambridge: Cambridge University Press, 1994.

———. *Miners and Merchants in Bourbon Mexico, 1763–1810*. Cambridge: Cambridge University Press, 1971.

Brennan, Denise. *What's Love Got to Do with It? Transnational Desires and Sex Tourism in the Dominican Republic*. Durham: Duke University Press, 2004.

Brenner, Anita. *Your Mexican Holiday*. New York: G. P. Putnam's Sons, 1932.

Briggs, Charles L. *The Wood Carvers of Córdova, New Mexico: Social Dimensions of an Artistic "Revival."* Knoxville: University of Tennessee Press, 1980.

Britton, John A. *Revolution and Ideology: Images of the Mexican Revolution in the United States*. Lexington: University Press of Kentucky, 1995.

Bruey, Alison J. "Neoliberalism and Repression in 'Poblaciones' of Santiago de Chile." *Stockholm Review of Latin American Studies*, no. 5 (September 2009): 17–27.

Buchenau, Jürgen, ed. *Mexico OtherWise: Modern Mexico in the Eyes of Foreign Observers*. Albuquerque: University of New Mexico Press, 2005.

———. "Small Numbers, Great Impact: Mexico and Its Immigrants, 1821–1973." *Journal of American Ethnic History* 20, no. 3 (Spring 2001): 23–49.

Burke, Flannery. *From Greenwich Village to Taos: Primitivism and Place at Mabel Dodge Luhan's*. Lawrence: University Press of Kansas, 2008.

———. "Spud Johnson and a Gay Man's Place in the Taos Creative Arts Community." *Pacific Historical Review* 79, no. 1 (February 2010): 86–113.

Burkey, Stan. *People First: A Guide to Self-Reliant, Participatory Rural Development*. London: Zed Books, 1993.

Butler, Matthew. "Introduction: A Revolution in Spirit? Mexico, 1910–1940." In *Faith and Impiety in Revolutionary Mexico*, edited by Matthew Butler, 1–20. New York: Palgrave Macmillan, 2007.

———. "Trouble Afoot? Pilgrimage in *Cristero* Mexico City." In *Faith and Impiety in Revolutionary Mexico*, edited by Matthew Butler, 149–66. New York: Palgrave Macmillan, 2007.

Byrnes, Dolores M. *Driving the State: Families and Public Policy in Central Mexico*. Ithaca: Cornell University Press, 2003.

Cadava, Geraldo. *Standing on Common Ground: The Making of a Sunbelt Borderland*. Cambridge MA: Harvard University Press, 2013.

Cantú, Lionel, Jr. *The Sexuality of Migration: Border Crossings and Mexican Immigrant Men*. Edited by Nancy A. Naples and Salvador Vidal-Ortiz. New York: New York University Press, 2009.

Carden, Mary Paniocia. "'Adventures in Auto-Eroticism': Economies of Traveling Masculinity in Autobiographical Texts by Jack Kerouac and Neal Cassady." *Journeys* 7, no. 1 (Summer 2006): 1–25.

Cárdenas, Nicolás, and Mauricio Tenorio. "Mexico 1920s–1940s: Revolutionary Government, Reactionary Politics." In *Fascism Outside Europe: The European Impulse against Domestic Conditions in the Diffusion of Global Fascism*, edited by Stein Ugelvik Larsen, 593–632. Boulder: Social Science Monographs, 2001.

Carey, Elaine. *Plaza of Sacrifices: Gender, Power, and Terror in 1968 Mexico*. Albuquerque: University of New Mexico Press, 2005.

———. "'Selling Is More of a Habit Than Using': Narcotraficante Lola La Chata and Her Threat to Civilization, 1930–1960." *Journal of Women's History* 21, no. 2 (Summer 2009): 62–89.

Castellanos, M. Bianet. "Adolescent Migration to Cancún: Reconfiguring Maya Households and Gender Relations in Mexico's Yucatán Peninsula." *Frontiers* 28, no. 3 (2007): 1–27.

———. "Cancún and the Campo: Indigenous Migration and Tourism Development in the Yucatán Peninsula." In *Holiday in Mexico: Critical Reflections on Tourism and Tourist Encounters*, edited by Dina Berger and Andrew G. Wood, 241–64. Durham: Duke University Press, 2010.

Cervantes, Fernando. "Mexico's 'Ritual Constant': Religion and Liberty from Colony to Post-Revolution." In *Faith and Impiety in Revolutionary Mexico*, edited by Matthew Butler, 57–73. New York: Palgrave Macmillan, 2007.

Cervantes Jáuregui, Beatriz, and Ana María Crespo, eds. *Fiesta y tradición en San Miguel de Allende: Memoria de don Félix Luna*. Guanajuato: Instituto Estatal de la Cultura de Guanajuato, Ediciones la Rana, 1999.

Chao Romero, Robert. *The Chinese in Mexico, 1882–1940*. Tucson: University of Arizona Press, 2011.

Chowning, Margaret. *Rebellious Nuns: The Troubled History of a Mexican Convent*. Oxford: Oxford University Press, 2006.

Clancy, Michael. *Exporting Paradise: Tourism and Development in Mexico*. London: Pergamon, 2001.

Clarke, Kamari Maxine. *Mapping Yoruba Networks: Power and Agency in the Making of Transnational Communities.* Durham: Duke University Press, 2004.

Coffey, Mary K. "Marketing Mexico's Great Masters: Folk Art Tourism and the Neoliberal Politics of Exhibition." In *Holiday in Mexico: Critical Reflections on Tourism and Tourist Encounters,* edited by Dina Berger and Andrew G. Wood, 265–91. Durham: Duke University Press, 2010.

Cohen, Deborah. *Braceros: Migrant Citizens and Transnational Subjects in the Postwar United States and Mexico.* Chapel Hill: University of North Carolina Press, 2011.

Corbin, Alain. *Village Bells: Sound and Meaning in the Nineteenth-Century French Countryside.* Translated by Martin Thom. New York: Columbia University Press, 1998.

Correa, Phyllis M. "Sharecropping and Agrarian Reform in the Township of Allende, Guanajuato." In *Memorias: San Miguel de Allende, Cruce de Caminos,* edited by Jorge F. Hernández and Don Patterson, 153–68. León, Gto.: Impresas ABC, 2006.

Cossío del Pomar, Felipe. *Cossío del Pomar en San Miguel de Allende.* Madrid: Playor, 1974.

———. *Iridiscencia: Crónica de un centro de arte.* Guanajuato: Gobierno del Estado de Guanajuato, 1988.

Covert, Lisa Pinley. "The GI Bill Abroad: A Postwar Experiment in International Relations." *Diplomatic History* 40, no. 2 (April 2016): 244–68.

———. "The Political Economy of Mexico's Independence Heroes: Selling Public History in San Miguel de Allende." *Latin Americanist* 54, no. 4 (December 2010): 29–46.

Cowan, Benjamin. "Sex and the Security State: Gender, Sexuality, and 'Subversion' at Brazil's Escola Superior de Guerra, 1964–1985." *Journal of the History of Sexuality* 16, no. 3 (September 2007): 459–81.

———. "'Why Hasn't This Teacher Been Shot?' Moral-Sex Panic, the Repressive Right, and Brazil's National Security State." *Hispanic American Historical Review* 92, no. 3 (2012): 403–36.

Croucher, Sheila. "Migrants of Privilege: The Political Transnationalism of Americans in Mexico." *Identities: Global Studies in Culture and Power* 16, no. 4 (2009): 463–91.

———. *The Other Side of the Fence: American Migrants in Mexico.* Austin: University of Texas Press, 2009.

Cruz López, Graciela. "Vínculos omnipotentes: El cabildo español de la villa de San Miguel el Grande, siglo XVIII." In *Memorias: San Miguel de Allende, Cruce de Caminos,* edited by Jorge F. Hernández and Don Patterson, 69–89. León, Gto.: Impresos ABC, 2006.

Curley, Robert. "'The First Encounter': Catholic Politics in Revolutionary Jalisco, 1917–19." In *Faith and Impiety in Revolutionary Mexico*, edited by Matthew Butler, 131–48. New York: Palgrave Macmillan, 2007.

de Grazia, Victoria. *Irresistible Empire: America's Advance through Twentieth-Century Europe*. Cambridge MA: Belknap Press of Harvard University Press, 2005.

de la Cadena, Marisol. *Indigenous Mestizos: Race and the Politics of Representation in Cuzco, 1919–1991*. Durham: Duke University Press, 2000.

de la Rosa, Natalia. "David Alfaro Siqueiros en el Instituto Politécnico Nacional: Amo o esclavo, herramientas modernas, y vehículos plásticos." In *(Ready) Media: Hacia una arqueología de los medios y la invención en México*, edited by Karla Jasso and Daniel Garza Usabiaga, 85–100. Mexico City: Instituto Nacional de Bellas Artes y Literatura/CONACULTA, 2012.

Dean, Douglas. *Douglas Dean's Gay Mexico*. San Francisco: Barbary Coast Publications, 1973.

de la Maza, Francisco. *San Miguel de Allende: Su historia, sus monumentos*. 2nd ed. Mexico City: Frente de Afirmación Hispanista, 1972.

Delpar, Helen. *The Enormous Vogue of Things Mexican: Cultural Relations between the United States and Mexico, 1920–1935*. Tuscaloosa: University of Alabama Press, 1992.

Denham, Alice. *Secrets of San Miguel*. Chapel Hill: Madeira Press, 2013.

Dennis, Philip A. "The Anti-Chinese Campaigns in Sonora, Mexico." *Ethnohistory* 26, no. 1 (Winter 1979): 65–80.

Dickerson, Grace Leslie. *Sketchbook of San Miguel de Allende*. New York: Vantage Press, 1964.

Dickinson, Stirling. Escuela Universitaria de Bellas Artes Catalog. N.p., 1940.

Dinius, Oliver, and Angela Vergara. "Company Towns in the Americas: An Introduction." In *Company Towns in the Americas: Landscape, Power, and Working-Class Communities*, edited by Angela Vergara and Oliver Dinius, 1–20. Athens: University of Georgia Press, 2011.

Dixon, David, Julie Murray, and Julia Gelatt. *America's Emigrants: U.S. Retirement Migration to Mexico and Panama*. Washington DC: Migration Policy Institute, 2006.

Dormady, Jason. *Primitive Revolution: Restorationist Religion and the Idea of the Mexican Revolution, 1940–1968*. Albuquerque: University of New Mexico Press, 2011.

Dunn, Timothy J. *The Militarization of the U.S.-Mexico Border, 1978–1992: Low-Intensity Conflict Doctrine Comes Home*. Austin: Center for Mexican American Studies, the University of Texas at Austin, 1996.

Durand, Jorge, ed. *Braceros: Las miradas mexicana y estadounidense (1945–1964)*. Mexico City: Miguel Ángel Porrúa, 2007.

Enloe, Cynthia. *Bananas, Beaches and Bases: Making Feminist Sense of International Politics*. Updated ed. Berkeley: University of California Press, 2000.

Faber, Sebastiaan. *Exile and Cultural Hegemony: Spanish Intellectuals in Mexico, 1939–1975*. Nashville: Vanderbilt University Press, 2002.

Fallaw, Ben. *Religion and State Formation in Postrevolutionary Mexico*. Durham: Duke University Press, 2013.

Farnsworth-Alvear, Ann. *Dulcinea in the Factory: Myths, Morals, Men, and Women in Colombia's Industrial Experiment*. Durham: Duke University Press, 2000.

Fein, Seth. "Culture across Borders in the Americas." *History Compass* (January 2003). doi:10.1111/1478-0542.025.

———. "From Collaboration to Containment: Hollywood and the International Political Economy of Mexican Cinema after the Second World War." In *Mexico's Cinema: A Century of Film and Filmmakers*, edited by Joanne Hershfield and David R. Maciel, 123–63. Wilmington DE: Scholarly Resources, 1999.

———. "Myths of Cultural Imperialism and Nationalism in Golden Age Mexican Cinema." In *Fragments of a Golden Age: The Politics of Culture in Mexico since 1940*, edited by Gilbert Joseph, Anne Rubenstein, and Eric Zolov, 159–98. Durham: Duke University Press, 2001.

———. "Producing the Cold War in Mexico: The Public Limits of Covert Communications." In *In from the Cold: Latin America's New Encounter with the Cold War*, edited by Gilbert M. Joseph and Daniela Spenser, 171–213. Durham: Duke University Press, 2008.

Friedman, Max Paul. *Nazis and Good Neighbors: The United States Campaign against the Germans of Latin America in World War II*. Cambridge: Cambridge University Press, 2003.

Galindo, Sergio. *Nudo*. Mexico City: Editorial Joaquín Mortiz, 1970.

Galloway, Margaret Cecilia. *Margaret Cecilia Galloway: Her Book*. San Miguel de Allende: n.p., 2004.

García y García, Enrique. *El agua en San Miguel de Allende: Ayer, hoy y mañana*. San Miguel de Allende: PTF, 2006.

Gauss, Susan M. *Made in Mexico: Regions, Nation, and the State in the Rise of Mexican Industrialism, 1920s–1940s*. University Park: Pennsylvania State University Press, 2010.

Gellman, Irwin F. *Good Neighbor Diplomacy: United States Policies in Latin America, 1933–1945*. Baltimore: Johns Hopkins University Press, 1979.

Gilbert, Alan. "The Housing of the Urban Poor." In *Cities, Poverty, and Development: Urbanization in the Third World*, edited by Alan Gilbert and Josef Gugler, 81–115. Oxford: Oxford University Press, 1982.

Gille, Judith L. *The View from Casa Chepitos: A Journey beyond the Border*. Seattle: Davis Bay Press, 2013.

Gillingham, Paul. *Cuauhtémoc's Bones: Forging National Identity in Modern Mexico*. Albuquerque: University of New Mexico Press, 2011.

Gillingham, Paul, and Benjamin T. Smith, eds. *Dictablanda: Politics, Work, and Culture in Mexico, 1938–1968*. Durham: Duke University Press, 2014.

Gillingham, Paul, and Benjamin T. Smith. "Introduction: The Paradoxes of Revolution." In *Dictablanda: Politics, Work, and Culture in Mexico, 1938–1968*, edited by Paul Gillingham and Benjamin T. Smith, 1–43. Durham: Duke University Press, 2014.

Gómez-Galvarriato, Aurora. "From Company Towns to Union Towns: Textile Workers and the Revolutionary State in Mexico." In *Company Towns in the Americas: Landscape, Power, and Working-Class Communities*, edited by Angela Vergara and Oliver Dinius, 45–67. Athens: University of Georgia Press, 2011.

——. *Industry and Revolution: Social and Economic Change in the Orizaba Valley, Mexico*. Cambridge MA: Harvard University Press, 2013.

González, Gilbert G. *Culture of Empire: American Writers, Mexico, and Mexican Immigrants, 1880–1930*. Austin: University of Texas Press, 2004.

González, Simón. *Síntesis histórica de San Miguel de Allende*. San Miguel de Allende: n.p., 1969.

González y González, Luis. *San José de Gracia: Mexican Village in Transition*. Translated by John Upton. Austin: University of Texas Press, 1974.

Gordillo, Luz María. *Mexican Women and the Other Side of Immigration: Engendering Transnational Ties*. Austin: University of Texas Press, 2010.

Gould, Jeffrey L. "Solidarity under Siege: The Latin American Left, 1968." *American Historical Review* 114, no. 2 (April 2009): 348–75.

Green, James N. *Beyond Carnival: Male Homosexuality in Twentieth-Century Brazil*. Chicago: University of Chicago Press, 1999.

——. "'Who Is the Macho Who Wants to Kill Me?' Male Homosexuality, Revolutionary Masculinity, and the Brazilian Armed Struggle of the 1960s and 1970s." *Hispanic American Historical Review* 92, no. 3 (August 2012): 437–69.

Green, Nancy L. "Expatriation, Expatriates, and Expats: The American Transformation of a Concept." *American Historical Review* 114, no. 2 (April 2009): 307–28.

Greenhaw, Wayne. *My Heart Is in the Earth: True Stories of Alabama and Mexico.* Montgomery AL: River City Publishing, 2001.

Guerra, Lillian. *Visions of Power in Cuba: Revolution, Redemption, and Resistance, 1959–1971.* Chapel Hill: University of North Carolina Press, 2012.

Guerrero Tarquín, Alfredo. *Memorias de un agrarista.* Mexico City: Instituto Nacional de Antropología e Historia, 1987.

Guevara Sanginés, María. "Participación de los africanos en el desarollo del Guanajuato colonial." In *Prescencia africana en México*, edited by Luz María Martínez Montiel, 133–98. Mexico City: Consejo Nacional para la Cultura y las Artes, 1997.

Gutmann, Matthew C. *The Meanings of Macho: Being a Man in Mexico City.* Berkeley: University of California Press, 1996.

Guy, Donna J. *Sex and Danger in Buenos Aires: Prostitution, Family, and Nation in Argentina.* Lincoln: University of Nebraska Press, 1991.

———. *Women Build the Welfare State: Performing Charity and Creating Rights in Argentina, 1880–1955.* Durham: Duke University Press, 2009.

Hail, John. *To Mexico with Love: San Miguel with Side Dishes.* New York: Exposition Press, 1966.

Hall, Catherine. *Civilising Subjects: Colony and Metropole in the English Imagination, 1830–1867.* Chicago: University of Chicago Press, 2002.

Hämäläinen, Pekka, and Samuel Truett. "On Borderlands." *Journal of American History* 98, no. 2 (September 2011): 338–61.

Hamill, Hugh M. "Experiments in International Living: American College Students, Mexicans for a Summer, Become Members of Households in Colonial Guanajuato." *National Geographic*, March 1953, 322–50.

Hart, John Mason. *Empire and Revolution: The Americans in Mexico since the Civil War.* Berkeley: University of California Press, 2002.

Hartwell, Nancy. *Señorita Okay.* New York: Holt, Rinehart and Winston, 1956.

Harvey, David. *A Brief History of Neoliberalism.* Oxford: Oxford University Press, 2005.

———. *The Condition of Postmodernity: An Enquiry into the Origins of Cultural Change.* Oxford: Blackwell, 1990.

Hayward, Ruth. "La Casa de la Turca." In *Solamente in San Miguel: Writings from the Authors' Sala of San Miguel de Allende*, edited by Cris K. A. Dimarco, 153–63. Port Orchard WA: Windstorm Creative, 2007.

Hernández, Jorge F. *La soledad del silencio: Microhistoria del santuario de Atotonilco.* Mexico City: Universidad de Guanajuato and Fondo de Cultura Económica, 1991.

Hernández, Jorge F., and Don Patterson, eds. *Memorias: San Miguel de Allende, Cruce de Caminos.* León, Gto.: Impresos ABC, 2006.

Herner, Irene. "Siqueiros, una lección mural en San Miguel de Allende." In *Cómo se pinta un mural*, by David Alfaro Siqueiros, 47–54. Guanajuato: Ediciones La Rana, 1998.

Hershfield, Joanne. *Imagining la Chica Moderna: Women, Nation, and Visual Culture in Mexico, 1917–1936*. Durham: Duke University Press, 2008.

Hoffnung-Garskof, Jesse. *A Tale of Two Cities: Santo Domingo and New York after 1950*. Princeton: Princeton University Press, 2008.

Hunt, Michael H. *Ideology and U.S. Foreign Policy*. New Haven: Yale University Press, 1987.

Huyssen, David. *Progressive Inequality: Rich and Poor in New York, 1890–1920*. Cambridge MA: Harvard University Press, 2014.

Ignatius of Loyola, Saint. *The Spiritual Exercises of St. Ignatius: Based on Studies in the Language of the Autograph*. Translated by Louis J. Puhl, S.J. 1545. New York: Vintage Books, 2000.

Irwin, Julia F. *Making the World Safe: The American Red Cross and a Nation's Humanitarian Awakening*. Oxford: Oxford University Press, 2013.

Jiménez Codinach, Guadalupe. "Memorias de una villa rebelde: San Miguel el Grande en la independencia de Nueva España." In *Memorias: San Miguel de Allende, Cruce de Caminos*, edited by Jorge F. Hernández and Don Patterson, 103–17. León, Gto.: Impresos ABC, 2006.

Johnson, David K. *The Lavender Scare: The Cold War Persecution of Gays and Lesbians in the Federal Government*. Chicago: University of Chicago Press, 2004.

Joseph, Gilbert, Catherine LeGrand, and Ricardo Salvatore, eds. *Close Encounters of Empire: Writing the Cultural History of U.S.-Latin American Relations*. Durham: Duke University Press, 1998.

Joseph, Gilbert M., Anne Rubenstein, and Eric Zolov. "Assembling the Fragments: Writing a Cultural History of Mexico since 1940." In *Fragments of a Golden Age: The Politics of Culture in Mexico since 1940*, edited by Gilbert M. Joseph, Anne Rubenstein, and Eric Zolov, 3–22. Durham: Duke University Press, 2001.

Joseph, Gilbert M., Anne Rubenstein, and Eric Zolov, eds. *Fragments of a Golden Age: The Politics of Culture in Mexico since 1940*. Durham: Duke University Press, 2001.

Kerouac, Jack. *On the Road*. 50th anniversary ed. New York: Viking Penguin, 2007.

Kesey, Ken. *Demon Box*. New York: Viking, 1986.

Klein, Christina. *Cold War Orientalism: Asia in the Middlebrow Imagination, 1945–1961*. Berkeley: University of California Press, 2003.

Knight, Alan. "The Mentality and Modus Operandi of Revolutionary Anticlericalism." In *Faith and Impiety in Revolutionary Mexico*, edited by Matthew Butler, 21–56. New York: Palgrave Macmillan, 2007.

———. *The Mexican Revolution.* Vol. 1, *Porfirians, Liberals and Peasants.* Cambridge: Cambridge University Press, 1986.

———. *The Mexican Revolution.* Vol. 2, *Counter-Revolution and Reconstruction.* Lincoln: University of Nebraska Press, 1986.

Kreitlow, Bert. "The Political Economy of Preserving the Past: The Rio Blanco Mill in Mexico." *Perspectives on History,* March 1999. https://www.historians.org/publications-and-directories/perspectives-on-history/march-1999/the-political-economy-of-preserving-the-past-the-rio-blanco-mill-in-mexico.

Kropp, Phoebe S. *California Vieja: Culture and Memory in a Modern American Place.* Berkeley: University of California Press, 2006.

La Fond, H. R. *How, When, and Where to Tour Mexico.* Oakland CA: Fontes Printing, 1951.

Langland, Victoria. "Birth Control Pills and Molotov Cocktails: Reading Sex and Revolution in 1968 Brazil." In *In from the Cold: Latin America's New Encounter with the Cold War,* edited by Gilbert Joseph and Daniela Spenser, 308–49. Durham: Duke University Press, 2008.

———. *Speaking of Flowers: Student Movements and the Making and Remembering of 1968 in Military Brazil.* Durham: Duke University Press, 2013.

Leach, Edmund. "Magical Hair." 1958. In *The Essential Edmund Leach,* edited by Stephen Hugh-Jones and James Laidlaw, 177–201. New Haven: Yale University Press, 2000.

Lears, T. J. Jackson. *No Place of Grace: Antimodernism and the Transformation of American Culture, 1880–1920.* New York: Pantheon, 1981.

Levinson, Bradley A. U. *We Are All Equal: Student Culture and Identity at a Mexican Secondary School, 1988–1998.* Durham: Duke University Press, 2001.

Lipman, Jana K. *Guantánamo: A Working-Class History between Empire and Revolution.* Berkeley: University of California Press, 2009.

Lomnitz, Claudio. *Death and the Idea of Mexico.* New York: Zone Books, 2008.

———. *Deep Mexico, Silent Mexico: An Anthropology of Nationalism.* Minneapolis: University of Minnesota Press, 2001.

———. "Narrating the Neoliberal Moment: History, Journalism, Historicity." *Public Culture* 20, no. 1 (Winter 2008): 39–56.

López, Rick A. *Crafting Mexico: Intellectuals, Artisans, and the State after the Revolution.* Durham: Duke University Press, 2010.

López Espinoza, José C. *Estampas sanmiguelenses.* Vol. 3. Mexico City: Presidencia Municipal de San Miguel de Allende, Guanajuato, 2006.

———. "Sucesos importantes en San Miguel de Allende en el siglo XX." In *Memorias: San Miguel de Allende, Cruce de Caminos,* edited by Jorge F. Hernández and Don Patterson, 239–43. León, Gto.: Impresos ABC, 2006.

Macías-González, Victor M. "The Transnational Homophile Movement and the Development of Domesticity in Mexico City's Homosexual Community, 1930–70." *Gender & History* 26, no. 3 (November 2014): 519–44.

Malo Zozaya, Miguel J. *Guía turista en San Miguel de Allende.* San Miguel de Allende: Instituto Allende, 1958.

Malo Zozaya, Miguel J., and F. León de Vivero. *San Miguel Allende: Guía oficial.* Mexico City: Instituto Nacional de Antropología e Historia, 1963.

Manzano, Valeria. "Sexualizing Youth: Morality Campaigns and Representations of Youth in Early 1960s Buenos Aires." *Journal of the History of Sexuality* 14, no. 4 (October 2005): 433–61.

Martin, Lawrence, and Sylvia Martin. *The Standard Guide to Mexico and the Caribbean.* New York: Funk & Wagnalls, 1954.

May, Elaine Tyler. *Homeward Bound: American Families in the Cold War Era.* New York: Basic Books, 1988.

McAlister, Melani. *Epic Encounters: Culture, Media, and U.S. Interests in the Middle East, 1945–2000.* Berkeley: University of California Press, 2001.

McNally, Andrew, and Evalyn McNally. *This Is Mexico.* New York: Dodd, Mead, 1947.

Mercadillo Miranda, José. *Anécdotas sin importancia.* San Miguel de Allende: Impresa San Miguel, 1960.

———. *El venerado e histórico Santuario de Atotonilco, Guanajuato.* 2nd ed. San Luis Potosí: Al Libro Mayor, 1984.

———. *La pintura mural del Santuario de Atotonilco.* Translated by Gladys J. Bonfiglio. Mexico City: Editorial Jus, 1950.

Merrill, Dennis. *Negotiating Paradise: U.S. Tourism and Empire in Twentieth-Century Latin America.* Chapel Hill: University of North Carolina Press, 2009.

Mexican National Railroad. *Mexico: Tropical Tours to Toltec Towns.* Chicago: Knight, Leonard, 1892.

Meyer, Jean. *The Cristero Rebellion: The Mexican People between Church and State.* Translated by Richard Southern. Cambridge: Cambridge University Press, 1976.

———. *El sinarquismo: ¿Un fascismo mexicano? 1937–1947.* Mexico City: Editorial Joaquín Mortiz, 1979.

———. "An Idea of Mexico: Catholics in the Revolution." In *The Eagle and the Virgin: Nation and Cultural Revolution in Mexico, 1920–1940,* edited by Mary Kay Vaughan and Stephen E. Lewis, 281–96. Durham: Duke University Press, 2006.

Missouri Pacific Lines. *Mexico: A Foreign Land a Step Away.* N.p., 1929.

Mojica, Fray José Francisco de Guadalupe. *I, a Sinner.* Translated by Fanchon Royer. Chicago: Franciscan Herald Press, 1963.

Montgomery, Charles H. *The Spanish Redemption: Heritage, Power, and Loss on New Mexico's Upper Rio Grande.* Berkeley: University of California Press, 2002.

Moreno, Julio. *Yankee Don't Go Home! Mexican Nationalism, American Business Culture, and the Shaping of Modern Mexico, 1920–1950.* Chapel Hill: University of North Carolina Press, 2003.

Morton, Ward M. *Woman Suffrage in Mexico.* Gainesville: University of Florida Press, 1962.

Mraz, John. "Today, Tomorrow, and Always: The Golden Age of Illustrated Magazines in Mexico, 1937–1960." In *Fragments of a Golden Age: The Politics of Culture in Mexico since 1940,* edited by Gilbert M. Joseph, Anne Rubenstein, and Eric Zolov, 116–57. Durham: Duke University Press, 2001.

Murphy, Gretchen. *Hemispheric Imaginings: The Monroe Doctrine and Narratives of U.S. Empire.* Durham: Duke University Press, 2005.

Newcomer, Daniel. *Reconciling Modernity: Urban State Formation in 1940s León, Mexico.* Lincoln: University of Nebraska Press, 2004.

Nieto Gamiño, Luis Felipe. "Los asentamientos prehispánicos de la cuenca central del río Laja." In *Memorias: San Miguel de Allende, Cruce de Caminos,* edited by Jorge F. Hernández and Don Patterson, 43–54. León, Gto.: Impresos ABC, 2006.

Ninkovich, Frank A. *The Diplomacy of Ideas: U.S. Foreign Policy and Cultural Relations, 1938–1950.* Cambridge: Cambridge University Press, 1981.

Norman, James. "Prologue." In *Mexican Hill Town.* Photographs by Allan W. Kahn. Santa Monica CA: Fisher-Edwards, 1963.

Oever, Roel van den. *Mama's Boy: Momism and Homophobia in Postwar American Culture.* New York: Palgrave Macmillan, 2012.

Olcott, Jocelyn. *Revolutionary Women in Postrevolutionary Mexico.* Durham: Duke University Press, 2005.

Olcott, Jocelyn, Mary Kay Vaughan, and Gabriela Cano, eds. *Sex in Revolution: Gender, Politics, and Power in Modern Mexico.* Durham: Duke University Press, 2006.

Oles, James. "Walls to Paint On: American Muralists in Mexico, 1933–1936." PhD diss., Yale University, 1995.

Olivé Negrete, Julio César, and Augusto Urteaga Castro-Pozo, eds. *INAH, una historia.* Mexico City: Instituto Nacional de Antropología e Historia, 1988.

Orozco, José. "'Esos Altos de Jalisco!' Emigration and the Idea of Alteño Exceptionalism, 1926–1952." PhD diss., Harvard University, 1998.

Otero, Lorena Melton Young. "U.S. Retired Persons in Mexico." *American Behavioral Scientist* 40, no. 7 (June–July 1997): 914–22.

Overmyer-Velázquez, Mark. *Visions of the Emerald City: Modernity, Tradition, and the Formation of Porfirian Oaxaca, Mexico.* Durham: Duke University Press, 2006.

Palacios, Joseph M. *The Catholic Social Imagination: Activism and the Just Society in Mexico and the United States.* Chicago: University of Chicago Press, 2007.

Palma Mora, Mónica. *De tierras extrañas: Un estudio sobre inmigración en México, 1950–1990.* Mexico City: Instituto Nacional de Antropología e Historia / Instituto Nacional de Migración / Centro de Estudios Migratorios, 2006.

———. *Veteranos de guerra norteamericanos en Guadalajara.* Mexico City: Instituto Nacional de Antropología e Historia, 1990.

Patterson, Don. *Journey to Xibalba: A Life in Archaeology.* Albuquerque: University of New Mexico Press, 2007.

Paz, Octavio. *The Labyrinth of Solitude and Other Writings.* Translated by Lysander Kemp, Yara Milos, and Rachel Philips Belash. New York: Grove Press, 1985.

Pells, Richard. *Not Like Us: How Europeans Have Loved, Hated, and Transformed American Culture since World War II.* New York: Basic Books, 1997.

Pensado, Jaime M. *Rebel Mexico: Student Unrest and Authoritarian Political Culture during the Long Sixties.* Stanford CA: Stanford University Press, 2013.

Pessar, Patricia. *From Fanatics to Folk: Brazilian Millenarianism and Popular Culture.* Durham: Duke University Press, 2004.

Pérez, Louis A. *On Becoming Cuban: Identity, Nationality, and Culture.* Chapel Hill: University of North Carolina, 1999.

Piccato, Pablo. *The Tyranny of Public Opinion: Honor in the Construction of the Mexican Public Sphere.* Durham: Duke University Press, 2010.

Piester, Kerianne. "Targeting the Poor: The Politics of Social Policy Reforms in Mexico." In *The New Politics of Inequality in Latin America: Rethinking Participation and Representation*, edited by Douglas A. Chalmers et al., 469–88. Oxford: Oxford University Press, 1997.

Pike, Fredrick. *FDR's Good Neighbor Policy: Sixty Years of Generally Gentle Chaos.* Austin: University of Texas Press, 1995.

Pilcher, Jeffrey M. *Cantinflas and the Chaos of Mexican Modernity.* Wilmington DE: SR Books, 2001.

———. "Mexico's Pepsi Challenge: Traditional Cooking, Mass Consumption, and National Identity." In *Fragments of a Golden Age: The Politics of Culture in Mexico since 1940*, edited by Gilbert Joseph, Anne Rubenstein, and Eric Zolov, 71–90. Durham: Duke University Press, 2001.

Plummer, Brenda Gayle. "Brown Babies: Race, Gender, and Policy after World War II." In *Window on Freedom: Race, Civil Rights, and Foreign Affairs, 1945–1988*, edited by Brenda Gayle Plummer, 67–91. Chapel Hill: University of North Carolina Press, 2003.

Poole, Deborah. "Landscape and the Imperial Subject: U.S. Images of the Andes, 1859–1930." In *Close Encounters of Empire: Writing the Cultural History of U.S.-Latin American Relations*, edited by Gilbert M. Joseph, Catherine C. LeGrand, and Ricardo D. Salvatore, 106–38. Durham: Duke University Press, 1998.

Potash, Robert. *Mexican Government and Industrial Development in the Early Republic: The Banco de Avío.* Amherst: University of Massachusetts Press, 1983.

Pratt, Mary Louise. *Imperial Eyes: Travel Writing and Transculturation.* New York: Routledge, 1992.

Purnell, Jennie. *Popular Movements and State Formation in Revolutionary Mexico: The Agraristas and Cristeros of Michoacán.* Durham: Duke University Press, 1999.

Rak, Mary Kidder. *Border Patrol.* Boston: Houghton Mifflin, 1938.

Ramírez, Catherine S. *The Woman in the Zoot Suit: Gender, Nationalism, and the Cultural Politics of Memory.* Durham: Duke University Press, 2009.

Reich, Peter Lester. *Mexico's Hidden Revolution: The Catholic Church in Law and Politics since 1929.* Notre Dame IN: University of Notre Dame Press, 1995.

Renda, Mary. *Taking Haiti: Military Occupation and the Culture of U.S. Imperialism, 1915–1940.* Chapel Hill: University of North Carolina Press, 2001.

Roorda, Eric Paul. *The Dictator Next Door: The Good Neighbor Policy and the Trujillo Regime in the Dominican Republic, 1930–1945.* Durham: Duke University Press, 1998.

Rosemblatt, Karin Alejandra. *Gendered Compromises: Political Cultures and the State in Chile, 1920–1950.* Chapel Hill: University of North Carolina Press, 2000.

Rosenberg, Emily S. *Spreading the American Dream: American Economic and Cultural Expansion, 1890–1945.* New York: Hill and Wang, 1982.

Rothman, Hal. *Devil's Bargains: Tourism in the Twentieth-Century American West.* Lawrence: University Press of Kansas, 1998.

Rowland, Donald W. *History of the Office of the Coordinator of Inter-American Affairs.* Historical Reports on War Administration. Washington DC: Government Printing Office, 1947.

Ruas, Eponina. *Ouro Preto: Sua história, seus templos e monumentos.* Rio de Janeiro: Departamento de Imprensa Nacional, 1950.

Rubenstein, Anne. *Bad Language, Naked Ladies, and Other Threats to the Nation: A Political History of Comic Books in Mexico.* Durham: Duke University Press, 1998.

———. "Bodies, Cities, Cinema: Pedro Infante's Death as Political Spectacle." In *Fragments of a Golden Age: The Politics of Culture in Mexico since 1940*, edited by Gilbert M. Joseph, Anne Rubenstein, and Eric Zolov, 199–233. Durham: Duke University Press, 2001.

———. "The War on 'Las Pelonas': Modern Women and Their Enemies, Mexico City, 1924." In *Sex in Revolution: Gender, Politics, and Power in Modern Mexico*, edited by Jocelyn Olcott, Mary Kay Vaughan, and Gabriela Cano, 57–80. Durham: Duke University Press, 2006.

Ruiz, Jason. *Americans in the Treasure House: Travel to Porfirian Mexico and the Cultural Politics of Empire*. Austin: University of Texas Press, 2014.

Ruíz Valenzuela, Antonio. *El reverendo Monseñor José Mercadillo Miranda, prelado de honor de su santidad, algo acerca de su actuación como bibliógrafo, literato, poeta, maestro en bellas artes, pintor y compositor musical*. San Miguel de Allende: n.p., 1977.

Sackett, Andrew. "The Making of Acapulco: People, Land, and the State in the Development of the Mexican Riviera, 1927–1973." PhD diss., Yale University, 2009.

———. "The Two Faces of Acapulco during the Golden Age." In *The Mexico Reader: History, Culture, Politics*, edited by Gilbert M. Joseph and Timothy J. Henderson, 500–510. Durham: Duke University Press, 2002.

Salvatore, Ricardo D. "The Enterprise of Knowledge: Representational Machines of Informal Empire." In *Close Encounters of Empire: Writing the Cultural History of U.S.-Latin American Relations*, edited by Gilbert M. Joseph, Catherine C. LeGrand, and Ricardo D. Salvatore, 69–104. Durham: Duke University Press, 1998.

Salvucci, Richard J. "Aspectos de un conflicto empresarial: El obraje de Balthasar de Sauto y la historia social de San Miguel el Grande, 1756–1771." *Anuario de Estudios Americanos* 36 (1979): 405–43.

———. *Textiles and Capitalism in Mexico: An Economic History of the Obrajes, 1539–1840*. Princeton: Princeton University Press, 1987.

Sánchez Díaz, Alfonso, ed. *La guerra cristera en Guanajuato*. Guanajuato: Ediciones La Rana, 2005.

Sánchez Rangel, Oscar. "La transición revolucionaria en San Miguel de Allende." In *Memorias: San Miguel de Allende, Cruce de Caminos*, edited by Jorge F. Hernández and Don Patterson, 129–37. León, Gto.: Impresos ABC, 2006.

Sanders, Nichole. *Gender and Welfare in Mexico: The Consolidation of a Postrevolutionary State*. University Park: Pennsylvania State University Press, 2011.

———. "Mothering Mexico: The Historiography of Mothers and Motherhood in 20th-Century Mexico." *History Compass* 7, no. 6 (2009): 1542–53.

Santiago, Myrna I. *The Ecology of Oil: Environment, Labor, and the Mexican Revolution, 1900–1938*. Cambridge: Cambridge University Press, 2006.

Santiago Silva, José de. *Atotonilco: Alfaro y Pocasangre*. Guanajuato: Ediciones La Rana, 2004.

Saragoza, Alex. "Golfing in the Desert: Los Cabos and Post-PRI Tourism in Mexico." In *Holiday in Mexico: Critical Reflections on Tourism and Tourist Encounters*, edited by Dina Berger and Andrew G. Wood, 295–319. Durham: Duke University Press, 2010.

———. "The Selling of Mexico: Tourism and the State, 1929–1952." In *Fragments of a Golden Age: The Politics of Culture in Mexico since 1940*, edited by Gilbert Joseph, Anne Rubenstein, and Eric Zolov, 91–115. Durham: Duke University Press, 2001.

Sassen, Saskia. *The Global City: New York, London, Tokyo*. 2nd ed. Princeton: Princeton University Press, 2001.

Scanlon, Arlene Patricia. *Un enclave cultural: Poder y etnicidad en el contexto de una escuela norteamericana en México*. Mexico City: Centro de Investigaciones y Estudios Superiores en Antropología Social, Ediciones de la Casa Chata, 1984.

Schell, Patience A. "Social Catholicism, Modern Consumption, and the Culture Wars in Postrevolutionary Mexico City." *History Compass* 5, no. 5 (2007): 1585–1603.

Schell, William, Jr. *Integral Outsiders: The American Colony in Mexico City, 1876–1911*. Wilmington DE: SR Books, 2001.

Schmidt, Arthur. "Making It Real Compared to What? Reconceptualizing Mexican History since 1940." In *Fragments of a Golden Age: The Politics of Culture in Mexico since 1940*, edited by Gilbert M. Joseph, Anne Rubenstein, and Eric Zolov, 21–68. Durham: Duke University Press, 2001.

Schmidt Camacho, Alicia. *Migrant Imaginaries: Latino Cultural Politics in the U.S.-Mexico Borderlands*. New York: New York University Press, 2008.

Schoultz, Lars. *Beneath the United States: A History of U.S. Policy toward Latin America*. Cambridge MA: Harvard University Press, 1998.

Schreiber, Rebecca Mina. *Cold War Exiles in Mexico: U.S. Dissidents and the Culture of Critical Resistance*. Minneapolis: University of Minnesota Press, 2008.

Schwartz, Rosalie. *Flying Down to Rio: Hollywood, Tourists, and Yankee Clippers*. College Station: Texas A&M University Press, 2004.

———. *Pleasure Island: Tourism and Temptation in Cuba*. Lincoln: University of Nebraska Press, 1997.

Sepúlveda Garza, Manola. "Historias rancheras: La lucha por la tierra en la hacienda Ciénega de Juana Ruiz, municipio de San Miguel de Allende." In *Guanajuato: Aportaciones recientes para su estudio*, edited by Patricia Moctezuma Yano, Juan Carlos Ruiz Guadalajara, and Jorge Uzeta Iturbide, 243–60. Guanajuato: Universidad de Guanajuato, 2004.

———. *Políticas agrarias y luchas sociales: San Diego de la Unión, Guanajuato, 1900–2000*. Mexico City: Procuraduría Agraria, Instituto Nacional de Antropología e Historia, 2000.

Serrano Álvarez, Pablo. *La batalla del espíritu: El movimiento sinarquista en el Bajío (1932–1951)*. Vols. 1 and 2. Mexico City: Consejo Nacional para la Cultura y las Artes, 1992.

Sherman, John W. *The Mexican Right: The End of Revolutionary Reform, 1929–1940*. Westport CT: Praeger, 1997.

Skehan, James W., S.J. *Place Me with Your Son: Ignatian Spirituality in Everyday Life*. 3rd ed. Washington DC: Georgetown University Press, 1991.

Smart, Charles Allen. *At Home in Mexico: How the Smarts Solved the Problem of Retiring on a Low Budget*. New York: Doubleday, 1957.

Smith, Stephanie. *Gender and the Mexican Revolution: Yucatán Women and the Realities of Patriarchy*. Chapel Hill: University of North Carolina Press, 2009.

Smith, Sherry. *Reimagining Indians: Native Americans through Anglo Eyes, 1880–1940*. Oxford: Oxford University Press, 2000.

Snodgrass, Michael. "The Golden Age of Charrismo: Workers, Braceros, and the Political Machinery of Postrevolutionary Mexico." In *Dictablanda: Politics, Work, and Culture in Mexico, 1938–1968*, edited by Paul Gillingham and Benjamin T. Smith, 175–95. Durham: Duke University Press, 2014.

———. "Patronage and Progress: The Bracero Program from the Perspective of Mexico." In *Workers across the Americas: The Transnational Turn in Labor History*, edited by Leon Fink, 245–66. Oxford: Oxford University Press, 2011.

Stansell, Christine. *American Moderns: Bohemian New York and the Creation of a New Century*. New York: Metropolitan Books, 2000.

Stein, Philip. *Siqueiros: His Life and Works*. New Yosrk: International Publishers, 1994.

Stephen, Lynn. "Epilogue: Rural Women's Grassroots Activism, 1980–2000; Reframing the Nation from Below." In *Sex in Revolution: Gender, Politics, and Power in Modern Mexico*, edited by Jocelyn Olcott, Mary Kay Vaughan, and Gabriela Cano, 241–60. Durham: Duke University Press, 2006.

Stern, Alexandra Minna. "Buildings, Boundaries, and Blood: Medicalization and Nation-Building on the U.S.-Mexico Border, 1910–1930." *Hispanic American Historical Review* 79, no. 1 (February 1999): 41–81.

Stoler, Ann Laura. *Carnal Knowledge and Imperial Power: Race and the Intimate in Colonial Rule*. Berkeley: University of California Press, 2002.

———. "Tense and Tender Ties: The Politics of Comparison in North American History and (Post)Colonial Studies." *Journal of American History* 88, no. 3 (December 2001): 829–65.

Streeby, Shelly. *American Sensations: Class, Empire, and the Production of Popular Culture*. Berkeley: University of California Press, 2002.

Strode, Hudson. *Now in Mexico*. New York: Harcourt, Brace, 1947.

Tenorio-Trillo, Mauricio. "The Cosmopolitan Mexican Summer, 1920–1949." *Latin American Research Review* 32, no. 3 (1997): 224–42.

Tomazos, Kostas, and William Cooper. "Volunteer Tourism: At the Crossroads of Commercialisation and Service?" *Current Issues in Tourism* 15, no. 5 (July 2012): 405–23.

Toor, Frances. *Frances Toor's Motorist Guide to Mexico*. Mexico City: Frances Toor Studios, 1938.

Topmiller, Michael, Frederick J. Conway, and James Gerber. "US Migration to Mexico: Numbers, Issues, and Scenarios." *Mexican Studies / Estudios Mexicanos* 27, no. 1 (Winter 2011): 45–71.

Torres, Blanca. *Hacia la utopía industrial*. Mexico City: El Colegio de México, 1984.

Torres, Rebecca Maria, and Janet D. Momsen. "Gringolandia: The Construction of a New Tourist Space in Mexico." *Annals of the Association of American Geographers* 95, no. 2 (2005): 314–35.

Toussaint, Manuel. *Tasco: Su historia, sus monumentos, características actuales y posibilidades turísticas*. Mexico City: Editorial Cultura, 1931.

Trouillot, Michel-Rolph. *Silencing the Past: Power and the Production of History*. Boston: Beacon Press, 1995

Truly, David. "The Lake Chapala Riviera: The Evolution of a Not So American Foreign Community." In *Adventures into Mexico: American Tourism beyond the Border*, edited by Nicholas Dagen Bloom, 167–90. Lanham MD: Rowman & Littlefield, 2006.

Tuñón, Julia. "Femininity, 'Indigenismo,' and Nation: Film Representation by Emilio 'El Indio' Fernández." In *Sex in Revolution: Gender, Politics, and*

Power in Modern Mexico, edited by Jocelyn Olcott, Mary Kay Vaughan, and Gabriela Cano, 81–96. Durham: Duke University Press, 2006.

Tutino, John. *From Insurrection to Revolution in Mexico: Social Bases of Agrarian Violence, 1750–1940*. Princeton: Princeton University Press, 1986.

———. *Making a New World: Founding Capitalism in the Bajío and Spanish North America*. Durham: Duke University Press, 2011.

Usabel, Gaizka S. de. *The High Noon of American Films in Latin America*. Ann Arbor MI: UMI Research Press, 1982.

Uzeta Iturbide, Jorge. "Ejidatarios y Chichimecas: Identidad india a través de la formación de un ejido guanajuatense." In *Guanajuato: Aportaciones recientes para su estudio*, edited by Patricia Moctezuma Yano, Juan Carlos Ruiz Guadalajara, and Jorge Uzeta Iturbide, 207–42. Guanajuato: Universidad de Guanajuato, 2004.

Valencia García, Guadalupe. *Guanajuato: Sociedad, economía, política, cultura*. Mexico City: Centro de Investigaciones Interdisciplinarias en Ciencias y Humanidades, Universidad Nacional Autónoma de México, 1998.

Vargas, Zaragosa. *Labor Rights Are Civil Rights: Mexican American Workers in Twentieth-Century America*. Princeton: Princeton University Press, 2005.

Vaughan, Mary Kay. "Modernizing Patriarchy: State Policies, Rural Households, and Women in Mexico, 1930–1940." In *Hidden Histories of Gender and the State in Latin America*, edited by Elizabeth Dore and Maxine Molyneux, 194–214. Durham: Duke University Press, 2000.

Vázquez Castillo, María Teresa. *Land Privatization in Mexico: Urbanization, Formation of Regions, and Globalization in Ejidos*. New York: Routledge, 2004.

Vázquez Soriano, Mario A. *Signos de identidad: Los espacios simbólicos de Dolores Hidalgo*. Mexico City: Instituto Mora, 1999.

Virtue, John. *Leonard and Reva Brooks: Artists in Exile in San Miguel de Allende*. Montreal: McGill-Queen's University Press, 2001.

———. *Model American Abroad: A Biography of Stirling Dickinson*. Port Orchard WA: Windstorm Creative, 2008.

Walker, Louise. *Waking from the Dream: Mexico's Middle Classes after 1968*. Stanford: Stanford University Press, 2013.

Weise, Julie M. *Corazón de Dixie: Mexicanos in the U.S. South since 1910*. Chapel Hill: University of North Carolina Press, 2015.

Whitaker, Arthur P. *The Western Hemisphere Idea: Its Rise and Decline*. Ithaca: Cornell University Press, 1954.

Winn, Peter. *Weavers of Revolution: The Yarur Workers and Chile's Road to Socialism*. New York: Oxford University Press, 1986.

Wright Carr, David Charles. *La conquista del Bajío y los orígenes de San Miguel de Allende*. Mexico City: Editorial de la Universidad del Valle de México and Fondo de Cultura Económica, 1999.

Wright-Rios, Edward. *Revolutions in Mexican Catholicism: Reform and Revelation in Oaxaca, 1887–1934*. Durham: Duke University Press, 2009.

Yuhl, Stephanie E. *A Golden Haze of Memory: The Making of Historic Charleston*. Chapel Hill: University of North Carolina Press, 2005.

Zavala, Leobino. *Tradiciones y leyendas sanmiguelenses*. Mexico City: Talleres Gráficos de México, 1990.

Zermeño P., Guillermo, and Rubén Aguilar V. "Dos razones para el estudio y la investigación de la Unión Nacional Sinarquista-Partido Demócrata Mexicano en Guanajuato." In *Guanajuato: Evolución social y política*, edited by José Arturo Salazar y García, 281–98. León, Gto.: El Colegio del Bajío, 1988.

Zolov, Eric. "Discovering a Land 'Mysterious and Obvious': The Renarrativizing of Postrevolutionary Mexico." In *Fragments of a Golden Age: The Politics of Culture in Mexico since 1940*, edited by Gilbert M. Joseph, Anne Rubenstein, and Eric Zolov, 234–72. Durham: Duke University Press, 2001.

———. "Expanding Our Conceptual Horizons: The Shift from an Old to a New Left in Latin America." *A Contracorriente* 5, no. 2 (Winter 2008): 47–73.

———. *Refried Elvis: The Rise of Mexican Counterculture*. Berkeley: University of California Press, 1999.

———. "Showcasing the 'Land of Tomorrow': Mexico and the 1968 Olympics." *The Americas* 61, no. 2 (October 2004): 159–88.

INDEX

The Plan de San Diego:
Tejano Rebellion, Mexican Intrigue
Charles H. Harris III
and Louis R. Sadler

The Inevitable Bandstand:
The State Band of Oaxaca
and the Politics of Sound
Charles V. Heath

Redeeming the Revolution:
The State and Organized Labor
in Post-Tlatelolco Mexico
Joseph U. Lenti

Gender and the Negotiation of
Daily Life in Mexico, 1750–1856
Sonya Lipsett-Rivera

Mexico's Crucial Century,
1810–1910: An Introduction
Colin M. MacLachlan and
William H. Beezley

The Civilizing Machine:
A Cultural History of Mexican
Railroads, 1876–1910
Michael Matthews

Street Democracy: Vendors,
Violence, and Public Space in
Late Twentieth-Century Mexico
Sandra C. Mendiola García

The Lawyer of the Church:
Bishop Clemente de Jesús Munguía
and the Clerical Response to the
Liberal Revolution in Mexico
Pablo Mijangos y González

¡México, la patria! Propaganda and
Production during World War II
Monica A. Rankin

Murder and Counterrevolution
in Mexico: The Eyewitness
Account of German Ambassador
Paul von Hintze, 1912–1914
Edited and with an introduction
by Friedrich E. Schuler

Deco Body, Deco City:
Female Spectacle and Modernity
in Mexico City, 1900–1939
Ageeth Sluis

Pistoleros and Popular Movements:
The Politics of State Formation
in Postrevolutionary Oaxaca
Benjamin T. Smith

Alcohol and Nationhood in
Nineteenth-Century Mexico
Deborah Toner

To order or obtain more information on these or other University of
Nebraska Press titles, visit nebraskapress.unl.edu.

Lightning Source UK Ltd.
Milton Keynes UK
UKOW03n0946270417

300008UK00008B/114/P

9 781496 200389